Tower Vortx Dual Air Fryer Cookbook

Super-easy, Affordable and Delicious Dual Basket Air Fryer

Recipes to Lose the fat not the flavour

Lula J. McKinney

Notice Of Disclaimer.

Please note that the information in this document is intended for educational and entertainment purposes only. Every effort has been made to provide accurate, up-to-date, reliable and complete information. No warranty of any kind is declared or implied. The reader acknowledges that the author does not engage in the provision of legal, financial, medical or professional advice. The content in this book has been obtained from a variety of sources. Please consult a licensed professional before attempting any of the techniques described in this book. By reading this document, the reader agrees that in no event shall the author be liable for any direct or indirect damages, including but not limited to errors, omissions or inaccuracies, resulting from the use of the information in this document.

CONTENTS

Snacks And Appetizers Recipes 78

Desserts Recipes 91

Breakfast Recipes

Morning Patties

Servings: 4
Cooking Time: 13 Minutes.
Ingredients:

- 1 lb. minced pork
- 1 lb. minced turkey
- 2 teaspoons dry rubbed sage
- 2 teaspoons fennel seeds
- 2 teaspoons garlic powder
- 1 teaspoon paprika
- 1 teaspoon of sea salt
- 1 teaspoon dried thyme

Directions:

1. In a mixing bowl, add turkey and pork, then mix them together.
2. Mix sage, fennel, paprika, salt, thyme, and garlic powder in a small bowl.
3. Drizzle this mixture over the meat mixture and mix well.
4. Take 2 tablespoons of this mixture at a time and roll it into thick patties.
5. Place half of the patties in Zone 1, and the other half in Zone 2, then spray them all with cooking oil.
6. Return the crisper plate to the Ninja Foodi Dual Zone Air Fryer.
7. Choose the Air Fry mode for Zone 1 and set the temperature to 390 degrees F and the time to 13 minutes.
8. Select the "MATCH" button to copy the settings for Zone 2.
9. Initiate cooking by pressing the START/STOP button.
10. Flip the patties in the drawers once cooked halfway through.
11. Serve warm and fresh.

Nutrition:

- (Per serving) Calories 305 | Fat 25g |Sodium 532mg | Carbs 2.3g | Fiber 0.4g | Sugar 2g | Protein 18.3g

Air Fryer Sausage Patties

Servings: 12
Cooking Time: 10 Minutes
Ingredients:

- 1-pound pork sausage or ready-made patties
- Fennel seeds or preferred seasonings

Directions:

1. Prepare the sausage by slicing it into patties, then flavor it with fennel seed or your favorite seasonings.
2. Install a crisper plate in both drawers. Place half the patties in zone 1 and half in zone 2, then insert the drawers into the unit.
3. Select zone 1, select AIR FRY, set temperature to 390 degrees F/ 200 degrees C, and set time to 10 minutes.
4. Select MATCH to match zone 2 settings to zone 1.
5. Press the START/STOP button to begin cooking.
6. When cooking is complete, remove the patties from the unit and serve with sauce or make a burger.

Nutrition:

- (Per serving) Calories 130 | Fat 10.5g | Sodium 284mg | Carbs 0.3g | Fiber 0.2g | Sugar 0g | Protein 7.4g

Sesame Bagels

Servings: 4
Cooking Time: 15 Minutes
Ingredients:

- 125g self-rising flour
- 240g non-fat plain Greek yoghurt
- 1 beaten egg
- 30g sesame seeds

Directions:

1. Combine the self-rising flour and Greek yoghurt in a medium mixing bowl using a wooden spoon.
2. Knead the dough for about 5 minutes on a lightly floured board.
3. Divide the dough into four equal pieces and roll each into a thin rope, securing the ends to form a bagel shape. Sprinkle the sesame seeds on it.
4. Press either "Zone 1" or "Zone 2" and then rotate the knob to select "Air Fryer".
5. Set the temperature to 140 degrees C, and then set the time for 3 minutes to preheat.
6. After preheating, arrange bagels into the basket.
7. Slide basket into Air Fryer and set the time for 15 minutes.
8. After cooking time is completed, remove both pans from Air Fryer.
9. Place the bagels onto a wire rack to cool for about 10 minutes and serve.

Hard Boiled Eggs

Servings: 6
Cooking Time: 18 Minutes
Ingredients:
- 6 eggs
- Cold water

Directions:
1. Press your chosen zone - "Zone 1" or "Zone 2" and then rotate the knob to select "Air Fryer".
2. Set the temperature to 120 degrees C, and then set the time for 5 minutes to preheat.
3. After preheating, arrange eggs into the basket of each zone.
4. Slide the baskets into Air Fryer and set the time for 18 minutes.
5. After cooking time is completed, transfer the eggs into cold water and serve.

Cauliflower Avocado Toast And All-in-one Toast

Servings: 3
Cooking Time: 10 Minutes
Ingredients:
- Cauliflower Avocado Toast:
- 1 (40 g) steamer bag cauliflower
- 1 large egg
- 120 ml shredded Mozzarella cheese
- 1 ripe medium avocado
- ½ teaspoon garlic powder
- ¼ teaspoon ground black pepper
- All-in-One Toast:
- 1 strip bacon, diced
- 1 slice 1-inch thick bread
- 1 egg
- Salt and freshly ground black pepper, to taste
- 60 ml grated Monterey Jack or Chedday cheese

Directions:
1. Make the Cauliflower Avocado Toast :
2. Cook cauliflower according to package instructions. Remove from bag and place into cheesecloth or clean towel to remove excess moisture.
3. Place cauliflower into a large bowl and mix in egg and Mozzarella. Cut a piece of parchment to fit your air fryer drawer. Separate the cauliflower mixture into two, and place it on the parchment in two mounds. Press out the cauliflower mounds into a ¼-inch-thick rectangle. Place the parchment into the zone 1 air fryer drawer.
4. Adjust the temperature to 204ºC and set the timer for 8 minutes.
5. Flip the cauliflower halfway through the cooking time.
6. When the timer beeps, remove the parchment and allow the cauliflower to cool 5 minutes.
7. Cut open the avocado and remove the pit. Scoop out the inside, place it in a medium bowl, and mash it with garlic powder and pepper. Spread onto the cauliflower. Serve immediately.
8. Make the All-in-One Toast :
9. Preheat the zone 2 air fryer drawer to 204ºC.
10. Air fry the bacon for 3 minutes, shaking the zone 2 drawer once or twice while it cooks. Remove the bacon to a paper towel lined plate and set aside.
11. Use a sharp paring knife to score a large circle in the middle of the slice of bread, cutting halfway through, but not all the way through to the cutting board. Press down on the circle in the center of the bread slice to create an indentation.
12. Transfer the slice of bread, hole side up, to the air fryer drawer. Crack the egg into the center of the bread, and season with salt and pepper.
13. Adjust the air fryer temperature to 192ºC and air fry for 5 minutes. Sprinkle the grated cheese around the edges of the bread, leaving the center of the yolk uncovered, and top with the cooked bacon. Press the cheese and bacon into the bread lightly to help anchor it to the bread and prevent it from blowing around in the air fryer.
14. Air fry for one or two more minutes, just to melt the cheese and finish cooking the egg. Serve immediately.

Bacon And Eggs For Breakfast

Servings:1
Cooking Time:12
Ingredients:
- 4 strips of thick-sliced bacon
- 2 small eggs
- Salt and black pepper, to taste
- Oil spray for greasing ramekins

Directions:
1. Take 2 ramekins and grease them with oil spray.
2. Crack eggs in a bowl and season it salt and black pepper.
3. Divide the egg mixture between two ramekins.
4. Put the bacon slices into Ninja Foodie 2-Basket Air Fryer zone 1 basket, and ramekins in zone 2 baskets.
5. Now for zone 1 set it to AIR FRY mode at 400 degrees F for 12 minutes.
6. And for zone 2 set it 350 degrees for 8 minutes using AIR FRY mode.
7. Press the Smart finish button and press start, it will finish both at the same time.
8. Once done, serve and enjoy.

Nutrition:
- (Per serving) Calories131 | Fat 10g| Sodium 187mg | Carbs0.6 g | Fiber 0g | Sugar 0.6g | Protein 10.7

Pork Sausage Eggs With Mustard Sauce

Servings: 8
Cooking Time: 12 Minutes
Ingredients:

- 450 g pork sausage meat
- 8 soft-boiled or hard-boiled eggs, peeled
- 1 large egg
- 2 tablespoons milk
- 235 ml crushed pork scratchings
- Smoky Mustard Sauce:
- 60 ml mayonnaise
- 2 tablespoons sour cream
- 1 tablespoon Dijon mustard
- 1 teaspoon chipotle hot sauce

Directions:

1. Divide the sausage into 8 portions. Take each portion of sausage, pat it down into a patty, and place 1 egg in the middle, gently wrapping the sausage around the egg until the egg is completely covered.

2. Repeat with the remaining eggs and sausage. In a small shallow bowl, whisk the egg and milk until frothy. In another shallow bowl, place the crushed pork scratchings. Working one at a time, dip a sausage-wrapped egg into the beaten egg and then into the pork scratchings, gently rolling to coat evenly. Repeat with the remaining sausage-wrapped eggs.

3. Put them half in zone 1, the remaining in zone 2. Lightly spray with olive oil. In zone 1 , select Air fry button, adjust temperature to 200°C, set time to 10 to 12 minutes. In zone 2, select Match Cook and press Start. Pause halfway through the baking time to turn the eggs, until the eggs are hot and the sausage is cooked through.

4. To make the sauce:

5. In a small bowl, combine the mayonnaise, sour cream, Dijon, and hot sauce. Whisk until thoroughly combined. Serve with the Scotch eggs.

Banana Bread

Servings: 8
Cooking Time: 35 Minutes
Ingredients:

- 95g flour
- 1 teaspoon ground cinnamon
- ¼ teaspoon ground nutmeg
- ½ teaspoon salt
- ¼ teaspoon baking soda
- 2 medium-sized ripe bananas mashed
- 2 large eggs lightly beaten
- 100g granulated sugar
- 2 tablespoons whole milk
- 1 tablespoon plain nonfat yoghurt
- 2 tablespoons vegetable oil
- 1 teaspoon vanilla
- 2 tablespoons walnuts roughly chopped

Directions:

1. Combine flour, cinnamon, nutmeg, baking soda, and salt in a large mixing basin.

2. Mash the banana in a separate dish before adding the eggs, sugar, milk, yoghurt, oil, and vanilla extract.

3. Combine the wet and dry ingredients in a mixing bowl and stir until just incorporated.

4. Pour the batter into the loaf pan and top with chopped walnuts.

5. Press either "Zone 1" and "Zone 2" and then rotate the knob select "Air Fryer".

6. Set the temperature to 155 degrees C, and then set the time for 3 minutes to preheat.

7. After preheating, arrange 1 loaf pan into the basket.

8. Slide basket into Air Fryer and set the time for 35 minutes.

9. After cooking time is completed, remove pan from Air Fryer.

10. Place the loaf pan onto a wire rack to cool for about 10 minutes.

11. Carefully invert the bread onto a wire rack to cool completely before slicing

12. Cut the bread into desired-sized slices and serve.

Parmesan Sausage Egg Muffins

Servings: 4
Cooking Time: 20 Minutes
Ingredients:

- 170 g Italian-seasoned sausage, sliced
- 6 eggs
- 30 ml double cream
- Salt and ground black pepper, to taste
- 85 g Parmesan cheese, grated

Directions:

1. Preheat the air fryer to 176°C. Grease a muffin pan.

2. Put the sliced sausage in the muffin pan.

3. Beat the eggs with the cream in a bowl and season with salt and pepper.

4. Pour half of the mixture over the sausages in the pan.

5. Sprinkle with cheese and the remaining egg mixture.

6. Bake in the preheated air fryer for 20 minutes or until set.

7. Serve immediately.

Egg In Bread Hole

Servings: 1
Cooking Time: 8 Minutes
Ingredients:

- 1 tablespoon butter, softened
- 2 eggs
- 2 slices of bread
- Salt and black pepper, to taste

Directions:

1. Line either basket of "Zone 1" and "Zone 2" with a greased piece of foil.
2. Press your chosen zone - "Zone 1" or "Zone 2" and then rotate the knob to select "Air Fryer".
3. Set the temperature to 160 degrees C, and then set the time for 3 minutes to preheat.
4. After preheating, place the butter on both sides of the bread. Cut a hole in the centre of the bread and crack the egg.
5. Slide the basket into the Air Fryer and set the time for 6 minutes.
6. After cooking time is completed, transfer the bread to a serving plate and serve.

Baked Eggs

Servings: 10
Cooking Time: 12 Minutes
Ingredients:

- 450g marinara sauce, divided
- 2 tablespoons capers, drained and divided
- 16 eggs
- 120g whipping cream, divided
- 50g Parmesan cheese, shredded and divided
- Salt and ground black pepper, as required

Directions:

1. Press "Zone 1" and "Zone 2" and then rotate the knob to select "Bake".
2. Set the temperature to 200 degrees C and then set the time for 5 minutes to preheat.
3. Divide the marinara sauce in the bottom of 8 greased ramekins evenly and top with capers.
4. Carefully crack 2 eggs over marinara sauce into each ramekin and top with cream, followed by the Parmesan cheese.
5. Sprinkle each ramekin with salt and black pepper.
6. After preheating, arrange the ramekins into the basket of each zone.
7. Slide the basket into the Air Fryer and set the time for 12 minutes.
8. After cooking time is completed, remove the ramekins from Air Fryer.

9. Serve hot.

Roasted Oranges

Servings: 4
Cooking Time: 6 Minutes
Ingredients:

- 2 oranges, halved
- 2 teaspoons honey
- 1 teaspoon cinnamon

Directions:

1. Place the oranges in each air fryer basket.
2. Drizzle honey and cinnamon over the orange halves.
3. Return the air fryer basket 1 to Zone 1, and basket 2 to Zone 2 of the Ninja Foodi 2-Basket Air Fryer.
4. Choose the "Air Fry" mode for Zone 1 at 395 degrees F temperature and 6 minutes of cooking time.
5. Select the "MATCH COOK" option to copy the settings for Zone 2.
6. Initiate cooking by pressing the START/PAUSE BUTTON.
7. Serve.

Nutrition:

- (Per serving) Calories 183 | Fat 15g |Sodium 402mg | Carbs 2.5g | Fiber 0.4g | Sugar 1.1g | Protein 10g

Mexican Breakfast Pepper Rings

Servings: 4
Cooking Time: 10 Minutes
Ingredients:

- Olive oil
- 1 large red, yellow, or orange pepper, cut into four ¾-inch rings
- 4 eggs
- Salt and freshly ground black pepper, to taste
- 2 teaspoons salsa

Directions:

1. Preheat the air fryer to 176°C. Lightly spray two baking pans with olive oil.
2. Place 4 bell pepper rings on the two pans. Crack one egg into each bell pepper ring. Season with salt and black pepper.
3. Spoon ½ teaspoon of salsa on top of each egg.
4. Place the two pans in the two air fryer drawers. Air fry until the yolk is slightly runny, 5 to 6 minutes or until the yolk is fully cooked, 8 to 10 minutes.
5. Serve hot.

Bacon Cinnamon Rolls

Servings: 8
Cooking Time: 10 Minutes
Ingredients:

- 8 bacon strips
- 180ml bourbon
- 1 tube (310g) refrigerated cinnamon rolls with icing
- 55g chopped pecans
- 2 tablespoons maple syrup

Directions:

1. In a small bowl, combine the bacon and the bourbon. Refrigerate overnight after sealing. Remove the bacon and pat it dry; toss out the bourbon.
2. Cook bacon in batches in a large frying pan over medium heat until nearly crisp but still flexible. Remove to a plate lined with paper towels to drain.
3. Separate the dough into 8 rolls and set aside the frosting packet. Spiral rolls should be unrolled into long strips.
4. Place 1 bacon strip on each dough strip, cut as necessary, and reroll to form a spiral. To seal the ends, pinch them together.
5. Press your chosen zone - "Zone 1" or "Zone 2" and then rotate the knob to select "Air Fry".
6. Set the temperature to 175 degrees C, and then set the time for 5 minutes to preheat.
7. After preheating, spray the Air-Fryer basket of each zone with cooking spray, line them with parchment paper, and place rolls.
8. Slide the basket into the Air Fryer and set the time for 5 minutes.
9. Turn the rolls over and cook for another 4 minutes, or until golden brown.
10. Meanwhile, combine the pecans and maple syrup in a mixing bowl. In a separate bowl, combine the contents of the icing packet.
11. Heat the remaining bacon drippings in the same frying pan over medium heat. Cook, stirring regularly until the pecan mixture is gently browned, about 2-3 minutes.
12. After cooking time is completed, transfer them onto serving plates and drizzle half the icing over warm cinnamon rolls; top with half the pecans.

Sausage And Cheese Balls

Servings: 16 Balls
Cooking Time: 12 Minutes
Ingredients:

- 450 g pork sausage meat, removed from casings
- 120 ml shredded Cheddar cheese
- 30 g full-fat cream cheese, softened
- 1 large egg

Directions:

1. Mix all ingredients in a large bowl. Form into sixteen balls. Place the balls into the two air fryer drawers.
2. Adjust the temperature to 204°C and air fry for 12 minutes.
3. Shake the drawers two or three times during cooking. Sausage balls will be browned on the outside and have an internal temperature of at least 64°C when completely cooked.
4. Serve warm.

Breakfast Sausage Omelet

Servings:2
Cooking Time:8
Ingredients:

- ¼ pound breakfast sausage, cooked and crumbled
- 4 eggs, beaten
- ½ cup pepper Jack cheese blend
- 2 tablespoons green bell pepper, sliced
- 1 green onion, chopped
- 1 pinch cayenne pepper
- Cooking spray

Directions:

1. Take a bowl and whisk eggs in it along with crumbled sausage, pepper Jack cheese, green onions, red bell pepper, and cayenne pepper.
2. Mix it all well.
3. Take two cake pans that fit inside the air fryer and grease it with oil spray.
4. Divide the omelet mixture between cake pans.
5. Put the cake pans inside both of the Ninja Foodie 2-Basket Air Fryer baskets.
6. Turn on the BAKE function of the zone 1 basket and let it cook for 15-20 minutes at 310 degrees F.
7. Select MATCH button for zone 2 basket.
8. Once the cooking cycle completes, take out, and serve hot, as a delicious breakfast.

Nutrition:

- (Per serving) Calories 691| Fat52.4g | Sodium1122 mg | Carbs 13.3g | Fiber 1.8g| Sugar 7g | Protein 42g

Donuts

Servings: 6

Cooking Time: 15 Minutes

Ingredients:

- 1 cup granulated sugar
- 2 tablespoons ground cinnamon
- 1 can refrigerated flaky buttermilk biscuits
- ¼ cup unsalted butter, melted

Directions:

1. Combine the sugar and cinnamon in a small shallow bowl and set aside.

2. Remove the biscuits from the can and put them on a chopping board, separated. Cut holes in the center of each biscuit with a 1-inch round biscuit cutter (or a similarly sized bottle cap).

3. Place a crisper plate in each drawer. In each drawer, place 4 biscuits in a single layer. Insert the drawers into the unit.

4. Select zone 1, then AIR FRY, then set the temperature to 360 degrees F/ 180 degrees C with a 10-minute timer. To match zone 2 settings to zone 1, choose MATCH. To begin cooking, select START/STOP.

5. Remove the donuts from the drawers after the timer has finished.

Nutrition:

- (Per serving) Calories 223 | Fat 8g | Sodium 150mg | Carbs 40g | Fiber 1.4g | Sugar 34.2g | Protein 0.8g

Breakfast Calzone And Western Frittata

Servings: 5

Cooking Time: 20 Minutes

Ingredients:

- Breakfast Calzone:
- 350 ml shredded Mozzarella cheese
- 120 ml blanched finely ground almond flour
- 30 g full-fat cream cheese
- 1 large whole egg
- 4 large eggs, scrambled
- 230 g cooked sausage meat, removed from casings and crumbled
- 8 tablespoons shredded mild Cheddar cheese
- Western Frittata:
- ½ red or green pepper, cut into ½-inch chunks
- 1 teaspoon olive oil
- 3 eggs, beaten
- 60 ml grated Cheddar cheese
- 60 ml diced cooked ham
- Salt and freshly ground black pepper, to taste
- 1 teaspoon butter
- 1 teaspoon chopped fresh parsley

Directions:

1. Make the Breakfast Calzone :

2. In a large microwave-safe bowl, add Mozzarella, almond flour, and cream cheese. Microwave for 1 minute. Stir until the mixture is smooth and forms a ball. Add the egg and stir until dough forms.

3. Place dough between two sheets of parchment and roll out to ¼-inch thickness. Cut the dough into four rectangles.

4. Mix scrambled eggs and cooked sausage together in a large bowl. Divide the mixture evenly among each piece of dough, placing it on the lower half of the rectangle. Sprinkle each with 2 tablespoons Cheddar.

5. Fold over the rectangle to cover the egg and meat mixture. Pinch, roll, or use a wet fork to close the edges completely.

6. Cut a piece of parchment to fit your air fryer drawer and place the calzones onto the parchment. Place parchment into the zone 1 air fryer drawer.

7. Adjust the temperature to 192ºC and air fry for 15 minutes.

8. Flip the calzones halfway through the cooking time. When done, calzones should be golden in color. Serve immediately.

9. Make the Western Frittata :

10. Preheat the zone 2 air fryer drawer to 204ºC.

11. Toss the peppers with the olive oil and air fry for 6 minutes, shaking the drawer once or twice during the cooking process to redistribute the ingredients.

12. While the vegetables are cooking, beat the eggs well in a bowl, stir in the Cheddar cheese and ham, and season with salt and freshly ground black pepper. Add the air-fried peppers to this bowl when they have finished cooking.

13. Place a cake pan into the zone 2 air fryer drawer with the butter, using an aluminum sling to lower the pan into the drawer. Air fry for 1 minute at 192ºC to melt the butter. Remove the cake pan and rotate the pan to distribute the butter and grease the pan. Pour the egg mixture into the cake pan and return the pan to the air fryer, using the aluminum sling.

14. Air fry at 192ºC for 12 minutes, or until the frittata has puffed up and is lightly browned. Let the frittata sit in the air fryer for 5 minutes to cool to an edible temperature and set up. Remove the cake pan from the air fryer, sprinkle with parsley and serve immediately.

Spinach Omelet And Bacon, Egg, And Cheese Roll Ups

Servings: 6
Cooking Time: 15 Minutes
Ingredients:

- Spinach Omelet:
- 4 large eggs
- 350 ml chopped fresh spinach leaves
- 2 tablespoons peeled and chopped brown onion
- 2 tablespoons salted butter, melted
- 120 ml shredded mild Cheddar cheese
- ¼ teaspoon salt
- Bacon, Egg, and Cheese Roll Ups:
- 2 tablespoons unsalted butter
- 60 ml chopped onion
- ½ medium green pepper, seeded and chopped
- 6 large eggs
- 12 slices bacon
- 235 ml shredded sharp Cheddar cheese
- 120 ml mild salsa, for dipping

Directions:

1. Make the Spinach Omelet :
2. In an ungreased round nonstick baking dish, whisk eggs. Stir in spinach, onion, butter, Cheddar, and salt.
3. Place dish into zone 1 air fryer basket. Adjust the temperature to 160°C and bake for 12 minutes. Omelet will be done when browned on the top and firm in the middle.
4. Slice in half and serve warm on two medium plates.
5. Make the Bacon, Egg, and Cheese Roll Ups :
6. In a medium skillet over medium heat, melt butter. Add onion and pepper to the skillet and sauté until fragrant and onions are translucent, about 3 minutes.
7. Whisk eggs in a small bowl and pour into skillet. Scramble eggs with onions and peppers until fluffy and fully cooked, about 5 minutes. Remove from heat and set aside.
8. On work surface, place three slices of bacon side by side, overlapping about ¼ inch. Place 60 ml scrambled eggs in a heap on the side closest to you and sprinkle 60 ml cheese on top of the eggs.
9. Tightly roll the bacon around the eggs and secure the seam with a toothpick if necessary. Place each roll into the zone 2 air fryer basket.
10. Adjust the temperature to 175°C and air fry for 15 minutes. Rotate the rolls halfway through the cooking time.
11. Bacon will be brown and crispy when completely cooked. Serve immediately with salsa for dipping.

Sausage With Eggs

Servings:2
Cooking Time:13
Ingredients:

- 4 sausage links, raw and uncooked
- 4 eggs, uncooked
- 1 tablespoon of green onion
- 2 tablespoons of chopped tomatoes
- Salt and black pepper, to taste
- 2 tablespoons of milk, dairy
- Oil spray, for greasing

Directions:

1. Take a bowl and whisk eggs in it.
2. Then pour milk, and add onions and tomatoes.
3. Whisk it all well.
4. Now season it with salt and black pepper.
5. Take one cake pan, that fit inside the air fryer and grease it with oil spray.
6. Pour the omelet in the greased cake pans.
7. Put the cake pan inside zone 1 air fryer basket of Ninja Foodie 2-Basket Air Fryer.
8. Now place the sausage link into the zone 2 basket.
9. Select bake for zone 1 basket and set the timer to 8-10 minutes at 300 degrees F.
10. For the zone 2 basket, select the AIR FRY button and set the timer to 12 minutes at 390 degrees.
11. Once the cooking cycle completes, serve by transferring it to plates.
12. Chop the sausage or cut it in round and then mix it with omelet.
13. Enjoy hot as a delicious breakfast.

Nutrition:

- (Per serving) Calories 240 | Fat 18.4g| Sodium 396mg | Carbs 2.8g | Fiber0.2g | Sugar 2g | Protein 15.6g

Sausage Breakfast Casserole

Servings: 4
Cooking Time: 10 Minutes
Ingredients:

- 455g hash browns
- 455g ground breakfast sausage
- 1 green capsicum diced
- 1 red capsicum diced
- 1 yellow capsicum diced
- ¼ cup sweet onion diced
- 4 eggs

Directions:

1. Layer each air fryer basket with parchment paper.
2. Place the hash browns in both the baskets.
3. Spread sausage, onion and peppers over the hash brown.
4. Return the air fryer basket 1 to Zone 1, and basket 2 to Zone 2 of the Ninja Foodi 2-Basket Air Fryer.
5. Choose the "Air Fry" mode for Zone 1 at 355 degrees F temperature and 10 minutes of cooking time.
6. Select the "MATCH COOK" option to copy the settings for Zone 2.
7. Initiate cooking by pressing the START/PAUSE BUTTON.
8. Beat eggs in a bowl and pour over the air fried veggies.
9. Continue air frying for 10 minutes.
10. Garnish with salt and black pepper.
11. Serve warm.

Nutrition:

- (Per serving) Calories 267 | Fat 12g |Sodium 165mg | Carbs 39g | Fiber 1.4g | Sugar 22g | Protein 3.3g

Eggs In Avocado Cups

Servings: 4
Cooking Time: 12 Minutes
Ingredients:

- 2 avocados, halved and pitted
- 4 eggs
- Salt and ground black pepper, as required

Directions:

1. Line either basket of "Zone 1" and "Zone 2" of Ninja Foodi 2-Basket Air Fryer with a greased square piece of foil.
2. Press your chosen zone - "Zone 1" and "Zone 2" and then rotate the knob to select "Bake".
3. Set the temperature to 200 degrees C and then set the time for 5 minutes to preheat.
4. Meanwhile, carefully scoop out about 2 teaspoons of flesh from each avocado half.

5. Crack 1 egg in each avocado half and sprinkle with salt and black pepper.
6. After preheating, arrange 2 avocado halves into the basket.
7. Slide the basket into the Air Fryer and set the time for 12 minutes.
8. After cooking time is completed, transfer the avocado halves and onto serving plates and serve hot.

Bacon And Egg Omelet

Servings:2
Cooking Time:10
Ingredients:

- 2 eggs, whisked
- ½ teaspoon of chopped tomatoes
- Sea Salt and black pepper, to taste
- 2 teaspoons of almond milk
- 1 teaspoon of cilantro, chopped
- 1 small green chili, chopped
- 4 slices of bacon

Directions:

1. Take a bowl and whisk eggs in it.
2. Then add green chili salt, black pepper, cilantro, almond milk, and chopped tomatoes.
3. Oil greases the ramekins.
4. Pour this into ramekins.
5. Put the bacon in the zone 1 basket and ramekins in zone 2 basket of the Ninja Foodie 2-Basket Air Fryer.
6. Now for zone 1, set it to AIR FRY mode at 400 degrees F for 10 minutes
7. And for zone 2, set it 350 degrees for 10 minutes in AIR FRY mode.
8. Press the Smart finish button and press start, it will finish both at the same time.
9. Once done, serve and enjoy.

Nutrition:

- (Per serving) Calories 285| Fat 21.5g| Sodium1000 mg | Carbs 2.2g | Fiber 0.1g| Sugar1 g | Protein 19.7g

Red Pepper And Feta Frittata

Servings: 4

Cooking Time: 20 Minutes

Ingredients:

- Olive oil cooking spray
- 8 large eggs
- 1 medium red pepper, diced
- ½ teaspoon salt
- ½ teaspoon black pepper
- 1 garlic clove, minced
- 120 ml feta, divided

Directions:

1. Lightly coat the inside of a 6-inch round cake pan with olive oil cooking spray. In a large bowl, beat the eggs for 1 to 2 minutes, or until well combined.

2. Add the red pepper, salt, black pepper, and garlic to the eggs, and mix together until the red pepper is distributed throughout. Fold in 60 ml the feta cheese.

3. Pour the egg mixture into the prepared cake pan, and sprinkle the remaining 60 ml feta over the top. Place into the zone 1 drawer. Select Bake button and adjust temperature to 180ºC, set time to 18 to 20 minutes and press Start.

4. Remove from the air fryer after the end and allow to cool for 5 minutes before serving.

Breakfast Pitta

Servings: 2

Cooking Time: 6 Minutes

Ingredients:

- 1 wholemeal pitta
- 2 teaspoons olive oil
- ½ shallot, diced
- ¼ teaspoon garlic, minced
- 1 large egg
- ¼ teaspoon dried oregano
- ¼ teaspoon dried thyme
- ⅛ teaspoon salt
- 2 tablespoons shredded Parmesan cheese

Directions:

1. Brush the top of the pitta with olive oil, then spread the diced shallot and minced garlic over the pitta. Crack the egg into a small bowl or ramekin, and season it with oregano, thyme, and salt.

2. Place the pitta into the zone 1 drawer, and gently pour the egg onto the top of the pitta. Sprinkle with cheese over the top.

3. Select Bake button and adjust temperature to 190ºC, set time to 6 minutes and press Start. After the end, allow to cool for 5 minutes before cutting into pieces for serving.

Mushroom-and-tomato Stuffed Hash Browns

Servings: 4

Cooking Time: 20 Minutes

Ingredients:

- Olive oil cooking spray
- 1 tablespoon plus 2 teaspoons olive oil, divided
- 110 g baby mushrooms, diced
- 1 spring onion, white parts and green parts, diced
- 1 garlic clove, minced
- 475 ml shredded potatoes
- ½ teaspoon salt
- ¼ teaspoon black pepper
- 1 plum tomato, diced
- 120 ml shredded mozzarella

Directions:

1. Lightly coat the inside of a 6-inch cake pan with olive oil cooking spray. In a small skillet, heat 2 teaspoons olive oil over medium heat. Add the mushrooms, spring onion, and garlic, and cook for 4 to 5 minutes, or until they have softened and are beginning to show some color.

2. Remove from heat. Meanwhile, in a large bowl, combine the potatoes, salt, pepper, and the remaining tablespoon olive oil. Toss until all potatoes are well coated. Pour half of the potatoes into the bottom of the cake pan.

3. Top with the mushroom mixture, tomato, and mozzarella. Spread the remaining potatoes over the top. Place the cake pan into the zone 1 drawer.

4. Select Bake button and adjust temperature to 190ºC, set time to 12 to 15 minutes and press Start. Until the top is golden brown, remove from the air fryer and allow to cool for 5 minutes before slicing and serving.

Egg With Baby Spinach

Servings:4
Cooking Time:12
Ingredients:

- Nonstick spray, for greasing ramekins
- 2 tablespoons olive oil
- 6 ounces baby spinach
- 2 garlic cloves, minced
- 1/3 teaspoon kosher salt
- 6-8 large eggs
- ½ cup half and half
- Salt and black pepper, to taste
- 8 Sourdough bread slices, toasted

Directions:

1. Grease 4 ramekins with oil spray and set aside for further use.
2. Take a skillet and heat oil in it.
3. Then cook spinach for 2 minutes and add garlic and salt black pepper.
4. Let it simmer for2more minutes.
5. Once the spinach is wilted, transfer it to a plate.
6. Whisk an egg into a small bowl.
7. Add in the spinach.
8. Whisk it well and then pour half and half.
9. Divide this mixture between 4 ramekins and remember not to overfill it to the top, leave a little space on top.
10. Put the ramekins in zone 1 and zone 2 baskets of the Ninja Foodie 2-Basket Air Fryer.
11. Press start and set zone 1 to AIR fry it at 350 degrees F for 8-12 minutes.
12. Press the MATCH button for zone 2.
13. Once it's cooked and eggs are done, serve with sourdough bread slices.

Nutrition:

- (Per serving) Calories 404| Fat 19.6g| Sodium 761mg | Carbs 40.1g | Fiber 2.5g| Sugar 2.5g | Protein 19.2g

Pepper Egg Cups

Servings: 4
Cooking Time: 18 Minutes.
Ingredients:

- 2 halved bell pepper, seeds removed
- 4 eggs
- 1 teaspoon olive oil
- 1 pinch salt and black pepper
- 1 pinch sriracha flakes

Directions:

1. Slice the bell peppers in half, lengthwise, and remove their seeds and the inner portion to get a cup-like shape.
2. Rub olive oil on the edges of the bell peppers.
3. Place them in the two crisper plates with their cut side up and crack 1 egg in each half of bell pepper.
4. Drizzle salt, black pepper, and sriracha flakes on top of the eggs.
5. Return the crisper plates to the Ninja Foodi Dual Zone Air Fryer.
6. Choose the Air Fry mode for Zone 1 and set the temperature to 390 degrees F and the time to 18 minutes.
7. Select the "MATCH" button to copy the settings for Zone 2.
8. Initiate cooking by pressing the START/STOP button.
9. Serve warm and fresh.

Nutrition:

- (Per serving) Calories 183 | Fat 15g |Sodium 402mg | Carbs 2.5g | Fiber 0.4g | Sugar 1.1g | Protein 10g

Air Fried Sausage

Servings: 4
Cooking Time: 13 Minutes.
Ingredients:

- 4 sausage links, raw and uncooked

Directions:

1. Divide the sausages in the two crisper plates.
2. Return the crisper plate to the Ninja Foodi Dual Zone Air Fryer.
3. Choose the Air Fry mode for Zone 1 and set the temperature to 390 degrees F and set the time to 13 minutes.
4. Select the "MATCH" button to copy the settings for Zone 2.
5. Initiate cooking by pressing the START/STOP button.
6. Serve warm and fresh.

Nutrition:

- (Per serving) Calories 267 | Fat 12g |Sodium 165mg | Carbs 39g | Fiber 1.4g | Sugar 22g | Protein 3.3g

Bacon And Spinach Egg Muffins

Servings: 6
Cooking Time: 12 To 14 Minutes
Ingredients:

- 6 large eggs
- 60 ml double (whipping) cream
- ½ teaspoon sea salt
- ¼ teaspoon freshly ground black pepper
- ¼ teaspoon cayenne pepper (optional)
- 180 ml frozen chopped spinach, thawed and drained
- 4 strips cooked bacon, crumbled
- 60 g shredded Cheddar cheese

Directions:

1. In a large bowl , whisk together the eggs, double cream, salt, black pepper, and cayenne pepper .
2. Divide the spinach and bacon among 6 silicone muffin cups. Place the muffin cups in the zone 1 air fryer drawer.
3. Divide the egg mixture among the muffin cups. Top with the cheese.
4. Set the temperature to 150ºC. Bake for 12 to 14 minutes, until the eggs are set and cooked through.

Bacon Cheese Egg With Avocado And Potato Nuggets

Servings: 8
Cooking Time: 20 Minutes
Ingredients:

- Bacon Cheese Egg with Avocado:
- 6 large eggs
- 60 ml double cream
- 350 ml chopped cauliflower
- 235 ml shredded medium Cheddar cheese
- 1 medium avocado, peeled and pitted
- 8 tablespoons full-fat sour cream
- 2 spring onions, sliced on the bias
- 12 slices bacon, cooked and crumbled
- Potato Nuggets:
- 1 teaspoon extra virgin olive oil
- 1 clove garlic, minced
- 1 L kale, rinsed and chopped
- 475 ml potatoes, boiled and mashed
- 30 ml milk
- Salt and ground black pepper, to taste
- Cooking spray

Directions:

1. Make the Bacon Cheese Egg with Avocado :
2. In a medium bowl, whisk eggs and cream together. Pour into a round baking dish.
3. Add cauliflower and mix, then top with Cheddar. Place dish into the zone 1 air fryer drawer.
4. Adjust the temperature to 160ºC and set the timer for 20 minutes.
5. When completely cooked, eggs will be firm and cheese will be browned. Slice into four pieces.
6. Slice avocado and divide evenly among pieces. Top each piece with 2 tablespoons sour cream, sliced spring onions, and crumbled bacon.
7. Make the Potato Nuggets :
8. Preheat the zone 2 air fryer drawer to 200ºC.
9. In a skillet over medium heat, sauté the garlic in the olive oil, until it turns golden brown. Sauté with the kale for an additional 3 minutes and remove from the heat.
10. Mix the mashed potatoes, kale and garlic in a bowl. Pour in the milk and sprinkle with salt and pepper.
11. Shape the mixture into nuggets and spritz with cooking spray.
12. Put in the zone 2 air fryer drawer and air fry for 15 minutes, flip the nuggets halfway through cooking to make sure the nuggets fry evenly.
13. Serve immediately.

Sweet Potatoes Hash

Servings:2
Cooking Time:25
Ingredients:

- 450 grams sweet potatoes
- 1/2 white onion, diced
- 3 tablespoons of olive oil
- 1 teaspoon smoked paprika
- 1/4 teaspoon cumin
- 1/3 teaspoon of ground turmeric
- 1/4 teaspoon of garlic salt
- 1 cup guacamole

Directions:

1. Peel and cut the potatoes into cubes.
2. Now, transfer the potatoes to a bowl and add oil, white onions, cumin, paprika, turmeric, and garlic salt.
3. Put this mixture between both the baskets of the Ninja Foodie 2-Basket Air Fryer.
4. Set it to AIR FRY mode for 10 minutes at 390 degrees F.
5. Then take out the baskets and shake them well.
6. Then again set time to 15 minutes at 390 degrees F.
7. Once done, serve it with guacamole.

Nutrition:

- (Per serving) Calories691 | Fat 49.7g| Sodium 596mg | Carbs 64g | Fiber15g | Sugar 19g | Protein 8.1g

Blueberry Muffins

Servings: 12
Cooking Time: 12 Minutes
Ingredients:

- 2 egg, beaten
- 2 ripe bananas, peeled and mashed
- 220g almond flour
- 4 tablespoons granulated sugar
- 1 teaspoon baking powder
- 2 tablespoons coconut oil, melted
- 80g maple syrup
- 2 teaspoons apple cider vinegar
- 2 teaspoons vanilla extract
- 2 teaspoons lemon zest, grated
- Pinch of ground cinnamon
- 150g fresh blueberries

Directions:

1. In a large bowl, add all the ingredients except blueberries and mix until well combined.
2. Gently fold in the blueberries.
3. Grease 2 muffin tins.
4. Place the mixture into prepared muffin cups about ¾ full.
5. Press your chosen zone - "Zone 1" or "Zone 2" and then rotate the knob to select "Bake".
6. Set the temperature to 190 degrees C and then set the time for 5 minutes to preheat.
7. After preheating, arrange 1 muffin tin into the basket of each zone.
8. Slide the basket into the Air Fryer and set the time for 12 minutes.
9. After cooking time is completed, remove the muffin tins from Air Fryer.
10. Place both tins onto a wire rack to cool for 10 minutes.
11. Invert the blueberry muffins onto the wire rack to cool completely before serving.

Biscuit Balls

Servings: 6
Cooking Time: 18 Minutes.
Ingredients:

- 1 tablespoon butter
- 2 eggs, beaten
- ¼ teaspoon pepper
- 1 can (10.2-oz) Pillsbury Buttermilk biscuits
- 2 ounces cheddar cheese, diced into ten cubes
- Cooking spray
- Egg Wash
- 1 egg
- 1 tablespoon water

Directions:

1. Place a suitable non-stick skillet over medium-high heat and cook the bacon until crispy, then place it on a plate lined with a paper towel.
2. Melt butter in the same skillet over medium heat. Beat eggs with pepper in a bowl and pour them into the skillet.
3. Stir cook for 5 minutes, then remove it from the heat.
4. Add bacon and mix well.
5. Divide the dough into 5 biscuits and slice each into 2 layers.
6. Press each biscuit into 4-inch round.
7. Add a tablespoon of the egg mixture at the center of each round and top it with a piece of cheese.
8. Carefully fold the biscuit dough around the filling and pinch the edges to seal.
9. Whisk egg with water in a small bowl and brush the egg wash over the biscuits.
10. Place half of the biscuit bombs in each of the crisper plate and spray them with cooking oil.
11. Return the crisper plate to the Ninja Foodi Dual Zone Air Fryer.
12. Choose the Air Fry mode for Zone 1 and set the temperature to 375 degrees F and the time to 14 minutes.
13. Select the "MATCH" button to copy the settings for Zone 2.
14. Initiate cooking by pressing the START/STOP button.
15. Flip the egg bombs when cooked halfway through, then resume cooking.
16. Serve warm.

Nutrition:

- (Per serving) Calories 102 | Fat 7.6g |Sodium 545mg | Carbs 1.5g | Fiber 0.4g | Sugar 0.7g | Protein 7.1g

Red Pepper And Feta Frittata And Bacon Eggs On The Go

Servings: 5
Cooking Time: 20 Minutes
Ingredients:

- Red Pepper and Feta Frittata:
- Olive oil cooking spray
- 8 large eggs
- 1 medium red pepper, diced
- ½ teaspoon salt
- ½ teaspoon black pepper
- 1 garlic clove, minced
- 120 ml feta, divided
- Bacon Eggs on the Go:
- 2 eggs
- 110 g bacon, cooked
- Salt and ground black pepper, to taste

Directions:

1. Make the Red Pepper and Feta Frittata :
2. Preheat the air fryer to 180°C. Lightly coat the inside of a 6-inch round cake pan with olive oil cooking spray.
3. In a large bowl, beat the eggs for 1 to 2 minutes, or until well combined.
4. Add the red pepper, salt, black pepper, and garlic to the eggs, and mix together until the red pepper is distributed throughout.
5. Fold in 60 ml the feta cheese.
6. Pour the egg mixture into the prepared cake pan, and sprinkle the remaining 60 ml feta over the top.
7. Place into the zone 1 air fryer basket and bake for 18 to 20 minutes, or until the eggs are set in the center.
8. Remove from the air fryer and allow to cool for 5 minutes before serving.
9. Make the Bacon Eggs on the Go :
10. Preheat the air fryer to 205°C. Put liners in a regular cupcake tin.
11. Crack an egg into each of the cups and add the bacon. Season with some pepper and salt.
12. Bake in the preheated zone 2 air fryer basket for 15 minutes, or until the eggs are set. Serve warm.

Honey Banana Oatmeal

Servings: 4
Cooking Time: 8 Minutes
Ingredients:

- 2 eggs
- 2 tbsp honey
- 1 tsp vanilla
- 45g quick oats
- 73ml milk
- 30g Greek yoghurt
- 219g banana, mashed

Directions:

1. In a bowl, mix eggs, milk, yoghurt, honey, vanilla, oats, and mashed banana until well combined.
2. Pour batter into the four greased ramekins.
3. Insert a crisper plate in the Ninja Foodi air fryer baskets.
4. Place ramekins in both baskets.
5. Select zone 1 then select "air fry" mode and set the temperature to 390 degrees F for 8 minutes. Press "match" to match zone 2 settings to zone 1. Press "start/stop" to begin.

Nutrition:

- (Per serving) Calories 228 | Fat 4.6g |Sodium 42mg | Carbs 40.4g | Fiber 4.2g | Sugar 16.1g | Protein 7.7g

Breakfast Potatoes

Servings: 6
Cooking Time: 20 Minutes
Ingredients:

- 3 russet potatoes, cut into bite-sized pieces with skin on
- 1 teaspoon garlic powder
- 1 teaspoon onion powder
- 2 teaspoons fine ground sea salt
- 1 teaspoon black pepper
- 1 tablespoon olive oil
- ½ red pepper, diced

Directions:

1. The potatoes should be washed and scrubbed before being sliced into bite-sized pieces with the skin on.
2. Using paper towels, dry them and place them in a large mixing bowl.
3. Toss in the spices and drizzle with olive oil. Stir in the pepper until everything is completely combined.
4. Line a basket with parchment paper.
5. Press either "Zone 1" or "Zone 2" and then rotate the knob to select "Air Fryer".
6. Set the temperature to 195 degrees C, and then set the time for 3 minutes to preheat.
7. After preheating, spread the potatoes in a single layer on the sheet.
8. Slide basket into Air Fryer and set the time for 15 minutes.
9. After cooking time is completed, remove basket from Air Fryer.
10. Place them on serving plates and serve.

Double-dipped Mini Cinnamon Biscuits

Servings: 8 Biscuits
Cooking Time: 13 Minutes
Ingredients:

- 475 ml blanched almond flour
- 120 ml liquid or powdered sweetener
- 1 teaspoon baking powder
- ½ teaspoon fine sea salt
- 60 ml plus 2 tablespoons (¾ stick) very cold unsalted butter
- 60 ml unsweetened, unflavoured almond milk
- 1 large egg
- 1 teaspoon vanilla extract
- 3 teaspoons ground cinnamon
- Glaze:
- 120 ml powdered sweetener
- 60 ml double cream or unsweetened, unflavoured almond milk

Directions:

1. Preheat the air fryer to 175⁰C. Line a pie pan that fits into your air fryer with parchment paper. 2. In a medium-sized bowl, mix together the almond flour, sweetener , baking powder, and salt. Cut the butter into ½-inch squares, then use a hand mixer to work the butter into the dry ingredients. When you are done, the mixture should still have chunks of butter. 3. In a small bowl, whisk together the almond milk, egg, and vanilla extract until blended. Using a fork, stir the wet ingredients into the dry ingredients until large clumps form. Add the cinnamon and use your hands to swirl it into the dough. 4. Form the dough into sixteen 1-inch balls and place them on the prepared pan, spacing them about ½ inch apart. Bake in the zone 1 air fryer basket until golden, 10 to 13 minutes. Remove from the air fryer and let cool on the pan for at least 5 minutes. 5. While the biscuits bake, make the glaze: Place the powdered sweetener in a small bowl and slowly stir in the heavy cream with a fork. 6. When the biscuits have cooled somewhat, dip the tops into the glaze, allow it to dry a bit, and then dip again for a thick glaze. 7. Serve warm or at room temperature. Store unglazed biscuits in an airtight container in the refrigerator for up to 3 days or in the freezer for up to a month. Reheat in a preheated 175⁰C air fryer for 5 minutes, or until warmed through, and dip in the glaze as instructed above.

Cheesy Scrambled Eggs And Egg And Bacon Muffins

Servings: 3
Cooking Time: 15 Minutes
Ingredients:

- Cheesy Scrambled Eggs:
- 1 teaspoon unsalted butter
- 2 large eggs
- 2 tablespoons milk
- 2 tablespoons shredded Cheddar cheese
- Salt and freshly ground black pepper, to taste
- Egg and Bacon Muffins:
- 2 eggs
- Salt and ground black pepper, to taste
- 1 tablespoon green pesto
- 85 g shredded Cheddar cheese
- 140 g cooked bacon
- 1 spring onion, chopped

Directions:

1. Make the Cheesy Scrambled Eggs :
2. Preheat the zone 1 air fryer basket to 150⁰C. Place the butter in a baking pan and cook for 1 to 2 minutes, until melted.
3. In a small bowl, whisk together the eggs, milk, and cheese. Season with salt and black pepper. Transfer the mixture to the pan.
4. Cook in the zone 1 basket for 3 minutes. Stir the eggs and push them toward the center of the pan.
5. Cook for another 2 minutes, then stir again. Cook for another 2 minutes, until the eggs are just cooked. Serve warm.
6. Make the Egg and Bacon Muffins :
7. Preheat the zone 2 air fryer basket to 175⁰C. Line a cupcake tin with parchment paper.
8. Beat the eggs with pepper, salt, and pesto in a bowl. Mix in the cheese.
9. Pour the eggs into the cupcake tin and top with the bacon and spring onion.
10. Bake in the preheated zone 2 air fryer basket for 15 minutes, or until the egg is set.
11. Serve immediately.

Asparagus And Bell Pepper Strata And Greek Bagels

Servings: 6
Cooking Time: 14 To 20 Minutes

Ingredients:

- Asparagus and Bell Pepper Strata:
- 8 large asparagus spears, trimmed and cut into 2-inch pieces
- 80 ml shredded carrot
- 120 ml chopped red pepper
- 2 slices wholemeal bread, cut into ½-inch cubes
- 3 egg whites
- 1 egg
- 3 tablespoons 1% milk
- ½ teaspoon dried thyme
- Greek Bagels:
- 120 ml self-raising flour, plus more for dusting
- 120 ml plain Greek yoghurt
- 1 egg
- 1 tablespoon water
- 4 teaspoons sesame seeds or za'atar
- Cooking oil spray
- 1 tablespoon butter, melted

Directions:

1. Make the Asparagus and Bell Pepper Strata :
2. In a baking pan, combine the asparagus, carrot, red bell pepper, and 1 tablespoon of water. Bake in the air fryer at 166ºC for 3 to 5 minutes, or until crisp-tender. Drain well.
3. Add the bread cubes to the vegetables and gently toss.
4. In a medium bowl, whisk the egg whites, egg, milk, and thyme until frothy.
5. Pour the egg mixture into the pan. Bake in the zone 1 drawer for 11 to 15 minutes, or until the strata is slightly puffy and set and the top starts to brown. Serve.
6. Make the Greek Bagels :
7. In a large bowl, using a wooden spoon, stir together the flour and yoghurt until a tacky dough forms. Transfer the dough to a lightly floured work surface and roll the dough into a ball.
8. Cut the dough into 2 pieces and roll each piece into a log. Form each log into a bagel shape, pinching the ends together.
9. In a small bowl, whisk the egg and water. Brush the egg wash on the bagels.
10. Sprinkle 2 teaspoons of the toppings on each bagel and gently press it into the dough.
11. Insert the crisper plate into the zone 2 drawer and the drawer into the unit. Preheat the drawer by selecting BAKE, setting the temperature to 166ºC, and setting the time to 3 minutes. Select START/STOP to begin.
12. Once the drawer is preheated, spray the crisper plate with cooking spray. Drizzle the bagels with the butter and place them into the drawer.
13. Select BAKE, set the temperature to 166ºC, and set the time to 10 minutes. Select START/STOP to begin.
14. When the cooking is complete, the bagels should be lightly golden on the outside. Serve warm.

Vegetables And Sides Recipes

Sweet Potatoes & Brussels Sprouts

Servings: 8
Cooking Time: 35 Minutes
Ingredients:

- 340g sweet potatoes, cubed
- 30ml olive oil
- 150g onion, cut into pieces
- 352g Brussels sprouts, halved
- Pepper
- Salt
- For glaze:
- 78ml ketchup
- 115ml balsamic vinegar
- 15g mustard
- 29 ml honey

Directions:

1. In a bowl, toss Brussels sprouts, oil, onion, sweet potatoes, pepper, and salt.
2. Insert a crisper plate in the Ninja Foodi air fryer baskets.
3. Add Brussels sprouts and sweet potato mixture in both baskets.
4. Select zone 1, then select "air fry" mode and set the temperature to 390 degrees F for 25 minutes. Press "match" to match zone 2 settings to zone 1. Press "start/stop" to begin. Stir halfway through.
5. Meanwhile, add vinegar, ketchup, honey, and mustard to a saucepan and cook over medium heat for 5-10 minutes.
6. Toss cooked sweet potatoes and Brussels sprouts with sauce.

Nutrition:

- (Per serving) Calories 142 | Fat 4.2g |Sodium 147mg | Carbs 25.2g | Fiber 4g | Sugar 8.8g | Protein 2.9g

Zucchini Cakes

Servings: 6
Cooking Time: 32 Minutes
Ingredients:

- 2 medium zucchinis, grated
- 1 cup corn kernel
- 1 medium potato cooked
- 2 tablespoons chickpea flour
- 2 garlic minced
- 2 teaspoons olive oil
- Salt and black pepper
- For Serving:
- Yogurt tahini sauce

Directions:

1. Mix grated zucchini with a pinch of salt in a colander and leave them for 15 minutes.
2. Squeeze out their excess water.
3. Mash the cooked potato in a large-sized bowl with a fork.
4. Add zucchini, corn, garlic, chickpea flour, salt, and black pepper to the bowl. 5. Mix these fritters' ingredients together and make 2 tablespoons-sized balls out of this mixture and flatten them lightly.
5. Divide the fritters in the two crisper plates in a single layer and spray them with cooking.
6. Return the crisper plates to the Ninja Foodi Dual Zone Air Fryer.
7. Choose the Air Fry mode for Zone 1 and set the temperature to 390 degrees F/ 200 degrees C and the time to 17 minutes.
8. Select the "MATCH" button to copy the settings for Zone 2.
9. Initiate cooking by pressing the START/STOP button.
10. Flip the fritters once cooked halfway through, then resume cooking.
11. Serve.

Broccoli, Squash, & Pepper

Servings: 4
Cooking Time: 12 Minutes
Ingredients:

- 175g broccoli florets
- 1 red bell pepper, diced
- 1 tbsp olive oil
- ½ tsp garlic powder
- ¼ onion, sliced
- 1 zucchini, sliced
- 2 yellow squash, sliced
- Pepper
- Salt

Directions:

1. In a bowl, toss veggies with oil, garlic powder, pepper, and salt.
2. Insert a crisper plate in the Ninja Foodi air fryer baskets.
3. Add the vegetable mixture in both baskets.
4. Select zone 1 then select "air fry" mode and set the temperature to 390 degrees F for 12 minutes. Press "match" to match zone 2 settings to zone 1. Press "start/stop" to begin. Stir halfway through.

Nutrition:

- (Per serving) Calories 75 | Fat 3.9g |Sodium 62mg | Carbs 9.6g | Fiber 2.8g | Sugar 4.8g | Protein 2.9g

Flavourful Mexican Cauliflower

Servings: 4
Cooking Time: 12 Minutes
Ingredients:

- 1 medium cauliflower head, cut into florets
- ½ tsp turmeric
- 1 tsp onion powder
- 2 tsp garlic powder
- 2 tsp parsley
- 1 lime juice
- 30ml olive oil
- 1 tsp chilli powder
- 1 tsp cumin
- Pepper
- Salt

Directions:

1. In a bowl, toss cauliflower florets with onion powder, garlic powder, parsley, oil, chilli powder, turmeric, cumin, pepper, and salt.
2. Insert a crisper plate in the Ninja Foodi air fryer baskets.
3. Add cauliflower florets in both baskets.
4. Select zone 1, then select "air fry" mode and set the temperature to 390 degrees F for 12 minutes. Press "match" to match zone 2 settings to zone 1. Press "start/stop" to begin. Stir halfway through.
5. Drizzle lime juice over cauliflower florets.

Nutrition:

- (Per serving) Calories 108 | Fat 7.4g |Sodium 91mg | Carbs 10g | Fiber 4.1g | Sugar 4.1g | Protein 3.4g

Curly Fries

Servings: 6
Cooking Time: 20 Minutes
Ingredients:

- 2 spiralized zucchinis
- 1 cup flour
- 2 tablespoons paprika
- 1 teaspoon cayenne pepper
- 1 teaspoon garlic powder
- 1 teaspoon black pepper
- 1 teaspoon salt
- 2 eggs
- Olive oil or cooking spray

Directions:

1. Mix flour with paprika, cayenne pepper, garlic powder, black pepper, and salt in a bowl.

2. Beat eggs in another bowl and dip the zucchini in the eggs.
3. Coat the zucchini with the flour mixture and divide it into two crisper plates. 4. Spray the zucchini with cooking oil.
4. Return the crisper plate to the Ninja Foodi Dual Zone Air Fryer.
5. Choose the Air Fry mode for Zone 1 and set the temperature to 400 degrees F/ 200 degrees C and the time to 20 minutes.
6. Select the "MATCH" button to copy the settings for Zone 2.
7. Initiate cooking by pressing the START/STOP button.
8. Toss the zucchini once cooked halfway through, then resume cooking.
9. Serve warm.

Mixed Air Fry Veggies

Servings: 4
Cooking Time: 25 Minutes
Ingredients:

- 2 cups carrots, cubed
- 2 cups potatoes, cubed
- 2 cups shallots, cubed
- 2 cups zucchini, diced
- 2 cups yellow squash, cubed
- Salt and black pepper, to taste
- 1 tablespoon Italian seasoning
- 2 tablespoons ranch seasoning
- 4 tablespoons olive oil

Directions:

1. Take a large bowl and add all the veggies to it.
2. Season the veggies with salt, pepper, Italian seasoning, ranch seasoning, and olive oil.
3. Toss all the ingredients well.
4. Divide the veggies into both the baskets of the air fryer.
5. Set zone 1 basket to AIR FRY mode at 360 degrees F for 25 minutes.
6. Select the MATCH button for the zone 2 basket.
7. Once it is cooked and done, serve, and enjoy.

Cheesy Potatoes With Asparagus

Servings: 2

Cooking Time: 35 Minutes

Ingredients:

- 1-½ pounds russet potato, wedges or cut in half
- 2 teaspoons mixed herbs
- 2 teaspoons chili flakes
- 2 cups asparagus
- 1 cup chopped onion
- 1 tablespoon Dijon mustard
- ¼ cup fresh cream
- 1 teaspoon olive oil
- 2 tablespoons butter
- ½ teaspoon salt and black pepper
- Water as required
- ½ cup Parmesan cheese

Directions:

1. Take a bowl and add asparagus and sweet potato wedges to it.

2. Season it with salt, black pepper, and olive oil.

3. Add the potato wedges to the zone 1 air fryer basket and asparagus to the zone 2 basket.

4. Set zone 1 to AIR FRY mode at 390 degrees F/ 200 degrees C for 12 minutes. 5. Set the zone 2 basket to AIR FRY mode at 390 degrees F/ 200 degrees C for 30-35 minutes. Click Sync button.

5. Meanwhile, take a skillet and add butter and sauté the onion in it for a few minutes.

6. Then add salt and Dijon mustard and chili flakes, Parmesan cheese, and fresh cream.

7. Once the veggies are cooked take them out and drizzle the cream mixture on top.

Sweet Potatoes With Honey Butter

Servings: 4

Cooking Time: 40 Minutes

Ingredients:

- 4 sweet potatoes, scrubbed
- 1 teaspoon oil
- Honey Butter
- 4 tablespoons unsalted butter
- 1 tablespoon Honey
- 2 teaspoons hot sauce
- ¼ teaspoon salt

Directions:

1. Rub the sweet potatoes with oil and place two potatoes in each crisper plate. 2. Return the crisper plate to the Ninja Foodi Dual Zone Air Fryer.

2. Choose the Air Fry mode for Zone 1 and set the temperature to 400 degrees F/ 200 degrees C and the time to 40 minutes.

3. Select the "MATCH" button to copy the settings for Zone 2.

4. Initiate cooking by pressing the START/STOP button.

5. Flip the potatoes once cooked halfway through, then resume cooking.

6. Mix butter with hot sauce, honey, and salt in a bowl.

7. When the potatoes are done, cut a slit on top and make a well with a spoon 9. Pour the honey butter in each potato jacket.

8. Serve.

Fresh Mix Veggies In Air Fryer

Servings: 4

Cooking Time: 12 Minutes

Ingredients:

- 1 cup cauliflower florets
- 1 cup carrots, peeled chopped
- 1 cup broccoli florets
- 2 tablespoons avocado oil
- Salt, to taste
- ½ teaspoon chili powder
- ½ teaspoon garlic powder
- ½ teaspoon herbs de Provence
- 1 cup Parmesan cheese

Directions:

1. Take a bowl, and add all the veggies to it.

2. Toss and then season the veggies with salt, chili powder, garlic powder, and herbs de Provence.

3. Toss it all well and then drizzle avocado oil.

4. Make sure the ingredients are coated well.

5. Distribute the veggies among both baskets of the air fryer.

6. Turn on the START/STOP button and set it to AIR FRY mode at 390 degrees F/ 200 degrees C for 10-12 minutes.

7. For the zone 2 basket setting, press the MATCH button.

8. After 8 minutes of cooking, press the START/STOP button and then take out the baskets and sprinkle Parmesan cheese on top of the veggies.

9. Then let the cooking cycle complete for the next 3-4 minutes.

10. Once done, serve.

Delicious Potatoes & Carrots

Servings: 8
Cooking Time: 25 Minutes
Ingredients:

- 453g carrots, sliced
- 2 tsp smoked paprika
- 21g sugar
- 30ml olive oil
- 453g potatoes, diced
- ¼ tsp thyme
- ½ tsp dried oregano
- 1 tsp garlic powder
- Pepper
- Salt

Directions:

1. In a bowl, toss carrots and potatoes with 1 tablespoon of oil.
2. Insert a crisper plate in the Ninja Foodi air fryer baskets.
3. Add carrots and potatoes to both baskets.
4. Select zone 1 then select "air fry" mode and set the temperature to 390 degrees F for 15 minutes. Press "match" to match zone 2 settings to zone 1. Press "start/stop" to begin.
5. In a mixing bowl, add cooked potatoes, carrots, smoked paprika, sugar, oil, thyme, oregano, garlic powder, pepper, and salt and toss well.
6. Return carrot and potato mixture into the air fryer basket and cook for 10 minutes more.

Nutrition:

- (Per serving) Calories 101 | Fat 3.6g |Sodium 62mg | Carbs 16.6g | Fiber 3g | Sugar 5.1g | Protein 1.6g

Lime Glazed Tofu

Servings: 6
Cooking Time: 14 Minutes
Ingredients:

- ⅔ cup coconut aminos
- 2 (14-oz) packages extra-firm, water-packed tofu, drained
- 6 tablespoons toasted sesame oil
- ⅔ cup lime juice

Directions:

1. Pat dry the tofu bars and slice into half-inch cubes.
2. Toss all the remaining ingredients in a small bowl.
3. Marinate for 4 hours in the refrigerator. Drain off the excess water.
4. Divide the tofu cubes in the two crisper plates.
5. Return the crisper plates to the Ninja Foodi Dual Zone Air Fryer.
6. Choose the Air Fry mode for Zone 1 and set the temperature to 400 degrees F/ 200 degrees C and the time to 14 minutes.
7. Select the "MATCH" button to copy the settings for Zone 2.
8. Initiate cooking by pressing the START/STOP button.
9. Toss the tofu once cooked halfway through, then resume cooking. 10. Serve warm.

Green Beans With Baked Potatoes

Servings: 2
Cooking Time: 45 Minutes
Ingredients:

- 2 cups green beans
- 2 large potatoes, cubed
- 3 tablespoons olive oil
- 1 teaspoon seasoned salt
- ½ teaspoon chili powder
- ⅙ teaspoon garlic powder
- ¼ teaspoon onion powder

Directions:

1. Take a large bowl and pour olive oil into it.
2. Add all the seasoning in the olive oil and whisk it well.
3. Toss the green beans in and mix well and then transfer to zone 1 basket of the air fryer.
4. Season the potatoes with the oil seasoning and add them to the zone 2 basket.
5. Press the Sync button.
6. Once the cooking cycle is complete, take out and serve.

Stuffed Tomatoes

Servings: 2
Cooking Time: 8 Minutes
Ingredients:

- 2 cups brown rice, cooked
- 1 cup tofu, grilled and chopped
- 4 large red tomatoes
- 4 tablespoons basil, chopped
- ¼ tablespoon olive oil
- Salt and black pepper, to taste
- 2 tablespoons lemon juice
- 1 teaspoon red chili powder
- ½ cup Parmesan cheese

Directions:

1. Take a large bowl and mix rice, tofu, basil, olive oil, salt, black pepper, lemon juice, and chili powder.
2. Core the center of the tomatoes.
3. Fill the cavity with the rice mixture.
4. Top them off with the cheese sprinkle.
5. Divide the tomatoes into two air fryer baskets.
6. Turn zone 1 to AIR FRY mode for 8 minutes at 400 degrees F/ 200 degrees C.
7. Select the MATCH button for zone 2.
8. Serve and enjoy.

Air-fried Radishes

Servings: 6
Cooking Time: 15 Minutes
Ingredients:
- 1020g radishes, quartered
- 3 tablespoons olive oil
- 1 tablespoon fresh oregano, minced
- ¼ teaspoon salt
- ⅛ teaspoon black pepper

Directions:
1. Toss radishes with oil, black pepper, salt and oregano in a bowl.
2. Divide the radishes into the Ninja Foodi 2 Baskets Air Fryer baskets.
3. Return the air fryer basket 1 to Zone 1, and basket 2 to Zone 2 of the Ninja Foodi 2-Basket Air Fryer.
4. Choose the "Air Fry" mode for Zone 1 at 375 degrees F and 15 minutes of cooking time.
5. Select the "MATCH COOK" option to copy the settings for Zone 2.
6. Initiate cooking by pressing the START/PAUSE BUTTON.
7. Toss the radishes once cooked halfway through.
8. Serve.

Nutrition:
- (Per serving) Calories 270 | Fat 14.6g |Sodium 394mg | Carbs 31.3g | Fiber 7.5g | Sugar 9.7g | Protein 6.4g

Breaded Summer Squash

Servings: 4
Cooking Time: 10 Minutes
Ingredients:
- 4 cups yellow summer squash, sliced
- 3 tablespoons olive oil
- ½ teaspoon salt
- ½ teaspoon pepper
- ⅛ teaspoon cayenne pepper
- ¾ cup panko bread crumbs
- ¾ cup grated Parmesan cheese

Directions:
1. Mix crumbs, cheese, cayenne pepper, black pepper, salt and oil in a bowl.
2. Coat the squash slices with the breadcrumb mixture.
3. Place these slices in the air fryer baskets.
4. Return the air fryer basket 1 to Zone 1, and basket 2 to Zone 2 of the Ninja Foodi 2-Basket Air Fryer.
5. Choose the "Air Fry" mode for Zone 1 at 350 degrees F and 10 minutes of cooking time.
6. Select the "MATCH COOK" option to copy the settings for Zone 2.
7. Initiate cooking by pressing the START/PAUSE BUTTON.
8. Flip the squash slices once cooked half way through.
9. Serve warm.

Nutrition:
- (Per serving) Calories 193 | Fat 1g |Sodium 395mg | Carbs 38.7g | Fiber 1.6g | Sugar 0.9g | Protein 6.6g

Falafel

Servings: 6
Cooking Time: 14 Minutes
Ingredients:
- 1 (15.5-oz) can chickpeas, rinsed and drained
- 1 small yellow onion, cut into quarters
- 3 garlic cloves, chopped
- ⅓ cup parsley, chopped
- ⅓ cup cilantro, chopped
- ⅓ cup scallions, chopped
- 1 teaspoon cumin
- ½ teaspoons salt
- ⅛ teaspoons crushed red pepper flakes
- 1 teaspoon baking powder
- 4 tablespoons all-purpose flour
- Olive oil spray

Directions:
1. Dry the chickpeas on paper towels.
2. Add onions and garlic to a food processor and chop them.
3. Add the parsley, salt, cilantro, scallions, cumin, and red pepper flakes.
4. Press the pulse button for 60 seconds, then toss in chickpeas and blend for 3 times until it makes a chunky paste.
5. Stir in baking powder and flour and mix well.
6. Transfer the falafel mixture to a bowl and cover to refrigerate for 3 hours.
7. Make 12 balls out of the falafel mixture.
8. Place 6 falafels in each of the crisper plate and spray them with oil.
9. Return the crisper plate to the Ninja Foodi Dual Zone Air Fryer.
10. Choose the Air Fry mode for Zone 1 and set the temperature to 350 degrees F/ 175 degrees C and the time to 14 minutes.
11. Select the "MATCH" button to copy the settings for Zone 2.
12. Initiate cooking by pressing the START/STOP button.
13. Toss the falafel once cooked halfway through, and resume cooking.
14. Serve warm.

Stuffed Sweet Potatoes

Servings: 4
Cooking Time: 55 Minutes
Ingredients:
- 2 medium sweet potatoes
- 1 teaspoon olive oil
- 1 cup cooked chopped spinach, drained
- 1 cup shredded cheddar cheese, divided
- 2 cooked bacon strips, crumbled
- 1 green onion, chopped
- ¼ cup fresh cranberries, coarsely chopped
- ⅓ cup chopped pecans, toasted
- 2 tablespoons butter
- ¼ teaspoon kosher salt
- ¼ teaspoon pepper

Directions:
1. Brush the sweet potatoes with the oil.
2. Place a crisper plate in both drawers. Add one sweet potato to each drawer. Place the drawers in the unit.
3. Select zone 1, then AIR FRY, then set the temperature to 360 degrees F/ 180 degrees C with a 40-minute timer. To match zone 2 settings to zone 1, choose MATCH. To begin, select START/STOP.
4. Remove the sweet potatoes from the drawers after the timer has finished. Cut them in half lengthwise. Scoop out the pulp, leaving a ¼-inch thick shell. 5. Put the pulp in a large bowl and stir in the spinach, ¾ cup of cheese, bacon, onion, pecans, cranberries, butter, salt, and pepper.
5. Spoon the mixture into the potato shells, mounding the mixture slightly.
6. Place a crisper plate in each drawer. Put one filled potato into each drawer and insert them into the unit.
7. Select zone 1, then AIR FRY, then set the temperature to 360 degrees F/ 180 degrees C with a 10-minute timer. To match zone 2 settings to zone 1, choose MATCH. To begin, select START/STOP.
8. Sprinkle with the remaining ¼ cup of cheese. Cook using the same settings until the cheese is melted .

Bacon Potato Patties

Servings: 2
Cooking Time: 15 Minutes
Ingredients:
- 1 egg
- 600g mashed potatoes
- 119g breadcrumbs
- 2 bacon slices, cooked & chopped
- 235g cheddar cheese, shredded
- 15g flour
- Pepper
- Salt

Directions:

1. In a bowl, mix mashed potatoes with remaining ingredients until well combined.
2. Make patties from potato mixture and place on a plate.
3. Place plate in the refrigerator for 10 minutes
4. Insert a crisper plate in the Ninja Foodi air fryer baskets.
5. Place the prepared patties in both baskets.
6. Select zone 1 then select "air fry" mode and set the temperature to 390 degrees F for 15 minutes. Press "match" to match zone 2 settings to zone 1. Press "start/stop" to begin. Turn halfway through.

Nutrition:
- (Per serving) Calories 702 | Fat 26.8g |Sodium 1405mg | Carbs 84.8g | Fiber 2.7g | Sugar 3.8g | Protein 30.5g

Air Fryer Vegetables

Servings: 2
Cooking Time: 15 Minutes
Ingredients:
- 1 courgette, diced
- 2 capsicums, diced
- 1 head broccoli, diced
- 1 red onion, diced
- Marinade
- 1 teaspoon smoked paprika
- 1 teaspoon garlic granules
- 1 teaspoon Herb de Provence
- Salt and black pepper, to taste
- 1½ tablespoon olive oil
- 2 tablespoons lemon juice

Directions:
1. Toss the veggies with the rest of the marinade ingredients in a bowl.
2. Spread the veggies in the air fryer baskets.
3. Return the air fryer basket 1 to Zone 1, and basket 2 to Zone 2 of the Ninja Foodi 2-Basket Air Fryer.
4. Choose the "Air Fry" mode for Zone 1 at 400 degrees F and 15 minutes of cooking time.
5. Select the "MATCH COOK" option to copy the settings for Zone 2.
6. Initiate cooking by pressing the START/PAUSE BUTTON.
7. Toss the veggies once cooked half way through.
8. Serve warm.

Nutrition:
- (Per serving) Calories 166 | Fat 3.2g |Sodium 437mg | Carbs 28.8g | Fiber 1.8g | Sugar 2.7g | Protein 5.8g

Caprese Panini With Zucchini Chips

Servings:4
Cooking Time: 20 Minutes
Ingredients:

- FOR THE PANINI
- 4 tablespoons pesto
- 8 slices Italian-style sandwich bread
- 1 tomato, diced
- 6 ounces fresh mozzarella cheese, shredded
- ¼ cup mayonnaise
- FOR THE ZUCCHINI CHIPS
- ½ cup all-purpose flour
- 2 large eggs
- ¼ teaspoon freshly ground black pepper
- ⅛ teaspoon kosher salt
- ½ cup panko bread crumbs
- ¼ cup grated Parmesan cheese
- 1 teaspoon Italian seasoning
- 1 medium zucchini, cut into ¼-inch-thick rounds
- 2 tablespoons vegetable oil

Directions:

1. To prep the panini: Spread 1 tablespoon of pesto each on 4 slices of the bread. Layer the diced tomato and shredded mozzarella on the other 4 slices of bread. Top the tomato/cheese mixture with the pesto-coated bread, pesto-side down, to form 4 sandwiches.
2. Spread the outside of each sandwich (both bread slices) with a thin layer of the mayonnaise.
3. To prep the zucchini chips: Set up a breading station with three small shallow bowls. Place the flour in the first bowl. In the second bowl, beat together the eggs, salt, and black pepper. Place the panko, Parmesan, and Italian seasoning in the third bowl.
4. Bread the zucchini in this order: First, dip the slices into the flour, coating both sides. Then, dip into the beaten egg. Finally, coat in the panko mixture. Drizzle the zucchini on both sides with the oil.
5. To cook the panini and zucchini chips: Install a crisper plate in each of the two baskets. Place 2 sandwiches in the Zone 1 basket and insert the basket in the unit. Place half of the zucchini chips in a single layer in the Zone 2 basket and insert the basket in the unit.
6. Select Zone 1, select AIR FRY, set the temperature to 375°F, and set the timer to 20 minutes.
7. Select Zone 2, select AIR FRY, set the temperature to 400°F, and set the timer to 20 minutes. Select SMART FINISH.
8. Press START/PAUSE to begin cooking.
9. When the Zone 1 timer reads 15 minutes, press START/PAUSE. Remove the basket, and use silicone-tipped tongs or a spatula to flip the sandwiches. Reinsert the basket and press START/PAUSE to resume cooking.
10. When both timers read 10 minutes, press START/PAUSE. Remove the Zone 1 basket and transfer the sandwiches to a plate. Place the remaining 2 sandwiches into the basket and insert the basket in the unit. Remove the Zone 2 basket and transfer the zucchini chips to a serving plate. Place the remaining zucchini chips in the basket. Reinsert the basket and press START/PAUSE to resume cooking.
11. When the Zone 1 timer reads 5 minutes, press START/PAUSE. Remove the basket and flip the sandwiches. Reinsert the basket and press START/PAUSE to resume cooking.
12. When cooking is complete, the panini should be toasted and the zucchini chips golden brown and crisp.
13. Cut each panini in half. Serve hot with zucchini chips on the side.

Nutrition:

- (Per serving) Calories: 751; Total fat: 39g; Saturated fat: 9.5g; Carbohydrates: 77g; Fiber: 3.5g; Protein: 23g; Sodium: 1,086mg

Herb And Lemon Cauliflower

Servings: 4
Cooking Time: 10 Minutes
Ingredients:

- 1 medium cauliflower, cut into florets (about 6 cups)
- 4 tablespoons olive oil, divided
- ¼ cup minced fresh parsley
- 1 tablespoon minced fresh rosemary
- 1 tablespoon minced fresh thyme
- 1 teaspoon grated lemon zest
- 2 tablespoons lemon juice
- ½ teaspoon salt
- ¼ teaspoon crushed red pepper flakes

Directions:

1. In a large bowl, combine the cauliflower florets and 2 tablespoons olive oil| toss to coat.
2. Put a crisper plate in both drawers, then put the cauliflower in a single layer in each. Insert the drawers into the unit.
3. Select zone 1, then AIR FRY, then set the temperature to 350 degrees F/ 175 degrees C with a 10-minute timer. To match zone 2 settings to zone 1, choose MATCH. To begin, select START/STOP.
4. Remove the cauliflower from the drawers after the timer has finished.
5. In a small bowl, combine the remaining ingredients. Stir in the remaining 2 tablespoons of oil.
6. Transfer the cauliflower to a large bowl and drizzle with the herb mixture. Toss to combine.

Veggie Burgers With "fried" Onion Rings

Servings:4
Cooking Time: 25 Minutes
Ingredients:

- FOR THE VEGGIE BURGERS
- 1 (15-ounce) can black beans, drained and rinsed
- ½ cup panko bread crumbs
- 1 large egg
- ¼ cup finely chopped red bell pepper
- ¼ cup frozen corn, thawed
- 1 tablespoon olive oil
- ½ teaspoon garlic powder
- ½ teaspoon ground cumin
- ¼ teaspoon smoked paprika
- Nonstick cooking spray
- 4 hamburger buns
- ¼ cup barbecue sauce, for serving
- FOR THE ONION RINGS
- 1 large sweet onion
- ½ cup all-purpose flour
- 2 large eggs
- 1 cup panko bread crumbs
- ½ teaspoon kosher salt
- Nonstick cooking spray

Directions:

1. To prep the veggie burgers: In a large bowl, mash the beans with a potato masher or a fork. Stir in the panko, egg, bell pepper, corn, oil, garlic powder, cumin, and smoked paprika. Mix well.
2. Shape the mixture into 4 patties. Spritz both sides of each patty with cooking spray.
3. To prep the onion rings: Cut the onion into ½-inch-thick rings.
4. Set up a breading station with three small shallow bowls. Place the flour in the first bowl. In the second bowl, beat the eggs. Place the panko and salt in the third bowl.
5. Bread the onions rings in this order: First, dip them into the flour, coating both sides. Then, dip into the beaten egg. Finally, coat them in the panko. Spritz each with cooking spray.
6. To cook the burgers and onion rings: Install a crisper plate in each of the two baskets. Place 2 veggie burgers in the Zone 1 basket. Place the onion rings in the Zone 2 basket and insert both baskets in the unit.
7. Select Zone 1, select AIR FRY, set the temperature to 390°F, and set the timer to 25 minutes.
8. Select Zone 2, select AIR FRY, set the temperature to 375°F, and set the timer to 10 minutes. Select SMART FINISH.
9. Press START/PAUSE to begin cooking.
10. When the Zone 1 timer reads 10 minutes, press START/PAUSE. Remove the basket and use a silicone spatula to flip burgers. Reinsert the basket and press START/PAUSE to resume cooking.
11. When the Zone 1 timer reads 10 minutes, press START/PAUSE. Remove the basket and transfer the burgers to a plate. Place the 2 remaining burgers in the basket. Reinsert the basket and press START/PAUSE to resume cooking.
12. When both timers read 5 minutes, press START/PAUSE. Remove the Zone 1 basket and flip the burgers, then reinsert the basket. Remove the Zone 2 basket and shake vigorously to rearrange the onion rings and separate any that have stuck together. Reinsert the basket and press START/PAUSE to resume cooking.
13. When cooking is complete, the veggie burgers should be cooked through and the onion rings golden brown.
14. Place 1 burger on each bun. Top with barbecue sauce and serve with onion rings on the side.

Nutrition:

- (Per serving) Calories: 538; Total fat: 16g; Saturated fat: 2g; Carbohydrates: 83g; Fiber: 10g; Protein: 19g; Sodium: 914mg

Lemon Herb Cauliflower

Servings: 4
Cooking Time: 10 Minutes
Ingredients:

- 384g cauliflower florets
- 1 tsp lemon zest, grated
- 1 tbsp thyme, minced
- 60ml olive oil
- 1 tbsp rosemary, minced
- ¼ tsp red pepper flakes, crushed
- 30ml lemon juice
- 25g parsley, minced
- ½ tsp salt

Directions:

1. In a bowl, toss cauliflower florets with the remaining ingredients until well coated.
2. Insert a crisper plate in the Ninja Foodi air fryer baskets.
3. Add cauliflower florets into both baskets.
4. Select zone 1, then select "air fry" mode and set the temperature to 360 degrees F for 10 minutes. Press "match" and "start/stop" to begin.

Nutrition:

- (Per serving) Calories 166 | Fat 14.4g |Sodium 340mg | Carbs 9.5g | Fiber 4.6g | Sugar 3.8g | Protein 3.3g

Potato And Parsnip Latkes With Baked Apples

Servings:4
Cooking Time: 20 Minutes
Ingredients:
- FOR THE LATKES
- 2 medium russet potatoes, peeled
- 1 large egg white
- 2 tablespoons all-purpose flour
- ¼ teaspoon garlic powder
- ¼ teaspoon kosher salt
- ¼ teaspoon freshly ground black pepper
- 1 medium parsnip, peeled and shredded
- 2 scallions, thinly sliced
- 2 tablespoons vegetable oil
- FOR THE BAKED APPLES
- 2 Golden Delicious apples, peeled and diced
- 2 tablespoons granulated sugar
- 2 teaspoons unsalted butter, cut into small pieces

Directions:
1. To prep the latkes: Grate the potatoes using the large holes of a box grater. Squeeze as much liquid out of the potatoes as you can into a large bowl. Set the potatoes aside in a separate bowl.
2. Let the potato liquid sit for 5 minutes, during which time the potato starch will settle to the bottom of the bowl. Pour off the water that has risen to the top, leaving the potato starch in the bowl.
3. Add the egg white, flour, salt, and black pepper to the potato starch to form a thick paste. Add the potatoes, parsnip, and scallions and mix well. Divide the mixture into 4 patties. Brush both sides of each patty with the oil.
4. To prep the baked apples: Place the apples in the Zone 2 basket. Sprinkle the sugar and butter over the top.
5. To cook the latkes and apples: Install a crisper plate in the Zone 1 basket. Place the latkes in the basket in a single layer, then insert the basket in the unit. Insert the Zone 2 basket in the unit.
6. Select Zone 1, select AIR FRY, set the temperature to 375°F, and set the timer to 15 minutes.
7. Select Zone 2, select BAKE, set the temperature to 330°F, and set the timer to 20 minutes. Select SMART FINISH.
8. Press START/PAUSE to begin cooking.
9. When both timers read 5 minutes, press START/PAUSE. Remove the Zone 1 basket and use silicone-tipped tongs or a spatula to flip the latkes.

Reinsert the basket in the unit. Remove the Zone 2 basket and gently mash the apples with a fork or the back of a spoon. Reinsert the basket and press START/PAUSE to resume cooking.
10. When cooking is complete, the latkes should be golden brown and cooked through and the apples very soft.
11. Transfer the latkes to a plate and serve with apples on the side.
Nutrition:
- (Per serving) Calories: 257; Total fat: 9g; Saturated fat: 2g; Carbohydrates: 42g; Fiber: 5.5g; Protein: 4g; Sodium: 91mg

Fried Patty Pan Squash

Servings: 6
Cooking Time: 15 Minutes
Ingredients:
- 5 cups small pattypan squash, halved
- 1 tablespoon olive oil
- 2 garlic cloves, minced
- ½ teaspoon salt
- ¼ teaspoon dried oregano
- ¼ teaspoon dried thyme
- ¼ teaspoon pepper
- 1 tablespoon minced parsley

Directions:
1. Rub the squash with oil, garlic and the rest of the ingredients.
2. Spread the squash in the air fryer baskets.
3. Return the air fryer basket 1 to Zone 1, and basket 2 to Zone 2 of the Ninja Foodi 2-Basket Air Fryer.
4. Choose the "Air Fry" mode for Zone 1 at 375 degrees F and 15 minutes of cooking time.
5. Select the "MATCH COOK" option to copy the settings for Zone 2.
6. Initiate cooking by pressing the START/PAUSE BUTTON.
7. Flip the squash once cooked halfway through.
8. Garnish with parsley.
9. Serve warm.
Nutrition:
- (Per serving) Calories 208 | Fat 5g |Sodium 1205mg | Carbs 34.1g | Fiber 7.8g | Sugar 2.5g | Protein 5.9g

Buffalo Seitan With Crispy Zucchini Noodles

Servings:4
Cooking Time: 12 Minutes

Ingredients:

- FOR THE BUFFALO SEITAN
- 1 (8-ounce) package precooked seitan strips
- 1 teaspoon garlic powder, divided
- ½ teaspoon onion powder
- ¼ teaspoon smoked paprika
- ¼ cup Louisiana-style hot sauce
- 2 tablespoons vegetable oil
- 1 tablespoon tomato paste
- ¼ teaspoon freshly ground black pepper
- FOR THE ZUCCHINI NOODLES
- 3 large egg whites
- 1¼ cups all-purpose flour
- 1 teaspoon kosher salt, divided
- 12 ounces seltzer water or club soda
- 5 ounces zucchini noodles
- Nonstick cooking spray

Directions:

1. To prep the Buffalo seitan: Season the seitan strips with ½ teaspoon of garlic powder, the onion powder, and smoked paprika.

2. In a large bowl, whisk together the hot sauce, oil, tomato paste, remaining ½ teaspoon of garlic powder, and the black pepper. Set the bowl of Buffalo sauce aside.

3. To prep the zucchini noodles: In a medium bowl, use a handheld mixer to beat the egg whites until stiff peaks form.

4. In a large bowl, combine the flour and ½ teaspoon of salt. Mix in the seltzer to form a thin batter. Fold in the beaten egg whites.

5. Add the zucchini to the batter and gently mix to coat.

6. To cook the seitan and zucchini noodles: Install a crisper plate in each of the two baskets. Place the seitan in the Zone 1 basket and insert the basket in the unit. Lift the noodles from the batter one at a time, letting the excess drip off, and place them in the Zone 2 basket. Insert the basket in the unit.

7. Select Zone 1, select BAKE, set the temperature to 370°F, and set the timer to 12 minutes.

8. Select Zone 2, select AIR FRY, set the temperature to 400°F, and set the timer to 12 minutes. Select SMART FINISH.

9. Press START/PAUSE to begin cooking.

10. When the Zone 1 timer reads 2 minutes, press START/PAUSE. Remove the basket and transfer the seitan to the bowl of Buffalo sauce. Turn to coat, then return the seitan to the basket. Reinsert the basket and press START/PAUSE to resume cooking.

11. When cooking is complete, the seitan should be warmed through and the zucchini noodles crisp and light golden brown.

12. Sprinkle the zucchini noodles with the remaining ½ teaspoon of salt. If desired, drizzle extra Buffalo sauce over the seitan. Serve hot.

Nutrition:

- (Per serving) Calories: 252; Total fat: 15g; Saturated fat: 1g; Carbohydrates: 22g; Fiber: 1.5g; Protein: 13g; Sodium: 740mg

Beets With Orange Gremolata And Goat's Cheese

Servings: 12
Cooking Time: 45 Minutes

Ingredients:

- 3 medium fresh golden beets (about 1 pound)
- 3 medium fresh beets (about 1 pound)
- 2 tablespoons lime juice
- 2 tablespoons orange juice
- ½ teaspoon fine sea salt
- 1 tablespoon minced fresh parsley
- 1 tablespoon minced fresh sage
- 1 garlic clove, minced
- 1 teaspoon grated orange zest
- 3 tablespoons crumbled goat's cheese
- 2 tablespoons sunflower kernels

Directions:

1. Scrub the beets and trim the tops by 1 inch.

2. Place the beets on a double thickness of heavy-duty foil . Fold the foil around the beets, sealing tightly.

3. Place a crisper plate in both drawers. Put the beets in a single layer in each drawer. Insert the drawers into the unit.

4. Select zone 1, then AIR FRY, then set the temperature to 360 degrees F/ 180 degrees C with a 45-minute timer. To match zone 2 settings to zone 1, choose MATCH. To begin, select START/STOP.

5. Remove the beets from the drawers after the timer has finished. Peel, halve, and slice them when they're cool enough to handle. Place them in a serving bowl.

6. Toss in the lime juice, orange juice, and salt to coat. Sprinkle the beets with the parsley, sage, garlic, and orange zest. The sunflower kernels and goat's cheese go on top.

Bacon Wrapped Corn Cob

Servings: 4
Cooking Time: 10 Minutes
Ingredients:
- 4 trimmed corns on the cob
- 8 bacon slices

Directions:
1. Wrap the corn cobs with two bacon slices.
2. Place the wrapped cobs into the Ninja Foodi 2 Baskets Air Fryer baskets.
3. Return the air fryer basket 1 to Zone 1, and basket 2 to Zone 2 of the Ninja Foodi 2-Basket Air Fryer.
4. Choose the "Air Fry" mode for Zone 1 and set the temperature to 355 degrees F and 10 minutes of cooking time.
5. Select the "MATCH COOK" option to copy the settings for Zone 2.
6. Initiate cooking by pressing the START/PAUSE BUTTON.
7. Flip the corn cob once cooked halfway through.
8. Serve warm.

Nutrition:
- (Per serving) Calories 350 | Fat 2.6g |Sodium 358mg | Carbs 64.6g | Fiber 14.4g | Sugar 3.3g | Protein 19.9g

Green Salad With Crispy Fried Goat Cheese And Baked Croutons

Servings:4
Cooking Time: 10 Minutes
Ingredients:
- FOR THE GOAT CHEESE
- 1 (4-ounce) log soft goat cheese
- ½ cup panko bread crumbs
- 2 tablespoons vegetable oil
- FOR THE CROUTONS
- 2 slices Italian-style sandwich bread
- 2 tablespoons vegetable oil
- 1 tablespoon poultry seasoning
- ½ teaspoon kosher salt
- ¼ teaspoon freshly ground black pepper
- FOR THE SALAD
- 8 cups green leaf lettuce leaves
- ½ cup store-bought balsamic vinaigrette

Directions:
1. To prep the goat cheese: Cut the goat cheese into 8 round slices.
2. Spread the panko on a plate. Gently press the cheese into the panko to coat on both sides. Drizzle with the oil.
3. To prep the croutons: Cut the bread into cubes and place them in a large bowl. Add the oil, poultry seasoning, salt, and black pepper. Mix well to coat the bread cubes evenly.
4. To cook the goat cheese and croutons: Install a crisper plate in each of the two baskets. Place the goat cheese in the Zone 1 basket and insert the basket in the unit. Place the croutons in the Zone 2 basket and insert the basket in the unit.
5. Select Zone 1, select AIR FRY, set the temperature to 400°F, and set the timer to 6 minutes.
6. Select Zone 2, select BAKE, set the temperature to 390°F, and set the timer to 10 minutes. Select SMART FINISH.
7. Press START/PAUSE to begin cooking.
8. When cooking is complete, the goat cheese will be golden brown and the croutons crisp.
9. Remove the Zone 1 basket. Let the goat cheese cool in the basket for 5 minutes; it will firm up as it cools.
10. To assemble the salad: In a large bowl, combine the lettuce, vinaigrette, and croutons. Toss well. Divide the salad among four plates. Top each plate with 2 pieces of goat cheese.

Nutrition:
- (Per serving) Calories: 578; Total fat: 40g; Saturated fat: 14g; Carbohydrates: 39g; Fiber: 3.5g; Protein: 24g; Sodium: 815mg

Fried Asparagus

Servings: 4
Cooking Time: 6 Minutes
Ingredients:
- ¼ cup mayonnaise
- 4 teaspoons olive oil
- 1½ teaspoons grated lemon zest
- 1 garlic clove, minced
- ½ teaspoon pepper
- ¼ teaspoon seasoned salt
- 1-pound fresh asparagus, trimmed
- 2 tablespoons shredded parmesan cheese
- Lemon wedges (optional)

Directions:
1. In a large bowl, combine the first 6 ingredients.
2. Add the asparagus| toss to coat.
3. Put a crisper plate in both drawers. Put the asparagus in a single layer in each drawer. Top with the parmesan cheese. Place the drawers into the unit.
4. Select zone 1, then AIR FRY, then set the temperature to 375 degrees F/ 190 degrees C with a 6-minute timer. To match zone 2 settings to zone 1, choose MATCH. To begin, select START/STOP.
5. Remove the asparagus from the drawers after the timer has finished.

Beef, Pork, And Lamb Recipes

Honey Glazed Bbq Pork Ribs

Servings: 4
Cooking Time: 30 Minutes
Ingredients:

- 2 pounds pork ribs
- ¼ cup honey, divided
- 1 cup BBQ sauce
- ½ teaspoon garlic powder
- 2 tablespoons tomato ketchup
- 1 tablespoon Worcestershire sauce
- 1 tablespoon low-sodium soy sauce
- Freshly ground white pepper, as required

Directions:

1. In a bowl, mix together honey and the remaining ingredients except pork ribs.
2. Add the pork ribs and coat with the mixture generously.
3. Refrigerate to marinate for about 20 minutes.
4. Grease each basket of "Zone 1" and "Zone 2" of Ninja Foodi 2-Basket Air Fryer.
5. Press "Zone 1" and "Zone 2" and then rotate the knob for each zone to select "Air Fry".
6. Set the temperature to 355 degrees F/ 180 degrees C for both zones and then set the time for 5 minutes to preheat.
7. After preheating, arrange the ribs into the basket of each zone.
8. Slide each basket into Air Fryer and set the time for 26 minutes.
9. While cooking, flip the ribs once halfway through.
10. After cooking time is completed, remove the ribs from Air Fryer and place onto serving plates.
11. Drizzle with the remaining honey and serve immediately.

Mustard Pork Chops

Servings: 4
Cooking Time: 15 Minutes
Ingredients:

- 450g pork chops, boneless
- 55g brown mustard
- 85g honey
- 57g mayonnaise
- 34g BBQ sauce
- Pepper
- Salt

Directions:

1. Coat pork chops with mustard, honey, mayonnaise, BBQ sauce, pepper, and salt in a bowl. Cover and place the bowl in the refrigerator for 1 hour.
2. Insert a crisper plate in the Ninja Foodi air fryer baskets.
3. Place the marinated pork chops in both baskets.
4. Select zone 1, then select "bake" mode and set the temperature to 380 degrees F for 15 minutes. Press "match" and then press "start/stop" to begin. Turn halfway through.

Bacon Wrapped Pork Tenderloin

Servings: 2
Cooking Time: 20 Minutes
Ingredients:

- ½ teaspoon salt
- ¼ teaspoon black pepper
- 1 pork tenderloin
- 6 center cut strips bacon
- cooking string

Directions:

1. Cut two bacon strips in half and place them on the working surface.
2. Place the other bacon strips on top and lay the tenderloin over the bacon strip.
3. Wrap the bacon around the tenderloin and tie the roast with a kitchen string.
4. Place the roast in the first air fryer basket.
5. Return the air fryer basket 1 to Zone 1, and basket 2 to Zone 2 of the Ninja Foodi 2-Basket Air Fryer.
6. Choose the "Air Fry" mode for Zone 1 and set the temperature to 400 degrees F and 20 minutes of cooking time.
7. Initiate cooking by pressing the START/PAUSE BUTTON.
8. Slice and serve warm.

Roast Souvlaki-style Pork With Lemon-feta Baby Potatoes

Servings:4
Cooking Time: 40 Minutes
Ingredients:
- FOR THE PORK
- 1½ pounds pork tenderloin, cut into bite-size cubes
- ¼ cup olive oil
- ¼ cup fresh lemon juice
- 2 teaspoons minced garlic
- 2 teaspoons honey
- 1½ teaspoons dried oregano
- ¼ teaspoon kosher salt
- ¼ teaspoon freshly ground black pepper
- FOR THE POTATOES
- 1 pound baby red or yellow potatoes, halved
- 1 tablespoon olive oil
- Grated zest and juice of 1 lemon
- ½ teaspoon kosher salt
- ¼ teaspoon freshly ground black pepper
- ⅓ cup crumbled feta cheese
- 2 tablespoons chopped fresh parsley

Directions:
1. To prep the pork: In a large bowl, combine the pork, oil, lemon juice, garlic, honey, oregano, salt, and black pepper. If desired, cover and refrigerate up to 24 hours.
2. To prep the potatoes: In a large bowl, combine the potatoes, oil, lemon zest, lemon juice, salt, and black pepper. Mix to coat the potatoes.
3. To cook the pork and potatoes: Install a crisper plate in each of the two baskets. Place the pork in the Zone 1 basket and insert the basket in the unit. Place the potatoes in the Zone 2 basket and insert the basket in the unit.
4. Select Zone 1, select ROAST, set the temperature to 390°F, and set the time to 20 minutes.
5. Select Zone 2, select AIR FRY, set the temperature to 400°F, and set the time to 40 minutes. Select SMART FINISH.
6. Press START/PAUSE to begin cooking.
7. When cooking is complete, the pork will be cooked through (an instant-read thermometer should read 145°F) and the potatoes will be tender and beginning to brown around the edges.
8. Stir the feta and parsley into the potatoes. Serve the pork and potatoes while hot.
Nutrition:

- (Per serving) Calories: 395; Total fat: 17g; Saturated fat: 4.5g; Carbohydrates: 24g; Fiber: 2g; Protein: 37g; Sodium: 399mg

Air Fried Lamb Chops

Servings: 4
Cooking Time: 10 Minutes
Ingredients:
- 700g lamb chops
- ½ teaspoon oregano
- 3 tablespoons parsley, minced
- ½ teaspoon black pepper
- 3 cloves garlic minced
- 2 tablespoons lemon juice
- 2 tablespoons olive oil
- Salt to taste

Directions:
1. Pat dry the chops and mix with lemon juice and the rest of the ingredients.
2. Place these chops in the air fryer baskets.
3. Return the air fryer basket 1 to Zone 1, and basket 2 to Zone 2 of the Ninja Foodi 2-Basket Air Fryer.
4. Choose the "Air Fry" mode for Zone 1and set the temperature to 400 degrees F and 10 minutes of cooking time.
5. Select the "MATCH COOK" option to copy the settings for Zone 2.
6. Initiate cooking by pressing the START/PAUSE BUTTON.
7. Flip the pork chops once cooked halfway through.
8. Serve warm.

Spice-rubbed Pork Loin

Servings: 6
Cooking Time: 20 Minutes
Ingredients:
- 1 teaspoon paprika
- ½ teaspoon ground cumin
- ½ teaspoon chili powder
- ½ teaspoon garlic powder
- 2 tablespoons coconut oil
- 1 (680 g) boneless pork loin
- ½ teaspoon salt
- ¼ teaspoon ground black pepper

Directions:
1. In a small bowl, mix paprika, cumin, chili powder, and garlic powder.
2. Drizzle coconut oil over pork. Sprinkle pork loin with salt and pepper, then rub spice mixture evenly on all sides.
3. Place pork loin into the two ungreased air fryer drawer. Adjust the temperature to 204ºC and air fry for 20 minutes, turning pork halfway through cooking. Pork loin will be browned and have an internal temperature of at least 64ºC when done. Serve warm.

New York Strip Steak

Servings: 2

Cooking Time: 10 Minutes

Ingredients:

- 1 (4½-ounce) New York strip steaks
- 1½ teaspoons olive oil
- Salt and ground black pepper, as required

Directions:

1. Grease each basket of "Zone 1" and "Zone 2" of Ninja Foodi 2-Basket Air Fryer.
2. Press "Zone 1" and "Zone 2" and then rotate the knob for each zone to select "Air Fry".
3. Set the temperature to 400 degrees F/ 200 degrees C for both zones and then set the time for 5 minutes to preheat.
4. Coat the steaks with oil and then sprinkle with salt and black pepper evenly.
5. After preheating, arrange the steak into the basket of each zone.
6. Slide each basket into Air Fryer and set the time for 10 minutes.
7. While cooking, flip the steak once halfway through.
8. After cooking time is completed, remove the steaks from Air Fryer and place onto a platter for about 10 minutes.
9. Cut each steak into desired size slices and serve immediately.

Bbq Pork Loin

Servings: 6

Cooking Time: 30 Minutes

Ingredients:

- 1 (1-pound) pork loin
- 2-3 tablespoons barbecue seasoning rub
- 2 tablespoons olive oil

Directions:

1. Coat each pork loin with oil and then rub with barbecue seasoning rub generously.
2. Grease each basket of "Zone 1" and "Zone 2" of Ninja Foodi 2-Basket Air Fryer.
3. Press "Zone 1" and "Zone 2" and then rotate the knob for each zone to select "Bake".
4. Set the temperature to 350 degrees F/ 175 degrees C for both zones and then set the time for 5 minutes to preheat.
5. After preheating, arrange pork loin into the basket of each zone.
6. Slide each basket into Air Fryer and set the time for 30 minutes.

7. After cooking time is completed, remove each pork loin from Air Fryer and place onto a platter for about 10 minutes before slicing.
8. With a sharp knife, cut each pork loin into desired-sized slices and serve.

Chinese Bbq Pork

Servings:35

Cooking Time:25

Ingredients:

- 4 tablespoons of soy sauce
- ¼ cup red wine
- 2 tablespoons of oyster sauce
- ¼ tablespoons of hoisin sauce
- ¼ cup honey
- ¼ cup brown sugar
- Pinch of salt
- Pinch of black pepper
- 1 teaspoon of ginger garlic, paste
- 1 teaspoon of five-spice powder
- 1.5 pounds of pork shoulder, sliced

Directions:

1. Take a bowl and mix all the ingredients listed under sauce ingredients.
2. Transfer half of it to a sauce pan and let it cook for 10 minutes.
3. Set it aside.
4. Let the pork marinate in the remaining sauce for 2 hours.
5. Afterward, put the pork slices in the basket and set it to AIRBORIL mode 450 degrees for 25 minutes.
6. Make sure the internal temperature is above 160 degrees F once cooked.
7. If not add a few more minutes to the overall cooking time.
8. Once done, take it out and baste it with prepared sauce.
9. Serve and Enjoy.

Nutrition:

- (Per serving) Calories 1239| Fat 73 g| Sodium 2185 mg | Carbs 57.3 g | Fiber 0.4g| Sugar53.7 g | Protein 81.5 g

Cheeseburgers With Barbecue Potato Chips

Servings:4
Cooking Time: 15 Minutes
Ingredients:
- FOR THE CHEESEBURGERS
- 1 pound ground beef (85 percent lean)
- ¼ teaspoon kosher salt
- ¼ teaspoon freshly ground black pepper
- ½ teaspoon olive oil
- 4 slices American cheese
- 4 hamburger rolls
- FOR THE POTATO CHIPS
- 2 large russet potatoes
- 2 teaspoons vegetable oil
- 1½ teaspoons smoked paprika
- 1 teaspoon light brown sugar
- ½ teaspoon garlic powder
- ½ teaspoon kosher salt
- ¼ teaspoon chili powder

Directions:
1. To prep the cheeseburgers: Season the beef with the salt and black pepper. Form the beef into 4 patties about 1 inch thick. Brush both sides of the beef patties with the oil.
2. To prep the potato chips: Fill a large bowl with ice water. Using a mandoline or sharp knife, cut the potatoes into very thin (⅛- to 1/16-inch) slices. Soak the potatoes in the ice water for 30 minutes.
3. Drain the potatoes and pat dry with a paper towel. Place in a large bowl and toss with the oil, smoked paprika, brown sugar, garlic powder, salt, and chili powder.
4. To cook the cheeseburgers and potato chips: Install a crisper plate in each of the two baskets. Place the burgers in the Zone 1 basket and insert the basket in the unit. Place the potato slices in the Zone 2 basket and insert the basket in the unit.
5. Select Zone 1, select AIR FRY, set the temperature to 390°F, and set the time to 12 minutes.
6. Select Zone 2, select AIR FRY, set the temperature to 390°F, and set the time to 15 minutes. Select SMART FINISH.
7. Press START/PAUSE to begin cooking.
8. At 5-minute intervals, press START/PAUSE. Remove the Zone 2 basket and shake the potato chips to keep them from sticking to each other. Reinsert the basket and press START/PAUSE to resume cooking.
9. When cooking is complete, the burgers should be cooked to your preferred doneness and the potato chips should be crisp and golden brown.
10. Top each burger patty in the basket with a slice of cheese. Turn the air fryer off and let the cheese melt inside the unit, or cover the basket with aluminum foil and let stand for 1 to 2 minutes, until the cheese is melted. Serve the cheeseburgers on buns with the chips on the side.

Nutrition:
- (Per serving) Calories: 475; Total fat: 22g; Saturated fat: 8g; Carbohydrates: 38g; Fiber: 2g; Protein: 32g; Sodium: 733mg

Beef Ribs I

Servings:2
Cooking Time:15
Ingredients:
- 4 tablespoons of barbecue spice rub
- 1 tablespoon kosher salt and black pepper
- 3 tablespoons brown sugar
- 2 pounds of beef ribs (3-3 1/2 pounds), cut in thirds
- 1 cup barbecue sauce

Directions:
1. In a small bowl, add salt, pepper, brown sugar, and BBQ spice rub.
2. Grease the ribs with oil spray from both sides and then rub it with a spice mixture.
3. Divide the ribs amongst the basket and set it to AIR FRY MODE at 375 degrees F for 15 minutes.
4. Hit start and let the air fryer cook the ribs.
5. Once done, serve with the coating BBQ sauce.

Nutrition:
- (Per serving) Calories1081 | Fat 28.6 g| Sodium 1701mg | Carbs 58g | Fiber 0.8g| Sugar 45.7g | Protein 138 g

Cinnamon-beef Kofta

Servings: 12 Koftas
Cooking Time: 13 Minutes
Ingredients:

- 680 g lean beef mince
- 1 teaspoon onion granules
- ¾ teaspoon ground cinnamon
- ¾ teaspoon ground dried turmeric
- 1 teaspoon ground cumin
- ¾ teaspoon salt
- ¼ teaspoon cayenne
- 12 (3½- to 4-inch-long) cinnamon sticks
- Cooking spray

Directions:

1. Preheat the air fryer to 192°C. Spritz the two air fryer drawers with cooking spray.
2. Combine all the ingredients, except for the cinnamon sticks, in a large bowl. Toss to mix well.
3. Divide and shape the mixture into 12 balls, then wrap each ball around each cinnamon stick and leave a quarter of the length uncovered.
4. Arrange the beef-cinnamon sticks in the preheated air fryer and spritz with cooking spray.
5. Air fry for 13 minutes or until the beef is browned. Flip the sticks halfway through.
6. Serve immediately.

Roast Beef

Servings: 4
Cooking Time: 35 Minutes
Ingredients:

- 2 pounds beef roast
- 1 tablespoon olive oil
- 1 medium onion (optional)
- 1 teaspoon salt
- 2 teaspoons rosemary and thyme, chopped (fresh or dried)

Directions:

1. Combine the sea salt, rosemary, and oil in a large, shallow dish.
2. Using paper towels, pat the meat dry. Place it on a dish and turn it to coat the outside with the oil-herb mixture.
3. Peel the onion and split it in half (if using).
4. Install a crisper plate in both drawers. Place half the beef roast and half an onion in the zone 1 drawer and half the beef and half the onion in zone 2's, then insert the drawers into the unit.
5. Select zone 1, select AIR FRY, set temperature to 360 degrees F/ 180 degrees C, and set time to 22 minutes. Select MATCH to match zone 2 settings to zone 1. Press the START/STOP button to begin cooking.
6. When the time reaches 11 minutes, press START/STOP to pause the unit. Remove the drawers and flip the roast. Re-insert the drawers into the unit and press START/STOP to resume cooking.

Nutrition:

- (Per serving) Calories 463 | Fat 17.8g | Sodium 732mg | Carbs 2.8g | Fiber 0.7g | Sugar 1.2g | Protein 69g

Panko Crusted Calf's Liver Strips

Servings: 4
Cooking Time: 23 To 25 Minutes
Ingredients:

- 450 g sliced calf's liver, cut into ½-inch wide strips
- 2 eggs
- 2 tablespoons milk
- 120 ml whole wheat flour
- 475 ml panko breadcrumbs
- Salt and ground black pepper, to taste
- Cooking spray

Directions:

1. Preheat the air fryer to 200°C and spritz with cooking spray.
2. Rub the calf's liver strips with salt and ground black pepper on a clean work surface.
3. Whisk the eggs with milk in a large bowl. Pour the flour in a shallow dish. Pour the panko on a separate shallow dish.
4. Dunk the liver strips in the flour, then in the egg mixture. Shake the excess off and roll the strips over the panko to coat well.
5. Arrange the liver strips in a single layer in the two preheated air fryer drawers and spritz with cooking spray.
6. Air fry for 5 minutes or until browned. Flip the strips halfway through.
7. Serve immediately.

Breaded Pork Chops

Servings: 4
Cooking Time: 10 Minutes
Ingredients:

- 4 boneless, center-cut pork chops, 1-inch thick
- 1 teaspoon Cajun seasoning
- 1½ cups cheese and garlic-flavored croutons
- 2 eggs
- Cooking spray

Directions:

1. Season both sides of the pork chops with the Cajun seasoning on a platter.
2. In a small food processor, pulse the croutons until finely chopped; transfer to a shallow plate.
3. In a separate shallow bowl, lightly beat the eggs.
4. Dip the pork chops in the egg, allowing any excess to drip off. Then place the chops in the crouton crumbs. Coat the chops in cooking spray.
5. Install a crisper plate in both drawers. Place half the pork chops in the zone 1 drawer and half in zone 2's, then insert the drawers into the unit.
6. Select zone 1, select ROAST, set temperature to 390 degrees F/ 200 degrees C, and set time to 10 minutes. Select MATCH to match zone 2 settings to zone 1. Press the START/STOP button to begin cooking.
7. When the time reaches 6 minutes, press START/STOP to pause the unit. Remove the drawers and flip the chops. Reinsert the drawers into the unit and press START/STOP to resume cooking.
8. When cooking is complete, serve and enjoy!

Nutrition:

- (Per serving) Calories 394 | Fat 18.1g | Sodium 428mg | Carbs 10g | Fiber 0.8g | Sugar 0.9g | Protein 44.7g

Lamb Chops With Dijon Garlic

Servings: 4
Cooking Time: 22 Minutes
Ingredients:

- 2 teaspoons Dijon mustard
- 2 teaspoons olive oil
- 1 teaspoon soy sauce
- 1 teaspoon garlic, minced
- 1 teaspoon cumin powder
- 1 teaspoon cayenne pepper
- 1 teaspoon Italian spice blend (optional)
- ¼ teaspoon salt
- 8 lamb chops

Directions:

1. Combine the Dijon mustard, olive oil, soy sauce, garlic, cumin powder, cayenne pepper, Italian spice blend (optional), and salt in a medium mixing bowl.
2. Put the marinade in a large Ziploc bag. Add the lamb chops. Seal the bag tightly after pressing out the air. Coat the lamb in the marinade by shaking the bag and pressing the chops into the mixture. Place in the fridge for at least 30 minutes, or up to overnight, to marinate.
3. Install a crisper plate in both drawers. Place half the lamb chops in the zone 1 drawer and half in zone 2's, then insert the drawers into the unit.
4. Select zone 1, select AIR FRY, set temperature to 390 degrees F/ 200 degrees C, and set time to 22 minutes. Select MATCH to match zone 2 settings to zone 1. Press the START/STOP button to begin cooking.
5. When the time reaches 11 minutes, press START/STOP to pause the unit. Remove the drawers and flip the lamb chops. Re-insert the drawers into the unit and press START/STOP to resume cooking.
6. Serve and enjoy!

Nutrition:

- (Per serving) Calories 343 | Fat 15.1g | Sodium 380mg | Carbs 0.9 g | Fiber 0.3g | Sugar 0.1g | Protein 48.9g

Spicy Lamb Chops

Servings:4
Cooking Time:15
Ingredients:

- 12 lamb chops, bone-in
- Salt and black pepper, to taste
- ½ teaspoon of lemon zest
- 1 tablespoon of lemon juice
- 1 teaspoon of paprika
- 1 teaspoon of garlic powder
- ½ teaspoon of Italian seasoning
- ¼ teaspoon of onion powder

Directions:

1. Add the lamb chops to the bowl and sprinkle salt, garlic powder, Italian seasoning, onion powder, black pepper, lemon zest, lemon juice, and paprika.
2. Rub the chops well, and divide it between both the baskets of the air fryer.
3. Set zone 1 basket to 400 degrees F, for 15 minutes at AIR FRY mode.
4. Select MATCH for zone2 basket.
5. After 10 minutes, take out the baskets and flip the chops cook for the remaining minutes, and then serve.

Nutrition:

- (Per serving) Calories 787| Fat 45.3g| Sodium1 mg | Carbs 16.1g | Fiber0.3g | Sugar 0.4g | Protein 75.3g

Bacon-wrapped Vegetable Kebabs

Servings: 4
Cooking Time: 10 To 12 Minutes
Ingredients:

- 110 g mushrooms, sliced
- 1 small courgette, sliced
- 12 baby plum tomatoes
- 110 g sliced bacon, halved
- Avocado oil spray
- Sea salt and freshly ground black pepper, to taste

Directions:

1. Stack 3 mushroom slices, 1 courgette slice, and 1 tomato. Wrap a bacon strip around the vegetables and thread them onto a skewer. Repeat with the remaining vegetables and bacon. Spray with oil and sprinkle with salt and pepper.
2. Set the air fryer to 204ºC. Place the skewers in the two air fryer drawers in a single layer and air fry for 5 minutes. Flip the skewers and cook for 5 to 7 minutes more, until the bacon is crispy and the vegetables are tender.
3. Serve warm.

Seasoned Lamb Steak

Servings: 2
Cooking Time: 10 Minutes
Ingredients:

- 2 lamb steaks
- ½ teaspoon kosher salt
- Drizzle of olive oil
- ½ teaspoon ground black pepper

Directions:

1. Take a bowl, add every ingredient except lamb steak. Mix well.
2. Rub lamb steaks with a little olive oil.
3. Press each side of steak into salt and pepper mixture.
4. Grease each basket of "Zone 1" and "Zone 2" of Ninja Foodi 2-Basket Air Fryer.
5. Press "Zone 1" and "Zone 2" and then rotate the knob for each zone to select "Air Fry".
6. Set the heat to 400 degrees F/ 200 degrees C for both zones and then set the time for 5 minutes to preheat.
7. After preheating, arrange steak into the basket of each zone.
8. Slide each basket into Air Fryer and set the time for 5 minutes.

9. While cooking, flip the steak once halfway through and cook for more 5 minutes.
10. After cooking time is completed, remove it from Air Fryer and place onto a platter for about 10 minutes before slicing.
11. With a sharp knife, cut each steak into desired-sized slices and serve.

Beef & Broccoli

Servings:4
Cooking Time:12
Ingredients:

- 12 ounces of teriyaki sauce, divided
- ½ tablespoon garlic powder
- ¼ cup of soy sauce
- 1 pound raw sirloin steak, thinly sliced
- 2 cups broccoli, cut into florets
- 2 teaspoons of olive oil
- Salt and black pepper, to taste

Directions:

1. Take a zip-lock plastic bag and mix teriyaki sauce, salt, garlic powder, black pepper, soy sauce, and olive oil.
2. Marinate the beef in it for 2 hours.
3. Then drain the beef from the marinade.
4. Now toss the broccoli with oil, teriyaki sauce, and salt and black pepper.
5. Put it in a zone 1 basket
6. Now for the zone, 1 basket set it to AIRFRY mode at 400 degrees F for 15 minutes.
7. Place the steak in a zone 2 basket and set it to AIR FRY mode at 375 degrees F for 10-12 minutes.
8. Hit start and let the cooking cycle completes.
9. Once it's done take out the beef and broccoli and
10. serve immediately with leftover teriyaki sauce and cooked rice.

Nutrition:

- (Per serving) Calories 344| Fat 10g| Sodium 4285mg | Carbs18.2 g | Fiber 1.5g| Sugar 13.3g | Protein42 g

Italian-style Meatballs With Garlicky Roasted Broccoli

Servings:4
Cooking Time: 15 Minutes
Ingredients:

- FOR THE MEATBALLS
- 1 large egg
- ¼ cup Italian-style bread crumbs
- 1 pound ground beef (85 percent lean)
- ¼ cup grated Parmesan cheese
- ¼ teaspoon kosher salt
- Nonstick cooking spray
- 2 cups marinara sauce
- FOR THE ROASTED BROCCOLI
- 4 cups broccoli florets
- 1 tablespoon olive oil
- ¼ teaspoon kosher salt
- ¼ teaspoon freshly ground pepper
- ¼ teaspoon red pepper flakes
- 1 tablespoon minced garlic

Directions:

1. To prep the meatballs: In a large bowl, beat the egg. Mix in the bread crumbs and let sit for 5 minutes.

2. Add the beef, Parmesan, and salt and mix until just combined. Form the meatball mixture into 8 meatballs, about 1 inch in diameter. Mist with cooking spray.

3. To prep the broccoli: In a large bowl, combine the broccoli, olive oil, salt, black pepper, and red pepper flakes. Toss to coat the broccoli evenly.

4. To cook the meatballs and broccoli: Install a crisper plate in the Zone 1 basket. Place the meatballs in the basket and insert the basket in the unit. Place the broccoli in the Zone 2 basket, sprinkle the garlic over the broccoli, and insert the basket in the unit.

5. Select Zone 1, select AIR FRY, set the temperature to 400°F, and set the time to 12 minutes.

6. Select Zone 2, select ROAST, set the temperature to 390°F, and set the time to 15 minutes. Select SMART FINISH.

7. Press START/PAUSE to begin cooking.

8. When the Zone 1 timer reads 5 minutes, press START/PAUSE. Remove the basket and pour the marinara sauce over the meatballs. Reinsert the basket and press START/PAUSE to resume cooking.

9. When cooking is complete, the meatballs should be cooked through and the broccoli will have begun to brown on the edges.

Nutrition:

- (Per serving) Calories: 493; Total fat: 33g; Saturated fat: 9g; Carbohydrates: 24g; Fiber: 3g; Protein: 31g; Sodium: 926mg

Meatloaf

Servings: 6
Cooking Time: 25 Minutes
Ingredients:

- For the meatloaf:
- 2 pounds ground beef
- 2 eggs, beaten
- 2 cups old-fashioned oats, regular or gluten-free
- ½ cup evaporated milk
- ½ cup chopped onion
- ½ teaspoon garlic salt
- For the sauce:
- 1 cup ketchup
- ¾ cup brown sugar, packed
- ¼ cup chopped onion
- ½ teaspoon liquid smoke
- ¼ teaspoon garlic powder
- Olive oil cooking spray

Directions:

1. In a large bowl, combine all the meatloaf ingredients.

2. Spray 2 sheets of foil with olive oil cooking spray.

3. Form the meatloaf mixture into a loaf shape, cut in half, and place each half on one piece of foil.

4. Roll the foil up a bit on the sides. Allow it to be slightly open.

5. Put all the sauce ingredients in a saucepan and whisk until combined on medium-low heat. This should only take 1–2 minutes

6. Install a crisper plate in both drawers. Place half the meatloaf in the zone 1 drawer and half in zone 2's, then insert the drawers into the unit.

7. Select zone 1, select AIR FRY, set temperature to 390 degrees F/ 200 degrees C, and set time to 25 minutes. Select MATCH to match zone 2 settings to zone 1. Press the START/STOP button to begin cooking.

8. When the time reaches 20 minutes, press START/STOP to pause the unit. Remove the drawers and coat the meatloaf with the sauce using a brush. Re-insert the drawers into the unit and press START/STOP to resume cooking.

9. Carefully remove and serve.

Nutrition:

- (Per serving) Calories 727 | Fat 34g | Sodium 688mg | Carbs 57g | Fiber 3g | Sugar 34g | Protein 49g

Goat Cheese-stuffed Bavette Steak

Servings: 6
Cooking Time: 14 Minutes
Ingredients:

- 450 g bavette or skirt steak
- 1 tablespoon avocado oil
- ½ teaspoon sea salt
- ½ teaspoon garlic powder
- ¼ teaspoon freshly ground black pepper
- 60 g goat cheese, crumbled
- 235 ml baby spinach, chopped

Directions:

1. Place the steak in a large zip-top bag or between two pieces of plastic wrap. Using a meat mallet or heavy-bottomed skillet, pound the steak to an even ¼-inch thickness.
2. Brush both sides of the steak with the avocado oil.
3. Mix the salt, garlic powder, and pepper in a small dish. Sprinkle this mixture over both sides of the steak.
4. Sprinkle the goat cheese over top, and top that with the spinach.
5. Starting at one of the long sides, roll the steak up tightly. Tie the rolled steak with kitchen string at 3-inch intervals.
6. Set the zone 1 air fryer drawer to 204°C. Place the steak roll-up in the zone 1 air fryer drawer. Air fry for 7 minutes. Flip the steak and cook for an additional 7 minutes, until an instant-read thermometer reads 49°C for medium-rare .

Zucchini Pork Skewers

Servings: 4
Cooking Time: 23 Minutes.
Ingredients:

- 1 large zucchini, cut 1" pieces
- 1 lb. boneless pork belly, cut into cubes
- 1 onion yellow, diced in squares
- 1 ½ cups grape tomatoes
- 1 garlic clove minced
- 1 lemon, juice only
- ¼ cup olive oil
- 2 tablespoons balsamic vinegar
- 1 teaspoon oregano
- olive oil spray

Directions:

1. Mix together balsamic vinegar, garlic, oregano lemon juice, and ¼ cup of olive oil in a suitable bowl.
2. Then toss in diced pork pieces and mix well to coat.

3. Leave the seasoned pork to marinate for 60 minutes in the refrigerator.
4. Take suitable wooden skewers for your Ninja Foodi Dual Zone Air Fryer's drawer, and then thread marinated pork and vegetables on each skewer in an alternating manner.
5. Place half of the skewers in each of the crisper plate and spray them with cooking oil.
6. Return the crisper plate to the Ninja Foodi Dual Zone Air Fryer.
7. Choose the Air Fry mode for Zone 1 and set the temperature to 390 degrees F and the time to 23 minutes.
8. Select the "MATCH" button to copy the settings for Zone 2.
9. Initiate cooking by pressing the START/STOP button.
10. Flip the skewers once cooked halfway through, and resume cooking.
11. Serve warm.

Nutrition:

- (Per serving) Calories 459 | Fat 17.7g |Sodium 1516mg | Carbs 1.7g | Fiber 0.5g | Sugar 0.4g | Protein 69.2g

Cheesesteak Taquitos

Servings: 8
Cooking Time: 12 Minutes
Ingredients:

- 1 pack soft corn tortillas
- 136g beef steak strips
- 2 green peppers, sliced
- 1 white onion, chopped
- 1 pkg dry Italian dressing mix
- 10 slices Provolone cheese
- Cooking spray or olive oil

Directions:

1. Mix beef with cooking oil, peppers, onion, and dressing mix in a bowl.
2. Divide the strips in the air fryer baskets.
3. Return the air fryer basket 1 to Zone 1, and basket 2 to Zone 2 of the Ninja Foodi 2-Basket Air Fryer.
4. Choose the "Air Fry" mode for Zone 1 at 375 degrees F and 12 minutes of cooking time.
5. Select the "MATCH COOK" option to copy the settings for Zone 2.
6. Initiate cooking by pressing the START/PAUSE BUTTON.
7. Flip the strips once cooked halfway through.
8. Divide the beef strips in the tortillas and top the beef with a beef slice.
9. Roll the tortillas and serve.

Roast Beef With Yorkshire Pudding

Servings:6
Cooking Time: 40 Minutes
Ingredients:

- FOR THE ROAST BEEF
- 3-pound beef roast, trimmed
- 1 tablespoon vegetable oil
- ½ teaspoon kosher salt
- ½ teaspoon freshly ground black pepper
- ½ teaspoon garlic powder
- ½ teaspoon onion powder
- ½ teaspoon dried thyme
- FOR THE YORKSHIRE PUDDING
- 3 large eggs
- ¾ cup whole milk
- 2 tablespoons beef broth
- ¾ cup all-purpose flour
- ½ teaspoon kosher salt
- 2 teaspoons unsalted butter

Directions:

1. To prep the roast beef: If necessary, trim the beef roast to fit in the Zone 1 basket. Rub the beef with the oil.
2. In a small bowl, combine the salt, black pepper, garlic powder, onion powder, and thyme. Rub the spice mixture all over the beef roast.
3. To prep the Yorkshire pudding: In a large bowl, whisk the eggs, milk, and beef broth until well combined. Whisk in the flour and salt to form a thin batter.
4. To cook the beef and Yorkshire pudding: Install a crisper plate in the Zone 1 basket. Place the beef roast in the basket and insert the basket in the unit. Place the butter in the Zone 2 basket and insert the basket in the unit.
5. Select Zone 1, select AIR FRY, set the temperature to 375°F, and set the time to 40 minutes for a medium-rare roast (set to 50 minutes for medium or 60 minutes for well done).
6. Select Zone 2, select BAKE, set the temperature to 400°F, and set the time to 20 minutes. Select SMART FINISH.
7. Press START/PAUSE to begin cooking.
8. When the Zone 2 timer reads 18 minutes, press START/PAUSE. Remove the basket and pour the batter into it. Reinsert the basket and press START/PAUSE to resume cooking.
9. When cooking is complete, the beef should be cooked to your liking and the Yorkshire pudding should be fluffy on the edges and set in the center.
10. Remove the beef from the basket and let rest for at least 15 minutes before slicing.
11. Cut the Yorkshire pudding into 6 servings and serve the sliced beef on top.

Nutrition:

- (Per serving) Calories: 517; Total fat: 26g; Saturated fat: 9.5g; Carbohydrates: 13g; Fiber: 0.5g; Protein: 52g; Sodium: 354mg

Sausage And Pork Meatballs

Servings: 8
Cooking Time: 8 To 12 Minutes
Ingredients:

- 1 large egg
- 1 teaspoon gelatin
- 450 g pork mince
- 230 g Italian-seasoned sausage, casings removed, crumbled
- 80 ml Parmesan cheese
- 60 ml finely diced onion
- 1 tablespoon tomato paste
- 1 teaspoon minced garlic
- 1 teaspoon dried oregano
- ¼ teaspoon red pepper flakes
- Sea salt and freshly ground black pepper, to taste
- Keto-friendly marinara sauce, for serving

Directions:

1. Beat the egg in a small bowl and sprinkle with the gelatin. Allow to sit for 5 minutes.
2. In a large bowl, combine the pork mince, sausage, Parmesan, onion, tomato paste, garlic, oregano, and red pepper flakes. Season with salt and black pepper.
3. Stir the gelatin mixture, then add it to the other ingredients and, using clean hands, mix to ensure that everything is well combined. Form into 1½-inch round meatballs.
4. Set the air fryer to 204°C. Place the meatballs in the two air fryer drawers in a single layer. Air fry for 5 minutes. Flip and cook for 3 to 7 minutes more, or until an instant-read thermometer reads 72°C.

Meat And Rice Stuffed Peppers

Servings: 4
Cooking Time: 18 Minutes
Ingredients:

- 340 g lean beef mince
- 110 g lean pork mince
- 60 ml onion, minced
- 1 (425 g) can finely-chopped tomatoes
- 1 teaspoon Worcestershire sauce
- 1 teaspoon barbecue seasoning
- 1 teaspoon honey
- ½ teaspoon dried basil
- 120 ml cooked brown rice
- ½ teaspoon garlic powder
- ½ teaspoon oregano
- ½ teaspoon salt
- 2 small peppers, cut in half, stems removed, deseeded
- Cooking spray

Directions:

1. Preheat the zone 1 air fryer drawer to 182ºC and spritz a baking pan with cooking spray.
2. Arrange the beef, pork, and onion in the baking pan and bake in the preheated air fryer drawer for 8 minutes. Break the ground meat into chunks halfway through the cooking.
3. Meanwhile, combine the tomatoes, Worcestershire sauce, barbecue seasoning, honey, and basil in a saucepan. Stir to mix well.
4. Transfer the cooked meat mixture to a large bowl and add the cooked rice, garlic powder, oregano, salt, and 60 ml of the tomato mixture. Stir to mix well.
5. Stuff the pepper halves with the mixture, then arrange the pepper halves in the zone 1 air fryer drawer and air fry for 10 minutes or until the peppers are lightly charred.
6. Serve the stuffed peppers with the remaining tomato sauce on top.

Garlic-rosemary Pork Loin With Scalloped Potatoes And Cauliflower

Servings:6
Cooking Time: 50 Minutes
Ingredients:

- FOR THE PORK LOIN
- 2 pounds pork loin roast
- 2 tablespoons vegetable oil
- 2 teaspoons dried thyme
- 2 teaspoons dried crushed rosemary
- 1 teaspoon minced garlic
- ¾ teaspoon kosher salt
- FOR THE SCALLOPED POTATOES AND CAULIFLOWER
- 1 teaspoon vegetable oil
- ¾ pound Yukon Gold potatoes, peeled and very thinly sliced
- 1½ cups cauliflower florets
- ¼ teaspoon kosher salt
- ¼ teaspoon freshly ground black pepper
- 1 tablespoon very cold unsalted butter, grated
- 3 tablespoons all-purpose flour
- 1 cup whole milk
- 1 cup shredded Gruyère cheese

Directions:

1. To prep the pork loin: Coat the pork with the oil. Season with thyme, rosemary, garlic, and salt.
2. To prep the potatoes and cauliflower: Brush the bottom and sides of the Zone 2 basket with the oil. Add one-third of the potatoes to the bottom of the basket and arrange in a single layer. Top with ½ cup of cauliflower florets. Sprinkle a third of the salt and black pepper on top. Scatter one-third of the butter on top and sprinkle on 1 tablespoon of flour. Repeat this step twice more for a total of three layers.
3. Pour the milk over the layered potatoes and cauliflower; it should just cover the top layer. Top with the Gruyère.
4. To cook the pork and scalloped vegetables: Install a crisper plate in the Zone 1 basket. Place the pork loin in the basket and insert the basket in the unit. Insert the Zone 2 basket in the unit.
5. Select Zone 1, select AIR FRY, set the temperature to 390°F, and set the time to 50 minutes.
6. Select Zone 2, select BAKE, set the temperature to 350°F, and set the time to 45 minutes. Select SMART FINISH.
7. Press START/PAUSE to begin cooking.
8. When cooking is complete, the pork will be cooked through (an instant-read thermometer should read 145°F) and the potatoes and cauliflower will be tender.
9. Let the pork rest for at least 15 minutes before slicing and serving with the scalloped vegetables.

Nutrition:

- (Per serving) Calories: 439; Total fat: 25g; Saturated fat: 10g; Carbohydrates: 17g; Fiber: 1.5g; Protein: 37g; Sodium: 431mg

Pork With Green Beans And Potatoes

Servings: 4
Cooking Time: 15 Minutes.
Ingredients:

- ¼ cup Dijon mustard
- 2 tablespoons brown sugar
- 1 teaspoon dried parsley flake
- ½ teaspoon dried thyme
- ¼ teaspoons salt
- ¼ teaspoons black pepper
- 1 ¼ lbs. pork tenderloin
- ¾ lb. small potatoes halved
- 1 (12-oz) package green beans, trimmed
- 1 tablespoon olive oil
- Salt and black pepper ground to taste

Directions:

1. Preheat your Air Fryer Machine to 400 degrees F.
2. Add mustard, parsley, brown sugar, salt, black pepper, and thyme in a large bowl, then mix well.
3. Add tenderloin to the spice mixture and coat well.
4. Toss potatoes with olive oil, salt, black pepper, and green beans in another bowl.
5. Place the prepared tenderloin in the crisper plate.
6. Return this crisper plate to the Zone 1 of the Ninja Foodi Dual Zone Air Fryer.
7. Choose the Air Fry mode for Zone 1 and set the temperature to 390 degrees F and the time to 15 minutes.
8. Add potatoes and green beans to the Zone 2.
9. Choose the Air Fry mode for Zone 2 with 350 degrees F and the time to 10 minutes.
10. Press the SYNC button to sync the finish time for both Zones.
11. Initiate cooking by pressing the START/STOP button.
12. Serve the tenderloin with Air Fried potatoes

Nutrition:

- (Per serving) Calories 400 | Fat 32g |Sodium 721mg | Carbs 2.6g | Fiber 0g | Sugar 0g | Protein 27.4g

Stuffed Beef Fillet With Feta Cheese

Servings: 4
Cooking Time: 10 Minutes
Ingredients:

- 680 g beef fillet, pounded to ¼ inch thick
- 3 teaspoons sea salt
- 1 teaspoon ground black pepper
- 60 g creamy goat cheese
- 120 ml crumbled feta cheese
- 60 ml finely chopped onions
- 2 cloves garlic, minced
- Cooking spray

Directions:

1. Preheat the air fryer to 204ºC. Spritz the two air fryer drawers with cooking spray. 2. Unfold the beef on a clean work surface. Rub the salt and pepper all over the beef to season. 3. Make the filling for the stuffed beef fillet: Combine the goat cheese, feta, onions, and garlic in a medium bowl. Stir until well blended. 4. Spoon the mixture in the center of the fillet. Roll the fillet up tightly like rolling a burrito and use some kitchen twine to tie the fillet. 5. Arrange the fillet in the two air fryer drawers and air fry for 10 minutes, flipping the fillet halfway through to ensure even cooking, or until an instant-read thermometer inserted in the center of the fillet registers 57ºC for medium-rare. 6. Transfer to a platter and serve immediately.

Steak Fajitas With Onions And Peppers

Servings: 6
Cooking Time: 15 Minutes
Ingredients:

- 1 pound steak
- 1 green bell pepper, sliced
- 1 yellow bell pepper, sliced
- 1 red bell pepper, sliced
- ½ cup sliced white onions
- 1 packet gluten-free fajita seasoning
- Olive oil spray

Directions:

1. Thinly slice the steak against the grain. These should be about ¼-inch slices.
2. Mix the steak with the peppers and onions.
3. Evenly coat with the fajita seasoning.
4. Install a crisper plate in both drawers. Place half the steak mixture in the zone 1 drawer and half in zone 2's, then insert the drawers into the unit.
5. Select zone 1, select AIR FRY, set temperature to 390 degrees F/ 200 degrees C, and set time to 15 minutes. Select MATCH to match zone 2 settings to zone 1. Press the START/STOP button to begin cooking.
6. When the time reaches 10 minutes, press START/STOP to pause the unit. Remove the drawers and flip the steak strips. Re-insert the drawers into the unit and press START/STOP to resume cooking.
7. Serve in warm tortillas.

Nutrition:

- (Per serving) Calories 305 | Fat 17g | Sodium 418mg | Carbs 15g | Fiber 2g | Sugar 4g | Protein 22g

Pork Katsu With Seasoned Rice

Servings:4
Cooking Time: 15 Minutes

Ingredients:

- FOR THE PORK KATSU
- 4 thin-sliced boneless pork chops (4 ounces each)
- 2 tablespoons all-purpose flour
- 2 large eggs
- 1 cup panko bread crumbs
- ¼ teaspoon kosher salt
- ¼ teaspoon freshly ground black pepper
- 1 teaspoon vegetable oil
- 3 tablespoons ketchup
- 3 tablespoons Worcestershire sauce
- 1 tablespoon oyster sauce
- ⅛ teaspoon granulated sugar
- FOR THE RICE
- 2 cups dried instant rice (not microwavable)
- 2½ cups water
- 1 tablespoon sesame oil
- 1 teaspoon soy sauce
- 1 tablespoon toasted sesame seeds
- 3 scallions, sliced

Directions:

1. To prep the pork katsu: Place the pork chops between two slices of plastic wrap. Using a meat mallet or rolling pin, pound the pork into ½-inch-thick cutlets.
2. Set up a breading station with three small shallow bowls. Place the flour in the first bowl. In the second bowl, whisk the eggs. Combine the panko, salt, and black pepper in the third bowl.
3. Bread the cutlets in this order: First, dip them in the flour, coating both sides. Then, dip them into the beaten egg. Finally, coat them in panko, gently pressing the bread crumbs to adhere to the pork. Drizzle both sides of the cutlets with the oil.
4. To prep the rice: In the Zone 2 basket, combine the rice, water, sesame oil, and soy sauce. Stir well to ensure all of the rice is submerged in the liquid.
5. To cook the pork and rice: Install a crisper plate in the Zone 1 basket. Place the pork in the basket and insert the basket in the unit. Insert the Zone 2 basket in the unit.
6. Select Zone 1, select AIR FRY, set the temperature to 390°F, and set the time to 15 minutes.
7. Select Zone 2, select BAKE, set the temperature to 350°F, and set the time to 10 minutes. Select SMART FINISH.
8. Press START/PAUSE to begin cooking.
9. When the Zone 1 timer reads 10 minutes, press START/PAUSE. Remove the basket and use silicone-tipped tongs to flip the pork. Reinsert the basket and press START/PAUSE to resume cooking.
10. When cooking is complete, the pork should be crisp and cooked through and the rice tender.
11. Stir the sesame seeds and scallions into the rice. For the sauce to go with the pork, in a small bowl, whisk together the ketchup, Worcestershire sauce, oyster sauce, and sugar. Drizzle the sauce over the pork and serve with the hot rice.

Nutrition:

- (Per serving) Calories: 563; Total fat: 20g; Saturated fat: 5.5g; Carbohydrates: 62g; Fiber: 1g; Protein: 34g; Sodium: 665mg

Smothered Chops

Servings: 4
Cooking Time: 30 Minutes

Ingredients:

- 4 bone-in pork chops (230 g each)
- 2 teaspoons salt, divided
- 1½ teaspoons freshly ground black pepper, divided
- 1 teaspoon garlic powder
- 235 ml tomato purée
- 1½ teaspoons Italian seasoning
- 1 tablespoon sugar
- 1 tablespoon cornflour
- 120 ml chopped onion
- 120 ml chopped green pepper
- 1 to 2 tablespoons oil

Directions:

1. Evenly season the pork chops with 1 teaspoon salt, 1 teaspoon pepper, and the garlic powder.
2. In a medium bowl, stir together the tomato purée, Italian seasoning, sugar, remaining 1 teaspoon of salt, and remaining ½ teaspoon of pepper.
3. In a small bowl, whisk 180 ml water and the cornflour until blended. Stir this slurry into the tomato purée, with the onion and green pepper. Transfer to a baking pan.
4. Preheat the air fryer to 176°C.
5. Place the sauce in the fryer and cook for 10 minutes. Stir and cook for 10 minutes more. Remove the pan and keep warm.
6. Increase the air fryer temperature to 204°C. Line the two air fryer drawers with parchment paper.
7. Place the pork chops on the parchment and spritz with oil.
8. Cook for 5 minutes. Flip and spritz the chops with oil and cook for 5 minutes more, until the internal temperature reaches 64°C. Serve with the tomato mixture spooned on top.

Green Pepper Cheeseburgers

Servings: 4
Cooking Time: 30 Minutes
Ingredients:
- 2 green peppers
- 680 g 85% lean beef mince
- 1 clove garlic, minced
- 1 teaspoon salt
- ½ teaspoon freshly ground black pepper
- 4 slices Cheddar cheese (about 85 g)
- 4 large lettuce leaves

Directions:
1. Preheat the air fryer to 204°C.
2. Arrange the peppers in the drawer of the air fryer. Pausing halfway through the cooking time to turn the peppers, air fry for 20 minutes, or until they are softened and beginning to char. Transfer the peppers to a large bowl and cover with a plate. When cool enough to handle, peel off the skin, remove the seeds and stems, and slice into strips. Set aside.
3. Meanwhile, in a large bowl, combine the beef with the garlic, salt, and pepper. Shape the beef into 4 patties.
4. Lower the heat on the air fryer to 182°C. Arrange the burgers in a single layer in the two drawers of the air fryer. Pausing halfway through the cooking time to turn the burgers, air fry for 10 minutes, or until a thermometer inserted into the thickest part registers 72°C.
5. Top the burgers with the cheese slices and continue baking for a minute or two, just until the cheese has melted. Serve the burgers on a lettuce leaf topped with the roasted peppers.

Nigerian Peanut-crusted Bavette Steak

Servings: 4
Cooking Time: 8 Minutes
Ingredients:
- Suya Spice Mix:
- 60 ml dry-roasted peanuts
- 1 teaspoon cumin seeds
- 1 teaspoon garlic powder
- 1 teaspoon smoked paprika
- ½ teaspoon ground ginger
- 1 teaspoon coarse or flaky salt
- ½ teaspoon cayenne pepper
- Steak:
- 450 g bavette or skirt steak
- 2 tablespoons vegetable oil

Directions:
1. For the spice mix: In a clean coffee grinder or spice mill, combine the peanuts and cumin seeds. Process until you get a coarse powder. 2. Pour the peanut mixture into a small bowl, add the garlic powder, paprika, ginger, salt, and cayenne, and stir to combine.

This recipe makes about 120 ml suya spice mix. Store leftovers in an airtight container in a cool, dry place for up to 1 month. 3. For the steak: Cut the steak into ½-inch-thick slices, cutting against the grain and at a slight angle. Place the beef strips in a resealable plastic bag and add the oil and 2½ to 3 tablespoons of the spice mixture. Seal the bag and massage to coat all of the meat with the oil and spice mixture. Marinate at room temperature for 30 minutes or in the refrigerator for up to 24 hours. 4. Place the beef strips in the zone 1 air fryer drawer. Set the temperature to 204°C for 8 minutes, turning the strips halfway through the cooking time. 5. Transfer the meat to a serving platter. Sprinkle with additional spice mix, if desired.

Ham Burger Patties

Servings:2
Cooking Time:17
Ingredients:
- 1 pound of ground beef
- Salt and pepper, to taste
- ½ teaspoon of red chili powder
- ¼ teaspoon of coriander powder
- 2 tablespoons of chopped onion
- 1 green chili, chopped
- Oil spray for greasing
- 2 large potato wedges

Directions:
1. Oil greases the air fryer baskets with oil spray.
2. Add potato wedges in the zone 1 basket.
3. Take a bowl and add minced beef in it and add salt, pepper, chili powder, coriander powder, green chili, and chopped onion.
4. mix well and make two burger patties with wet hands place the two patties in the air fryer zone 2 basket.
5. put the basket inside the air fryer.
6. now, set time for zone 1 for 12 minutes using AIR FRY mode at 400 degrees F.
7. Select the MATCH button for zone 2.
8. once the time of cooking complete, take out the baskets.
9. flip the patties and shake the potatoes wedges.
10. again, set time of zone 1 basket for 4 minutes at 400 degrees F
11. Select the MATCH button for the second basket.
12. Once it's done, serve and enjoy.
Nutrition:
- (Per serving) Calories875 | Fat21.5g | Sodium 622mg | Carbs 88g | Fiber10.9 g| Sugar 3.4g | Protein 78.8g

Pork Chops With Broccoli

Servings: 2
Cooking Time: 13 Minutes.
Ingredients:
- 2 (5 ounces) bone-in pork chops
- 2 tablespoons avocado oil
- ½ teaspoon paprika
- ½ teaspoon onion powder
- ½ teaspoon garlic powder
- 1 teaspoon salt
- 2 cups broccoli florets
- 2 garlic cloves, minced

Directions:
1. Rub the pork chops with avocado oil, garlic, paprika, and spices.
2. Add pork chop to the crisper plate of Zone 1 in the Ninja Foodi Dual Zone Air Fryer.
3. Return the crisper plate to the Air Fryer.
4. Choose the Air Fry mode for Zone 1 and set the temperature to 400 degrees F and the time to 12 minutes.
5. Add the broccoli to the Zone 2 drawer and return it to the unit.
6. Choose the Air Fry mode for Zone 2 with 375 degrees F and the time to 13 minutes.
7. Press the SYNC button to sync the finish time for both Zones.
8. Initiate cooking by pressing the START/STOP button.
9. Flip the pork once cooked halfway through.
10. Cut the hardened butter into the cubes and place them on top of the pork chops.
11. Serve warm with crispy broccoli florets

Nutrition:
- (Per serving) Calories 410 | Fat 17.8g |Sodium 619mg | Carbs 21g | Fiber 1.4g | Sugar 1.8g | Protein 38.4g

Jerk-rubbed Pork Loin With Carrots And Sage

Servings: 4
Cooking Time: 35 Minutes
Ingredients:
- 1½ pounds pork loin
- 3 teaspoons canola oil, divided
- 2 tablespoons jerk seasoning
- 1-pound carrots, peeled, cut into 1-inch pieces
- 1 tablespoon honey
- ½ teaspoon kosher salt
- ½ teaspoon chopped fresh sage

Directions:
1. Place the pork loin in a pan or a dish with a high wall. Using a paper towel, pat the meat dry.
2. Rub 2 teaspoons of canola oil evenly over the pork with your hands. Then spread the jerk seasoning evenly over it with your hands.
3. Allow the pork loin to marinate for at least 10 minutes or up to 8 hours in the refrigerator after wrapping it in plastic wrap or sealing it in a plastic bag.
4. Toss the carrots with the remaining canola oil and ½ teaspoon of salt in a medium mixing bowl.

5. Place a crisper plate in each of the drawers. Put the marinated pork loin in the zone 1 drawer and place it in the unit. Place the carrots in the zone 2 drawer and place the drawer in the unit.
6. Select zone 1 and select AIR FRY. Set the temperature to 390 degrees F/ 200 degrees C and the time setting to 25 minutes. Select zone 2 and select AIR FRY. Set the temperature to 390 degrees F/ 200 degrees C and the time setting to 16 minutes. Select SYNC. Press START/STOP to begin cooking.
7. Check the pork loin for doneness after the zones have finished cooking. When the internal temperature of the loin hits 145°F on an instant-read thermometer, the pork is ready.
8. Allow the pork loin to rest for at least 5 minutes on a plate or cutting board.
9. Combine the carrots and sage in a mixing bowl.
10. When the pork loin has rested, slice it into the desired thickness of slices and serve with the carrots.

Nutrition:
- (Per serving) Calories 500 | Fat 19.8g | Sodium 680mg | Carbs 50.1g | Fiber 4.1g | Sugar 0g | Protein 27.9g

Parmesan Pork Chops

Servings: 4
Cooking Time: 15 Minutes.
Ingredients:
- 4 boneless pork chops
- 2 tablespoons olive oil
- ½ cup freshly grated Parmesan
- 1 teaspoon salt
- 1 teaspoon paprika
- 1 teaspoon garlic powder
- 1 teaspoon onion powder
- ½ teaspoon black pepper

Directions:
1. Pat dry the pork chops with a paper towel and rub them with olive oil.
2. Mix parmesan with spices in a medium bowl.
3. Rub the pork chops with Parmesan mixture.
4. Place 2 seasoned pork chops in each of the two crisper plate
5. Return the crisper plate to the Ninja Foodi Dual Zone Air Fryer.
6. Choose the Air Fry mode for Zone 1 and set the temperature to 390 degrees F and the time to 15 minutes.
7. Select the "MATCH" button to copy the settings for Zone 2.
8. Initiate cooking by pressing the START/STOP button.
9. Flip the pork chops when cooked halfway through, then resume cooking.
10. Serve warm.

Nutrition:
- (Per serving) Calories 396 | Fat 23.2g |Sodium 622mg | Carbs 0.7g | Fiber 0g | Sugar 0g | Protein 45.6g

Fish And Seafood Recipes

Dukkah-crusted Halibut

Servings: 2
Cooking Time: 17 Minutes
Ingredients:
- Dukkah:
- 1 tablespoon coriander seeds
- 1 tablespoon sesame seeds
- 1½ teaspoons cumin seeds
- 50 g roasted mixed nuts
- ¼ teaspoon kosher or coarse sea salt
- ¼ teaspoon black pepper
- Fish:
- 2 halibut fillets, 140 g each
- 2 tablespoons mayonnaise
- Vegetable oil spray
- Lemon wedges, for serving

Directions:
1. For the Dukkah: Combine the coriander, sesame seeds, and cumin in a small baking pan. Place the pan in the zone 1 air fryer basket. Set the air fryer to 205°C for 5 minutes. Toward the end of the cooking time, you will hear the seeds popping. Transfer to a plate and let cool for 5 minutes. 2. Transfer the toasted seeds to a food processor or spice grinder and add the mixed nuts. Pulse until coarsely chopped. Add the salt and pepper and stir well.
2. 3. For the fish: Spread each fillet with 1 tablespoon of the mayonnaise. Press a heaping tablespoon of the Dukkah into the mayonnaise on each fillet, pressing lightly to adhere. 4. Spray the zone 2 air fryer basket with vegetable oil spray. Place the fish in the zone 2 basket. Cook for 12 minutes, or until the fish flakes easily with a fork. 5. Serve the fish with lemon wedges.

Orange-mustard Glazed Salmon

Servings: 2
Cooking Time: 10 Minutes
Ingredients:
- 1 tablespoon orange marmalade
- ¼ teaspoon grated orange zest plus 1 tablespoon juice
- 2 teaspoons whole-grain mustard
- 2 (230 g) skin-on salmon fillets, 1½ inches thick
- Salt and pepper, to taste
- Vegetable oil spray

Directions:
1. Preheat the zone 1 air fryer drawer to 204°C.
2. Make foil sling for air fryer drawer by folding 1 long sheet of aluminum foil so it is 4 inches wide. Lay sheet of foil widthwise across drawer, pressing foil into and up sides of drawer. Fold excess foil as needed so that edges of foil are flush with top of drawer. Lightly spray foil and drawer with vegetable oil spray.
3. Combine marmalade, orange zest and juice, and mustard in bowl. Pat salmon dry with paper towels and season with salt and pepper. Brush tops and sides of fillets evenly with glaze. Arrange fillets skin side down on sling in prepared drawer, spaced evenly apart. Air fry salmon until center is still translucent when checked with the tip of a paring knife and registers 52°C , 10 to 14 minutes, using sling to rotate fillets halfway through cooking.
4. Using the sling, carefully remove salmon from air fryer. Slide fish spatula along underside of fillets and transfer to individual serving plates, leaving skin behind. Serve.

Brown Sugar Garlic Salmon

Servings: 4
Cooking Time: 10 Minutes
Ingredients:
- 455g salmon
- Salt and black pepper, to taste
- 2 tablespoons brown sugar
- 1 teaspoon chili powder
- ½ teaspoon paprika
- 1 teaspoon Italian seasoning
- 1 teaspoon garlic powder

Directions:
1. Mix brown sugar with garlic powder, Italian seasoning, paprika, and chili powder in a bowl.
2. Rub this mixture over the salmon along with black pepper and salt.
3. Place the salmon in the air fryer baskets.
4. Return the air fryer basket 1 to Zone 1, and basket 2 to Zone 2 of the Ninja Foodi 2-Basket Air Fryer.
5. Choose the "Air Fry" mode for Zone 1 and set the temperature to 400 degrees F and 10 minutes of cooking time.
6. Select the "MATCH COOK" option to copy the settings for Zone 2.
7. Initiate cooking by pressing the START/PAUSE BUTTON.
8. Flip the salmon once cooked halfway through.
9. Serve warm.

Nutrition:
- (Per serving) Calories 275 | Fat 1.4g |Sodium 582mg | Carbs 31.5g | Fiber 1.1g | Sugar 0.1g | Protein 29.8g

Tilapia Sandwiches With Tartar Sauce

Servings: 4
Cooking Time: 17 Minutes
Ingredients:

- 160 g mayonnaise
- 2 tablespoons dried minced onion
- 1 dill pickle spear, finely chopped
- 2 teaspoons pickle juice
- ¼ teaspoon salt
- ⅛ teaspoon freshly ground black pepper
- 40 g plain flour
- 1 egg, lightly beaten
- 200 g panko bread crumbs
- 2 teaspoons lemon pepper
- 4 (170 g) tilapia fillets
- Olive oil spray
- 4 soft sub rolls
- 4 lettuce leaves

Directions:

1. To make the tartar sauce, in a small bowl, whisk the mayonnaise, dried onion, pickle, pickle juice, salt, and pepper until blended. Refrigerate while you make the fish.
2. Scoop the flour onto a plate; set aside.
3. Put the beaten egg in a medium shallow bowl.
4. On another plate, stir together the panko and lemon pepper.
5. Preheat the air fryer to 205ºC.
6. Dredge the tilapia fillets in the flour, in the egg, and press into the panko mixture to coat.
7. Once the unit is preheated, spray the zone 1 basket with olive oil and place a baking paper liner into the basket. Place the prepared fillets on the liner in a single layer. Lightly spray the fillets with olive oil.
8. cook for 8 minutes, remove the basket, carefully flip the fillets, and spray them with more olive oil. Reinsert the basket to resume cooking.
9. When the cooking is complete, the fillets should be golden and crispy and a food thermometer should register 65ºC. Place each cooked fillet in a sub roll, top with a little bit of tartar sauce and lettuce, and serve.

Salmon With Coconut

Servings:2
Cooking Time:15
Ingredients:

- Oil spray, for greasing
- 2 salmon fillets, 6ounces each
- Salt and ground black pepper, to taste
- 1 tablespoon butter, for frying
- 1 tablespoon red curry paste
- 1 cup of coconut cream
- 2 tablespoons fresh cilantro, chopped
- 1 cup of cauliflower florets
- ½ cup Parmesan cheese, hard

Directions:

1. Take a bowl and mix salt, black pepper, butter, red curry paste, coconut cream in a bowl and marinate the salmon in it.
2. Oil sprays the cauliflower florets and then seasons it with salt and freshly ground black pepper.
3. Put the florets in the zone 1 basket.
4. Layer the parchment paper over the zone 2 baskets, and then place the salmon fillet on it.
5. Set the zone 2 basket to AIR FRY mod at 15 minutes for4 00 degrees F
6. Hit the smart finish button to finish it at the same time.
7. Once the time for cooking is over, serve the salmon with cauliflower floret with Parmesan cheese drizzle on top.

Nutrition:

- (Per serving) Calories 774 | Fat 59g| Sodium 1223mg | Carbs 12.2g | Fiber 3.9g | Sugar5.9 g | Protein53.5 g

Fried Prawns

Servings: 4
Cooking Time: 5 Minutes
Ingredients:

- 70 g self-raising flour
- 1 teaspoon paprika
- 1 teaspoon salt
- ½ teaspoon freshly ground black pepper
- 1 large egg, beaten
- 120 g finely crushed panko bread crumbs
- 20 frozen large prawns (about 900 g), peeled and deveined
- Cooking spray

Directions:

1. In a shallow bowl, whisk the flour, paprika, salt, and pepper until blended. Add the beaten egg to a second shallow bowl and the bread crumbs to a third.
2. One at a time, dip the prawns into the flour, the egg, and the bread crumbs, coating thoroughly.
3. Preheat the air fryer to 205ºC. Line the two air fryer baskets with baking paper.
4. Place the prawns on the baking paper and spritz with oil.
5. Air fry for 2 minutes. Shake the baskets, spritz the prawns with oil, and air fry for 3 minutes more until lightly browned and crispy. Serve hot.

Blackened Mahimahi With Honey-roasted Carrots

Servings:4
Cooking Time: 30 Minutes
Ingredients:
- FOR THE MAHIMAHI
- 4 mahimahi fillets (4 ounces each)
- 1 tablespoon olive oil
- 1 tablespoon blackening seasoning
- Lemon wedges, for serving
- FOR THE CARROTS
- 1 pound carrots, peeled and cut into ½-inch rounds
- 2 teaspoons vegetable oil
- ½ teaspoon kosher salt
- ¼ teaspoon freshly ground black pepper
- 1 tablespoon salted butter, cut into small pieces
- 1 tablespoon honey
- 2 tablespoons chopped fresh parsley

Directions:
1. To prep the mahimahi: Brush both sides of the fish with the oil and sprinkle with the blackening seasoning.
2. To prep the carrots: In a large bowl, combine the carrots, oil, salt, and black pepper. Stir well to coat the carrots with the oil.
3. To cook the mahimahi and carrots: Install a crisper plate in each of the two baskets. Place the fish in the Zone 1 basket and insert the basket in the unit. Place the carrots in the Zone 2 basket and insert the basket in the unit.
4. Select Zone 1, select AIR FRY, set the temperature to 380°F, and set the timer to 14 minutes.
5. Select Zone 2, select ROAST, set the temperature to 400°F, and set the timer to 30 minutes. Select SMART FINISH.
6. Press START/PAUSE to begin cooking.
7. When the Zone 2 timer reads 15 minutes, press START/PAUSE. Remove the basket and scatter the butter over the carrots, then drizzle them with the honey. Reinsert the basket and press START/PAUSE to resume cooking.
8. When cooking is complete, the fish should be cooked through and the carrots soft.
9. Stir the parsley into the carrots. Serve the fish with lemon wedges.

Nutrition:
- (Per serving) Calories: 235; Total fat: 9.5g; Saturated fat: 3g; Carbohydrates: 15g; Fiber: 3g; Protein: 22g; Sodium: 672mg

Crusted Tilapia

Servings: 4
Cooking Time: 17 Minutes
Ingredients:
- ¾ cup breadcrumbs
- 1 packet dry ranch-style dressing
- 2 ½ tablespoons vegetable oil
- 2 eggs beaten
- 4 tilapia fillets
- Herbs and chilies to garnish

Directions:
1. Thoroughly mix ranch dressing with panko in a bowl.
2. Whisk eggs in a shallow bowl.
3. Dip each fish fillet in the egg, then coat evenly with the panko mixture.
4. Set two coated fillets in each of the crisper plate.
5. Return the crisper plates to the Ninja Foodi Dual Zone Air Fryer.
6. Choose the Air Fry mode for Zone 1 and set the temperature to 390 degrees F and the time to 17 minutes|
7. Select the "MATCH" button to copy the settings for Zone 2.
8. Initiate cooking by pressing the START/STOP button.
9. Serve warm with herbs and chilies.

Fried Lobster Tails

Servings: 4
Cooking Time: 18 Minutes
Ingredients:
- 4 (4-oz) lobster tails
- 8 tablespoons butter, melted
- 2 teaspoons lemon zest
- 2 garlic cloves, grated
- Salt and black pepper, ground to taste
- 2 teaspoons fresh parsley, chopped
- 4 wedges lemon

Directions:
1. Spread the lobster tails into Butterfly, slit the top to expose the lobster meat while keeping the tail intact.
2. Place two lobster tails in each of the crisper plate with their lobster meat facing up.
3. Mix melted butter with lemon zest and garlic in a bowl.
4. Brush the butter mixture on top of the lobster tails.
5. And drizzle salt and black pepper on top.
6. Return the crisper plate to the Ninja Foodi Dual Zone Air Fryer.
7. Choose the Air Fry mode for Zone 1 and set the temperature to 390 degrees F and the time to 18 minutes|
8. Select the "MATCH" button to copy the settings for Zone 2.
9. Initiate cooking by pressing the START/STOP button.
10. Garnish with parsley and lemon wedges.
11. Serve warm.

Bacon-wrapped Shrimp

Servings: 8
Cooking Time: 10 Minutes

Ingredients:

- 24 jumbo raw shrimp, deveined with tail on, fresh or thawed from frozen
- 8 slices bacon, cut into thirds
- 1 tablespoon olive oil
- 1 teaspoon paprika
- 1–2 cloves minced garlic
- 1 tablespoon finely chopped fresh parsley

Directions:

1. Combine the olive oil, paprika, garlic, and parsley in a small bowl.
2. If necessary, peel the raw shrimp, leaving the tails on.
3. Add the shrimp to the oil mixture. Toss to coat well.
4. Wrap a piece of bacon around the middle of each shrimp and place seam-side down on a small baking dish.
5. Refrigerate for 30 minutes before cooking.
6. Place a crisper plate in each drawer. Put the shrimp in a single layer in each drawer. Insert the drawers into the unit.
7. Select zone 1, then AIR FRY, then set the temperature to 360 degrees F/ 180 degrees C with a 10-minute timer. To match zone 2 settings to zone 1, choose MATCH. To begin, select START/STOP.
8. Remove the shrimp from the drawers when the cooking time is over.

Nutrition:

- (Per serving) Calories 479 | Fat 15.7g | Sodium 949mg | Carbs 0.6g | Fiber 0.1g | Sugar 0g | Protein 76.1g

Herb Lemon Mussels

Servings: 6
Cooking Time: 10 Minutes

Ingredients:

- 1kg mussels, steamed & half shell
- 1 tbsp thyme, chopped
- 1 tbsp parsley, chopped
- 1 tsp dried parsley
- 1 tsp garlic, minced
- 60ml olive oil
- 45ml lemon juice
- Pepper
- Salt

Directions:

1. In a bowl, mix mussels with the remaining ingredients.
2. Insert a crisper plate in the Ninja Foodi air fryer baskets.
3. Add the mussels to both baskets.
4. Select zone 1 then select "air fry" mode and set the temperature to 360 degrees F for 10 minutes. Press "match" to match zone 2 settings to zone 1. Press "start/stop" to begin.

Nutrition:

- (Per serving) Calories 206 | Fat 11.9g |Sodium 462mg | Carbs 6.3g | Fiber 0.3g | Sugar 0.2g | Protein 18.2g

Scallops

Servings: 4
Cooking Time: 5 Minutes

Ingredients:

- ½ cup Italian breadcrumbs
- ½ teaspoon garlic powder
- ¼ teaspoon salt
- ½ teaspoon black pepper
- 2 tablespoons butter, melted
- 1 pound sea scallops, rinsed and pat dry

Directions:

1. Combine the breadcrumbs, garlic powder, salt, and pepper in a small bowl. Pour the melted butter into another shallow bowl.
2. Dredge each scallop in the melted butter, then roll it in the breadcrumb mixture until well covered.
3. Place a crisper plate in each drawer. Put the scallops in a single layer in each drawer. Insert the drawers into the unit.
4. Select zone 1, then AIR FRY, then set the temperature to 360 degrees F/ 180 degrees C with a 5-minute timer. To match zone 2 settings to zone 1, choose MATCH. To begin, select START/STOP.
5. Press START/STOP to pause the unit when the timer reaches 3 minutes. Remove the drawers. Use tongs to carefully flip the scallops over. To resume cooking, re-insert the drawers into the unit and press START/STOP.
6. Remove the scallops from the drawers after the timer has finished.

Nutrition:

- (Per serving) Calories 81 | Fat 6g | Sodium 145mg | Carbs 3g | Fiber 4g | Sugar 1g | Protein 3g

Delicious Haddock

Servings: 4
Cooking Time: 10 Minutes
Ingredients:

- 1 egg
- 455g haddock fillets
- 1 tsp seafood seasoning
- 136g flour
- 15ml olive oil
- 119g breadcrumbs
- Pepper
- Salt

Directions:

1. In a shallow dish, whisk egg. Add flour to a plate.
2. In a separate shallow dish, mix breadcrumbs, pepper, seafood seasoning, and salt.
3. Brush fish fillets with oil.
4. Coat each fish fillet with flour, then dip in egg and finally coat with breadcrumbs.
5. Insert a crisper plate in the Ninja Foodi air fryer baskets.
6. Place coated fish fillets in both baskets.
7. Select zone 1, then select "air fry" mode and set the temperature to 360 degrees F for 10 minutes. Press "match" to match zone 2 settings to zone 1. Press "start/stop" to begin.

Nutrition:

- (Per serving) Calories 393 | Fat 7.4g |Sodium 351mg | Carbs 43.4g | Fiber 2.1g | Sugar 1.8g | Protein 35.7g

Honey Pecan Shrimp

Servings: 4
Cooking Time: 10 Minutes
Ingredients:

- ¼ cup cornstarch
- ¾ teaspoon salt
- ¼ teaspoon black pepper
- 2 egg whites
- ⅔ cup pecans, chopped
- 455g shrimp, peeled, and deveined
- ¼ cup honey
- 2 tablespoons mayonnaise

Directions:

1. Mix cornstarch with ½ teaspoon black pepper, and ½ teaspoon salt in a bowl.
2. Mix pecans and ¼ teaspoon salt in another bowl.
3. Beat egg whites in another bowl.
4. Dredge the shrimp through the cornstarch mixture then dip in the egg whites.
5. Coat the shrimp with pecans mixture.
6. Divide the coated shrimp in the air fryer baskets.

7. Return the air fryer basket 1 to Zone 1, and basket 2 to Zone 2 of the Ninja Foodi 2-Basket Air Fryer.
8. Choose the "Air Fry" mode for Zone 1 at 330 degrees F and 10 minutes of cooking time.
9. Select the "MATCH COOK" option to copy the settings for Zone 2.
10. Initiate cooking by pressing the START/PAUSE BUTTON.
11. Flip the shrimps once cooked halfway through.
12. Serve.

Nutrition:

- (Per serving) Calories 155 | Fat 4.2g |Sodium 963mg | Carbs 21.5g | Fiber 0.8g | Sugar 5.7g | Protein 8.1g

Codfish With Herb Vinaigrette

Servings:2
Cooking Time:16
Ingredients:

- Vinaigrette Ingredients:
- 1/2 cup parsley leaves
- 1 cup basil leaves
- ½ cup mint leaves
- 2 tablespoons thyme leaves
- 1/4 teaspoon red pepper flakes
- 2 cloves of garlic
- 4 tablespoons of red wine vinegar
- ¼ cup of olive oil
- Salt, to taste
- Other Ingredients:
- 1.5 pounds fish fillets, cod fish
- 2 tablespoons olive oil
- Salt and black pepper, to taste
- 1 teaspoon of paprika
- 1teasbpoon of Italian seasoning

Directions:

1. Blend the entire vinaigrette ingredient in a high-speed blender and pulse into a smooth paste.
2. Set aside for drizzling overcooked fish.
3. Rub the fillets with salt, black pepper, paprika, Italian seasoning, and olive oil.
4. Divide it between two baskets of the air fryer.
5. Set the zone 1 to 16 minutes at 390 degrees F, at AIR FRY mode.
6. Press the MATCH button for the second basket.
7. Once done, serve the fillets with the drizzle of blended vinaigrette

Nutrition:

- (Per serving) Calories 1219| Fat 81.8g| Sodium 1906mg | Carbs64.4 g | Fiber5.5 g | Sugar 0.4g | Protein 52.1g

Shrimp Skewers

Servings: 4
Cooking Time: 10minutes
Ingredients:

- 453g shrimp
- 15ml lemon juice
- 15ml olive oil
- 1 tbsp old bay seasoning
- 1 tsp garlic, minced

Directions:

1. Toss shrimp with old bay seasoning, garlic, lemon juice, and olive oil in a bowl.
2. Thread shrimp onto the soaked skewers.
3. Insert a crisper plate in the Ninja Foodi air fryer baskets.
4. Place the shrimp skewers in both baskets.
5. Select zone 1, then select "air fry" mode and set the temperature to 390 degrees F for 10 minutes. Press "match" to match zone 2 settings to zone 1. Press "start/stop" to begin.

Nutrition:

- (Per serving) Calories 167 | Fat 5.5g |Sodium 758mg | Carbs 2g | Fiber 0g | Sugar 0.1g | Protein 25.9g

Parmesan Mackerel With Coriander And Garlic Butter Prawns Scampi

Servings: 6
Cooking Time: 8 Minutes
Ingredients:

- Parmesan Mackerel with Coriander:
- 340 g mackerel fillet
- 60 g Parmesan, grated
- 1 teaspoon ground coriander
- 1 tablespoon olive oil
- Garlic Butter Prawns Scampi:
- Sauce:
- 60 g unsalted butter
- 2 tablespoons fish stock or chicken broth
- 2 cloves garlic, minced
- 2 tablespoons chopped fresh basil leaves
- 1 tablespoon lemon juice
- 1 tablespoon chopped fresh parsley, plus more for garnish
- 1 teaspoon red pepper flakes
- Prawns:
- 455 g large prawns, peeled and deveined, tails removed
- Fresh basil sprigs, for garnish

Directions:

1. Make the Parmesan Mackerel with Coriander :
2. Sprinkle the mackerel fillet with olive oil and put it in the zone 1 air fryer drawer.
3. Top the fish with ground coriander and Parmesan.
4. Cook the fish at 200ºC for 7 minutes.
5. Make the Garlic Butter Prawns Scampi :
6. Preheat the zone 2 air fryer drawer to 176ºC.
7. Put all the ingredients for the sauce in a baking pan and stir to incorporate.
8. Transfer the baking pan to the zone 2 air fryer drawer and air fry for 3 minutes, or until the sauce is heated through.
9. Once done, add the prawns to the baking pan, flipping to coat in the sauce.
10. Return to the air fryer and cook for another 5 minutes, or until the prawns are pink and opaque. Stir the prawns twice during cooking.
11. Serve garnished with the parsley and basil sprigs.

Smoked Salmon

Servings:4
Cooking Time:12
Ingredients:

- 2 pounds of salmon fillets, smoked
- 6 ounces cream cheese
- 4 tablespoons mayonnaise
- 2 teaspoons of chives, fresh
- 1 teaspoon of lemon zest
- Salt and freshly ground black pepper, to taste
- 2 tablespoons of butter

Directions:

1. Cut the salmon into very small and uniform bite-size pieces.
2. Mix cream cheese, chives, mayonnaise, black pepper, and lemon zest, in a small mixing bowl.
3. Let it sit aside for further use.
4. Coat the salmon pieces with salt and butter.
5. Divide the bite-size pieces into both zones of the air fryer.
6. Set it on AIRFRY mode at 400 degrees F for 12 minutes.
7. Select MATCH for zone 2 basket.
8. Hit start, so the cooking start.
9. Once the salmon is done, top it with a bowl creamy mixture and serve.
10. Enjoy hot.

Nutrition:

- (Per serving) Calories 557| Fat 15.7 g| Sodium 371mg | Carbs 4.8 g | Fiber 0g | Sugar 1.1g | Protein 48 g

Herb Tuna Patties

Servings: 10
Cooking Time: 12 Minutes
Ingredients:

- 2 eggs
- 425g can tuna, drained & diced
- ½ tsp garlic powder
- ½ small onion, minced
- 1 celery stalk, chopped
- 42g parmesan cheese, grated
- 50g breadcrumbs
- ½ tsp dried oregano
- ½ tsp dried basil
- ½ tsp dried thyme
- 15ml lemon juice
- 1 lemon zest
- Pepper
- Salt

Directions:

1. In a bowl, mix tuna with remaining ingredients until well combined.
2. Insert a crisper plate in the Ninja Foodi air fryer baskets.
3. Make patties from the tuna mixture and place them in both baskets.
4. Select zone 1, then select "bake" mode and set the temperature to 380 degrees F for 12 minutes. Press "match" to match zone 2 settings to zone 1. Press "start/stop" to begin. Turn halfway through.

Nutrition:

- (Per serving) Calories 86 | Fat 1.5g |Sodium 90mg | Carbs 4.5g | Fiber 0.4g | Sugar 0.6g | Protein 12.8g

Roasted Halibut Steaks With Parsley

Servings: 4
Cooking Time: 10 Minutes
Ingredients:

- 455 g halibut steaks
- 60 ml vegetable oil
- 2½ tablespoons Worcester sauce
- 2 tablespoons honey
- 2 tablespoons vermouth or white wine vinegar
- 1 tablespoon freshly squeezed lemon juice
- 1 tablespoon fresh parsley leaves, coarsely chopped
- Salt and pepper, to taste
- 1 teaspoon dried basil

Directions:

1. Preheat the air fryer to 200°C.
2. Put all the ingredients in a large mixing dish and gently stir until the fish is coated evenly.
3. Transfer the fish to the zone 1 air fryer drawer and roast for 10 minutes, flipping the fish halfway through, or until the fish reaches an internal temperature of at least 64°C on a meat thermometer.
4. Let the fish cool for 5 minutes and serve.

Chili Lime Tilapia

Servings: 4
Cooking Time: 10 Minutes
Ingredients:

- 340g tilapia fillets
- 2 teaspoons chili powder
- 1 teaspoon cumin
- 1 teaspoon garlic powder
- ½ teaspoon oregano
- ½ teaspoon sea salt
- ¼ teaspoon black pepper
- Lime zest from 1 lime
- Juice of ½ lime

Directions:

1. Mix chili powder and other spices with lime juice and zest in a bowl.
2. Rub this spice mixture over the tilapia fillets.
3. Place two fillets in each air basket.
4. Return the air fryer basket to the Ninja Foodi 2 Baskets Air Fryer.
5. Choose the "Air Fry" mode for Zone 1 at 400 degrees F and 10 minutes of cooking time.
6. Select the "MATCH COOK" option to copy the settings for Zone 2.
7. Initiate cooking by pressing the START/PAUSE BUTTON.
8. Flip the tilapia fillets once cooked halfway through.
9. Serve warm.

Nutrition:

- (Per serving) Calories 275 | Fat 1.4g |Sodium 582mg | Carbs 31.5g | Fiber 1.1g | Sugar 0.1g | Protein 29.8g

Snapper With Fruit

Servings: 4
Cooking Time: 9 To 13 Minutes
Ingredients:
- 4 red snapper fillets, 100 g each
- 2 teaspoons olive oil
- 3 nectarines, halved and pitted
- 3 plums, halved and pitted
- 150 g red grapes
- 1 tablespoon freshly squeezed lemon juice
- 1 tablespoon honey
- ½ teaspoon dried thyme

Directions:
1. Put the red snapper in the two air fryer baskets and drizzle with the olive oil. Air fry at 200ºC for 4 minutes.
2. Remove the baskets and add the nectarines and plums. Scatter the grapes over all.
3. Drizzle with the lemon juice and honey and sprinkle with the thyme.
4. Return the baskets to the air fryer and air fry for 5 to 9 minutes more, or until the fish flakes when tested with a fork and the fruit is tender. Serve immediately.

Scallops And Spinach With Cream Sauce And Confetti Salmon Burgers

Servings: 6
Cooking Time: 12 Minutes
Ingredients:
- Scallops and Spinach with Cream Sauce:
- Vegetable oil spray
- 280 g frozen spinach, thawed and drained
- 8 jumbo sea scallops
- Kosher or coarse sea salt, and black pepper, to taste
- 180 ml heavy cream
- 1 tablespoon tomato paste
- 1 tablespoon chopped fresh basil
- 1 teaspoon minced garlic
- Confetti Salmon Burgers:
- 400 g cooked fresh or canned salmon, flaked with a fork
- 40 g minced spring onions, white and light green parts only
- 40 g minced red bell pepper
- 40 g minced celery
- 2 small lemons
- 1 teaspoon crab boil seasoning such as Old Bay
- ½ teaspoon kosher or coarse sea salt
- ½ teaspoon black pepper
- 1 egg, beaten
- 30 g fresh bread crumbs
- Vegetable oil, for spraying

Directions:
1. Make the Scallops and Spinach with Cream Sauce :
2. Spray a baking pan with vegetable oil spray. Spread the thawed spinach in an even layer in the bottom of the pan.
3. Spray both sides of the scallops with vegetable oil spray. Season lightly with salt and pepper. Arrange the scallops on top of the spinach.
4. In a small bowl, whisk together the cream, tomato paste, basil, garlic, ½ teaspoon salt, and ½ teaspoon pepper. Pour the sauce over the scallops and spinach.
5. Place the pan in the zone 1 air fryer drawer. Set the temperature to 176ºC for 10 minutes. Use a meat thermometer to ensure the scallops have an internal temperature of 56ºC.
6. Make the Confetti Salmon Burgers :
7. In a large bowl, combine the salmon, vegetables, the zest and juice of 1 of the lemons, crab boil seasoning, salt, and pepper. Add the egg and bread crumbs and stir to combine. Form the mixture into 4 patties weighing approximately 140 g each. Chill until firm, about 15 minutes.
8. Preheat the 2 air fryer drawer to 204ºC.
9. Spray the salmon patties with oil on all sides and spray the zone 2 air fryer drawer to prevent sticking. Air fry for 12 minutes, flipping halfway through, until the burgers are browned and cooked through. Cut the remaining lemon into 4 wedges and serve with the burgers.

Sweet & Spicy Fish Fillets

Servings: 4
Cooking Time: 8 Minutes
Ingredients:
- 4 salmon fillets
- 1 tsp smoked paprika
- 1 tsp chilli powder
- ½ tsp red pepper flakes, crushed
- ½ tsp garlic powder
- 85g honey
- Pepper
- Salt

Directions:
1. In a small bowl, mix honey, garlic powder, chilli powder, paprika, red pepper flakes, pepper, and salt.
2. Brush fish fillets with honey mixture.
3. Insert a crisper plate in the Ninja Foodi air fryer baskets.
4. Place fish fillets in both baskets.
5. Select zone 1, then select "air fry" mode and set the temperature to 390 degrees F for 8 minutes. Press "match" and then"start/stop" to begin.

Nutrition:
- (Per serving) Calories 305 | Fat 11.2g |Sodium 125mg | Carbs 18.4g | Fiber 0.6g | Sugar 17.5g | Protein 34.8g

Parmesan-crusted Fish Sticks With Baked Macaroni And Cheese

Servings:4
Cooking Time: 25 Minutes
Ingredients:

- FOR THE FISH STICKS
- 1 pound cod or haddock fillets
- ½ cup all-purpose flour
- 2 large eggs
- ¼ teaspoon kosher salt
- ¼ teaspoon freshly ground black pepper
- ¾ cup panko bread crumbs
- ¼ cup grated Parmesan cheese
- Nonstick cooking spray
- FOR THE MACARONI AND CHEESE
- 1½ cups elbow macaroni
- 1 cup whole milk
- ½ cup heavy (whipping) cream
- 8 ounces shredded Colby-Jack cheese
- 4 ounces cream cheese, at room temperature
- 1 teaspoon Dijon mustard
- ½ teaspoon kosher salt
- ½ teaspoon freshly ground black pepper

Directions:

1. To prep the fish sticks: Cut the fish into sticks about 3 inches long and ¾ inch wide.
2. Set up a breading station with three small shallow bowls. Place the flour in the first bowl. In the second bowl, whisk the eggs and season with the salt and black pepper. Combine the panko and Parmesan in the third bowl.
3. Bread the fish sticks in this order: First, dip them into the flour, coating all sides. Then, dip into the beaten egg. Finally, coat them in the panko mixture, gently pressing the bread crumbs into the fish. Spritz each fish stick all over with cooking spray.
4. To prep the macaroni and cheese: Place the macaroni in the Zone 2 basket. Add the milk, cream, Colby-Jack, cream cheese, mustard, salt, and black pepper. Stir well to combine, ensuring the pasta is completely submerged in the liquid.
5. To cook the fish sticks and macaroni and cheese: Install a crisper plate in the Zone 1 basket. Arrange the fish sticks in a single layer in the basket (use a rack or cook in batches if necessary) and insert the basket in the unit. Insert the Zone 2 basket in the unit.
6. Select Zone 1, select AIR FRY, set the temperature to 390°F, and set the timer to 18 minutes.
7. Select Zone 2, select BAKE, set the temperature to 360°F, and set the timer to 25 minutes. Select SMART FINISH.
8. Press START/PAUSE to begin cooking.
9. When the Zone 1 timer reads 3 minutes, press START/PAUSE. Remove the basket and use silicone-tipped tongs to gently flip over the fish sticks. Reinsert the basket and press START/PAUSE to resume cooking.
10. When cooking is complete, the fish sticks should be crisp and the macaroni tender.
11. Stir the macaroni and cheese and let stand for 5 minutes before serving. The sauce will thicken as it cools.

Nutrition:

- (Per serving) Calories: 903; Total fat: 51g; Saturated fat: 25g; Carbohydrates: 60g; Fiber: 2.5g; Protein: 48g; Sodium: 844mg

Cajun Scallops

Servings: 6
Cooking Time: 6 Minutes
Ingredients:

- 6 sea scallops
- Cooking spray
- Salt to taste
- Cajun seasoning

Directions:

1. Season the scallops with Cajun seasoning and salt.
2. Place them in one air fryer basket and spray them with cooking oil.
3. Return the air fryer basket 1 to Zone 1 of the Ninja Foodi 2-Basket Air Fryer.
4. Choose the "Air Fry" mode for Zone 1 and set the temperature to 400 degrees F and 6 minutes of cooking time.
5. Initiate cooking by pressing the START/PAUSE BUTTON.
6. Flip the scallops once cooked halfway through.
7. Serve warm.

Nutrition:

- (Per serving) Calories 266 | Fat 6.3g |Sodium 193mg | Carbs 39.1g | Fiber 7.2g | Sugar 5.2g | Protein 14.8g

Coconut Cream Mackerel

Servings: 4
Cooking Time: 6 Minutes
Ingredients:

- 900 g mackerel fillet
- 240 ml coconut cream
- 1 teaspoon ground coriander
- 1 teaspoon cumin seeds
- 1 garlic clove, peeled, chopped

Directions:

1. Chop the mackerel roughly and sprinkle it with coconut cream, ground coriander, cumin seeds, and garlic.
2. Then put the fish in the two air fryer drawers and cook at 204ºC for 6 minutes.

Prawns Curry And Paprika Crab Burgers

Servings: 7
Cooking Time: 14 Minutes
Ingredients:

- Prawns Curry:
- 180 ml unsweetened full-fat coconut milk
- 10 g finely chopped yellow onion
- 2 teaspoons garam masala
- 1 tablespoon minced fresh ginger
- 1 tablespoon minced garlic
- 1 teaspoon ground turmeric
- 1 teaspoon salt
- ¼ to ½ teaspoon cayenne pepper
- 455 g raw prawns (21 to 25 count), peeled and deveined
- 2 teaspoons chopped fresh coriander
- Paprika Crab Burgers:
- 2 eggs, beaten
- 1 shallot, chopped
- 2 garlic cloves, crushed
- 1 tablespoon olive oil
- 1 teaspoon yellow mustard
- 1 teaspoon fresh coriander, chopped
- 280 g crab meat
- 1 teaspoon smoked paprika
- ½ teaspoon ground black pepper
- Sea salt, to taste
- 70 g Parmesan cheese

Directions:

1. Make the Prawns Curry :

2. In a large bowl, stir together the coconut milk, onion, garam masala, ginger, garlic, turmeric, salt and cayenne, until well blended.
3. Add the prawns and toss until coated with sauce on all sides. Marinate at room temperature for 30 minutes.
4. Transfer the prawns and marinade to a baking pan. Place the pan in the zone 1 air fryer basket. Set the air fryer to 190ºC for 10 minutes, stirring halfway through the cooking time.
5. Transfer the prawns to a serving bowl or platter. Sprinkle with the cilantro and serve.
6. Make the Paprika Crab Burgers :
7. In a mixing bowl, thoroughly combine the eggs, shallot, garlic, olive oil, mustard, coriander, crab meat, paprika, black pepper, and salt. Mix until well combined.
8. Shape the mixture into 6 patties. Roll the crab patties over grated Parmesan cheese, coating well on all sides. Place in your refrigerator for 2 hours.
9. Spritz the crab patties with cooking oil on both sides. Cook in the preheated zone 2 air fryer basket at 180ºC for 14 minutes. Serve on dinner rolls if desired. Bon appétit!

Lemon Pepper Fish Fillets

Servings: 4
Cooking Time: 10 Minutes
Ingredients:

- 4 tilapia fillets
- 30ml olive oil
- 2 tbsp lemon zest
- ⅛ tsp paprika
- 1 tsp garlic, minced
- 1 ½ tsp ground peppercorns
- Pepper
- Salt

Directions:

1. In a small bowl, mix oil, peppercorns, paprika, garlic, lemon zest, pepper, and salt.
2. Brush the fish fillets with oil mixture.
3. Insert a crisper plate in the Ninja Foodi air fryer baskets.
4. Place fish fillets in both baskets.
5. Select zone 1 then select "air fry" mode and set the temperature to 390 degrees F for 10 minutes. Press "match" to match zone 2 settings to zone 1. Press "start/stop" to begin.

Nutrition:

- (Per serving) Calories 203 | Fat 9g |Sodium 99mg | Carbs 0.9g | Fiber 0.2g | Sugar 0.2g | Protein 32.1g

Two-way Salmon

Servings:2
Cooking Time:18
Ingredients:

- 2 salmon fillets, 8 ounces each
- 2 tablespoons of Cajun seasoning
- 2 tablespoons of jerk seasoning
- 1 lemon cut in half
- oil spray, for greasing

Directions:

1. First, drizzle lemon juice over the salmon and wash it with tap water.
2. Rinse and pat dry the fillets with a paper towel.
3. Now rub o fillet with Cajun seasoning and grease it with oil spray.
4. Take the second fillet and rub it with jerk seasoning.
5. Grease the second fillet of salmon with oil spray.
6. now put the salmon fillets in both the baskets.
7. Set the Zone 1 basket to 390 degrees F for 16-18 minutes
8. Select MATCH button for zone 2 basket.
9. hit the start button to start cooking.
10. Once the cooking is done, serve the fish hot with mayonnaise.

Nutrition:

- (Per serving) Calories 238| Fat 11.8g| Sodium 488mg | Carbs 9g | Fiber 0g | Sugar8 g | Protein 35g

Orange-mustard Glazed Salmon And Cucumber And Salmon Salad

Servings: 4
Cooking Time: 10 Minutes
Ingredients:

- Orange-Mustard Glazed Salmon:
- 1 tablespoon orange marmalade
- ¼ teaspoon grated orange zest plus 1 tablespoon juice
- 2 teaspoons whole-grain mustard
- 2 (230 g) skin-on salmon fillets, 1½ inches thick
- Salt and pepper, to taste
- Vegetable oil spray
- Cucumber and Salmon Salad:
- 455 g salmon fillet
- 1½ tablespoons olive oil, divided
- 1 tablespoon sherry vinegar
- 1 tablespoon capers, rinsed and drained
- 1 seedless cucumber, thinly sliced
- ¼ white onion, thinly sliced
- 2 tablespoons chopped fresh parsley
- Salt and freshly ground black pepper, to taste

Directions:

1. Make the Orange-Mustard Glazed Salmon :
2. Preheat the air fryer to 205°C.
3. Make foil sling for air fryer basket by folding 1 long sheet of aluminum foil so it is 4 inches wide. Lay sheet of foil widthwise across zone 1 basket, pressing foil into and up sides of basket. Fold excess foil as needed so that edges of foil are flush with top of basket. Lightly spray foil and basket with vegetable oil spray.
4. Combine marmalade, orange zest and juice, and mustard in bowl. Pat salmon dry with paper towels and season with salt and pepper. Brush tops and sides of fillets evenly with glaze. Arrange fillets skin side down on sling in prepared zone 1 basket, spaced evenly apart. Air fry salmon until center is still translucent when checked with the tip of a paring knife and registers 50°C , 10 to 14 minutes, using sling to rotate fillets halfway through cooking.
5. Using the sling, carefully remove salmon from air fryer. Slide fish spatula along underside of fillets and transfer to individual serving plates, leaving skin behind. Serve.
6. Make the Cucumber and Salmon Salad :
7. Preheat the air fryer to 205°C.
8. Lightly coat the salmon with ½ tablespoon of the olive oil. Place skin-side down in the zone 2 air fryer basket and air fry for 8 to 10 minutes until the fish is opaque and flakes easily with a fork. Transfer the salmon to a plate and let cool to room temperature. Remove the skin and carefully flake the fish into bite-size chunks.
9. In a small bowl, whisk the remaining 1 tablespoon olive oil and the vinegar until thoroughly combined. Add the flaked fish, capers, cucumber, onion, and parsley. Season to taste with salt and freshly ground black pepper. Toss gently to coat. Serve immediately or cover and refrigerate for up to 4 hours.

Stuffed Mushrooms With Crab

Servings: 4
Cooking Time: 18 Minutes
Ingredients:
- 907g baby bella mushrooms
- cooking spray
- 2 teaspoons tony chachere's salt blend
- ¼ red onion, diced
- 2 celery ribs, diced
- 227g lump crab
- ½ cup seasoned bread crumbs
- 1 large egg
- ½ cup parmesan cheese, shredded
- 1 teaspoon oregano
- 1 teaspoon hot sauce

Directions:
1. Mix all the ingredients except the mushrooms in a bowl.
2. Divide the crab filling into the mushroom caps.
3. Place the caps in the air fryer baskets.
4. Return the air fryer basket 1 to Zone 1, and basket 2 to Zone 2 of the Ninja Foodi 2-Basket Air Fryer.
5. Choose the "Air Fry" mode for Zone 1 at 400 degrees F and 18 minutes of cooking time.
6. Select the "MATCH COOK" option to copy the settings for Zone 2.
7. Initiate cooking by pressing the START/PAUSE BUTTON.
8. Serve warm.

Nutrition:
- (Per serving) Calories 399 | Fat 16g |Sodium 537mg | Carbs 28g | Fiber 3g | Sugar 10g | Protein 35g

Fish Fillets With Lemon-dill Sauce

Servings: 4
Cooking Time: 7 Minutes
Ingredients:
- 455 g snapper, grouper, or salmon fillets
- Sea salt and freshly ground black pepper, to taste
- 1 tablespoon avocado oil
- 60 g sour cream
- 60 g mayonnaise
- 2 tablespoons fresh dill, chopped, plus more for garnish
- 1 tablespoon freshly squeezed lemon juice
- ½ teaspoon grated lemon zest

Directions:
1. Pat the fish dry with paper towels and season well with salt and pepper. Brush with the avocado oil. 2. Set the air fryer to 204ºC. Place the fillets in the two air fryer drawers and air fry for 1 minute. 3. Lower the air fryer temperature to 164ºC and continue cooking for 5 minutes. Flip the fish and cook for 1 minute more or until an instant-read thermometer reads 64ºC. 4.

While the fish is cooking, make the sauce by combining the sour cream, mayonnaise, dill, lemon juice, and lemon zest in a medium bowl. Season with salt and pepper and stir until combined. Refrigerate until ready to serve. 5. Serve the fish with the sauce, garnished with the remaining dill.

Roasted Salmon And Parmesan Asparagus

Servings: 4
Cooking Time: 27 Minutes
Ingredients:
- 2 tablespoons Montreal steak seasoning
- 3 tablespoons brown sugar
- 3 uncooked salmon fillets (6 ounces each)
- 2 tablespoons canola oil, divided
- 1-pound asparagus, ends trimmed
- Kosher salt, as desired
- Ground black pepper, as desired
- ¼ cup shredded parmesan cheese, divided

Directions:
1. Combine the steak spice and brown sugar in a small bowl.
2. Brush 1 tablespoon of oil over the salmon fillets, then thoroughly coat with the sugar mixture.
3. Toss the asparagus with the remaining 1 tablespoon of oil, salt, and pepper in a mixing bowl.
4. Place a crisper plate in both drawers. Put the fillets skin-side down in the zone 1 drawer, then place the drawer in the unit. Insert the zone 2 drawer into the device after placing the asparagus in it.
5. Select zone 1, then ROAST, then set the temperature to 390 degrees F/ 200 degrees C with a 17-minute timer. To match the zone 2 settings to zone 1, choose MATCH. To begin cooking, press the START/STOP button.
6. When the zone 2 timer reaches 7 minutes, press START/STOP. Remove the zone 2 drawer from the unit. Flip the asparagus with silicone-tipped tongs. Re-insert the drawer into the unit. Continue cooking by pressing START/STOP.
7. When the zone 2 timer has reached 14 minutes, press START/STOP. Remove the zone 2 drawer from the unit. Sprinkle half the parmesan cheese over the asparagus, and mix lightly. Re-insert the drawer into the unit. Continue cooking by pressing START/STOP.
8. Transfer the fillets and asparagus to a serving plate once they've finished cooking. Serve with the remaining parmesan cheese on top of the asparagus.

Nutrition:
- (Per serving) Calories 293 | Fat 15.8g | Sodium 203mg | Carbs 11.1g | Fiber 2.4g | Sugar 8.7g | Protein 29g

Tuna-stuffed Quinoa Patties

Servings: 4

Cooking Time: 15 Minutes

Ingredients:

- 35 g quinoa
- 4 slices white bread with crusts removed
- 120 ml milk
- 3 eggs
- 280 g tuna packed in olive oil, drained
- 2 to 3 lemons
- Kosher or coarse sea salt, and pepper, to taste
- 150 g panko bread crumbs
- Vegetable oil, for spraying
- Lemon wedges, for serving

Directions:

1. Rinse the quinoa in a fine-mesh sieve until the water runs clear. Bring 1 liter of salted water to a boil. Add the quinoa, cover, and reduce heat to low. Simmer the quinoa covered until most of the water is absorbed and the quinoa is tender, 15 to 20 minutes. Drain and allow to cool to room temperature. Meanwhile, soak the bread in the milk.

2. Mix the drained quinoa with the soaked bread and 2 of the eggs in a large bowl and mix thoroughly. In a medium bowl, combine the tuna, the remaining egg, and the juice and zest of 1 of the lemons. Season well with salt and pepper. Spread the panko on a plate.

3. Scoop up approximately 60 g of the quinoa mixture and flatten into a patty. Place a heaping tablespoon of the tuna mixture in the center of the patty and close the quinoa around the tuna. Flatten the patty slightly to create an oval-shaped croquette. Dredge both sides of the croquette in the panko. Repeat with the remaining quinoa and tuna.

4. Spray the two air fryer baskets with oil to prevent sticking, and preheat the air fryer to 205ºC. Arrange 4 or 5 of the croquettes in each basket, taking care to avoid overcrowding. Spray the tops of the croquettes with oil. Air fry for 8 minutes until the top side is browned and crispy. Carefully turn the croquettes over and spray the second side with oil. Air fry until the second side is browned and crispy, another 7 minutes.

5. Serve the croquetas warm with plenty of lemon wedges for spritzing.

Butter-wine Baked Salmon

Servings: 4

Cooking Time: 10 Minutes

Ingredients:

- 4 tablespoons butter, melted
- 2 cloves garlic, minced
- Sea salt and ground black pepper, to taste
- 60 ml dry white wine or apple cider vinegar
- 1 tablespoon lime juice
- 1 teaspoon smoked paprika
- ½ teaspoon onion powder
- 4 salmon steaks
- Cooking spray

Directions:

1. Place all the ingredients except the salmon and oil in a shallow dish and stir to mix well.

2. Add the salmon steaks, turning to coat well on both sides. Transfer the salmon to the refrigerator to marinate for 30 minutes.

3. Preheat the air fryer to 182ºC.

4. Place the salmon steaks in the two air fryer drawers, discarding any excess marinade. Spray the salmon steaks with cooking spray.

5. Air fry for about 10 minutes, flipping the salmon steaks halfway through, or until cooked to your preferred doneness.

6. Divide the salmon steaks among four plates and serve.

Italian Baked Cod

Servings: 4

Cooking Time: 12 Minutes

Ingredients:

- 4 cod fillets, 170 g each
- 2 tablespoons salted butter, melted
- 1 teaspoon Italian seasoning
- ¼ teaspoon salt
- 120 ml tomato-based pasta sauce

Directions:

1. Place cod into an ungreased round nonstick baking dish. Pour butter over cod and sprinkle with Italian seasoning and salt. Top with pasta sauce.

2. Place dish into the two air fryer drawers. Adjust the temperature to 176ºC and bake for 12 minutes. Fillets will be lightly browned, easily flake, and have an internal temperature of at least 64ºC when done. Serve warm.

Salmon Fritters With Courgette & Cajun And Lemon Pepper Cod

Servings: 6
Cooking Time: 12 Minutes
Ingredients:
- Salmon Fritters with Courgette:
- 2 tablespoons almond flour
- 1 courgette, grated
- 1 egg, beaten
- 170 g salmon fillet, diced
- 1 teaspoon avocado oil
- ½ teaspoon ground black pepper
- Cajun and Lemon Pepper Cod:
- 1 tablespoon Cajun seasoning
- 1 teaspoon salt
- ½ teaspoon lemon pepper
- ½ teaspoon freshly ground black pepper
- 2 cod fillets, 230 g each, cut to fit into the air fryer basket
- Cooking spray
- 2 tablespoons unsalted butter, melted
- 1 lemon, cut into 4 wedges

Directions:
1. Make the Salmon Fritters with Courgette :
2. Mix almond flour with courgette, egg, salmon, and ground black pepper.
3. Then make the fritters from the salmon mixture.
4. Sprinkle the zone 1 air fryer basket with avocado oil and put the fritters inside.
5. Cook the fritters at 190ºC for 6 minutes per side.
6. Make the Cajun and Lemon Pepper Cod :
7. Preheat the air fryer to 180ºC. Spritz the zone 2 air fryer basket with cooking spray.
8. Thoroughly combine the Cajun seasoning, salt, lemon pepper, and black pepper in a small bowl. Rub this mixture all over the cod fillets until completely coated.
9. Put the fillets in the air fryer basket and brush the melted butter over both sides of each fillet.
10. Bake in the preheated air fryer for 12 minutes, flipping the fillets halfway through, or until the fish flakes easily with a fork.
11. Remove the fillets from the basket and serve with fresh lemon wedges.

Panko-crusted Fish Sticks

Servings: 4
Cooking Time: 15 Minutes
Ingredients:
- Tartar Sauce:
- 470 ml mayonnaise
- 2 tablespoons dill pickle relish
- 1 tablespoon dried minced onions
- Fish Sticks:
- Olive or vegetable oil, for spraying
- 455 g tilapia fillets
- 75 g plain flour
- 120 g panko bread crumbs
- 2 tablespoons Creole seasoning
- 2 teaspoons garlic granules
- 1 teaspoon onion powder
- ½ teaspoon salt
- ¼ teaspoon freshly ground black pepper
- 1 large egg

Directions:
1. Make the Tartar Sauce: In a small bowl, whisk together the mayonnaise, pickle relish, and onions. Cover with plastic wrap and refrigerate until ready to serve. You can make this sauce ahead of time; the flavors will intensify as it chills. Make the Fish Sticks: 2. Preheat the air fryer to 175ºC. Line the two air fryer baskets with baking paper and spray lightly with oil. 3. Cut the fillets into equal-size sticks and place them in a zip-top plastic bag. 4. Add the flour to the bag, seal, and shake well until evenly coated. 5. In a shallow bowl, mix together the bread crumbs, Creole seasoning, garlic, onion powder, salt, and black pepper. 6. In a small bowl, whisk the egg. 7. Dip the fish sticks in the egg, then dredge in the bread crumb mixture until completely coated. 8. Place the fish sticks in the two prepared baskets. Do not overcrowd. Spray lightly with oil. 9. Cook for 12 to 15 minutes, or until browned and cooked through. Serve with the tartar sauce.

Shrimp Po'boys With Sweet Potato Fries

Servings:4
Cooking Time: 30 Minutes

Ingredients:

- FOR THE SHRIMP PO'BOYS
- ½ cup buttermilk
- 1 tablespoon Louisiana-style hot sauce
- ¾ cup all-purpose flour
- ½ cup cornmeal
- ½ teaspoon kosher salt
- ½ teaspoon paprika
- ½ teaspoon garlic powder
- ½ teaspoon freshly ground black pepper
- 1 pound peeled medium shrimp, thawed if frozen
- Nonstock cooking spray
- ½ cup store-bought rémoulade sauce
- 4 French bread rolls, halved lengthwise
- ½ cup shredded lettuce
- 1 tomato, sliced
- FOR THE SWEET POTATO FRIES
- 2 medium sweet potatoes
- 2 teaspoons vegetable oil
- ¼ teaspoon garlic powder
- ¼ teaspoon paprika
- ¼ teaspoon kosher salt

Directions:

1. To prep the shrimp: In a medium bowl, combine the buttermilk and hot sauce. In a shallow bowl, combine the flour, cornmeal, salt, paprika, garlic powder, and black pepper.

2. Add the shrimp to the buttermilk and stir to coat. Remove the shrimp, letting the excess buttermilk drip off, then add to the cornmeal mixture to coat.

3. Spritz the breaded shrimp with cooking spray, then let sit for 10 minutes.

4. To prep the sweet potatoes: Peel the sweet potatoes and cut them lengthwise into ¼-inch-thick sticks (like shoestring fries).

5. In a large bowl, combine the sweet potatoes, oil, garlic powder, paprika, and salt. Toss to coat.

6. To cook the shrimp and fries: Install a crisper plate in each of the two baskets. Place the shrimp in the Zone 1 basket and insert the basket in the unit. Place the sweet potatoes in a single layer in the Zone 2 basket and insert the basket in the unit.

7. Select Zone 1, select AIR FRY, set the temperature to 390°F, and set the timer to 13 minutes.

8. Select Zone 2, select AIR FRY, set the temperature to 400°F, and set the timer to 30 minutes. Select SMART FINISH.

9. Press START/PAUSE to begin cooking.

10. When cooking is complete, the shrimp should be golden and cooked through and the sweet potato fries crisp.

11. Spread the rémoulade on the cut sides of the rolls. Divide the lettuce and tomato among the rolls, then top with the fried shrimp. Serve with the sweet potato fries on the side.

Nutrition:

- (Per serving) Calories: 669; Total fat: 22g; Saturated fat: 2g; Carbohydrates: 86g; Fiber: 3.5g; Protein: 33g; Sodium: 1,020mg

Poultry Recipes

Air-fried Turkey Breast With Roasted Green Bean Casserole

Servings: 4
Cooking Time: 50 Minutes
Ingredients:
- FOR THE TURKEY BREAST
- 2 teaspoons unsalted butter, at room temperature
- 1 bone-in split turkey breast (3 pounds), thawed if frozen
- 1 teaspoon poultry seasoning
- ½ teaspoon kosher salt
- ⅓ teaspoon freshly ground black pepper
- FOR THE GREEN BEAN CASSEROLE
- 1 (10.5-ounce) can condensed cream of mushroom soup
- ½ cup whole milk
- 1 cup store-bought crispy fried onions, divided
- ¼ teaspoon kosher salt
- ¼ teaspoon freshly ground black pepper
- 1 pound green beans, trimmed
- ¼ cup panko bread crumbs
- Nonstick cooking spray

Directions:
1. To prep the turkey breast: Spread the butter over the skin side of the turkey. Season with the poultry seasoning, salt, and black pepper.
2. To prep the green bean casserole: In a medium bowl, combine the soup, milk, ½ cup of crispy onions, the salt, and black pepper.
3. To cook the turkey and beans:
4. Install a crisper plate in the Zone 1 basket. Place the turkey skin-side up in the basket and insert the basket in the unit. Place the green beans in the Zone 2 basket and insert the basket in the unit.
5. Select Zone 1, select AIR FRY, set the temperature to 360°F, and set the time to 50 minutes.
6. Select Zone 2, select ROAST, set the temperature to 350°F, and set the time to 40 minutes. Select SMART FINISH.
7. Press START/PAUSE to begin cooking.
8. When the Zone 2 timer reads 30 minutes, press START/PAUSE. Remove the basket and stir the soup mixture into the beans. Scatter the panko and remaining ½ cup of crispy onions over the top, then spritz with cooking spray. Reinsert the basket and press START/PAUSE to resume cooking.
9. When cooking is complete, the turkey will be cooked through and the green bean casserole will be bubbling and golden brown on top.
10. Let the turkey and casserole rest for at least 15 minutes before serving.
11. Per serving
12. Calories: 577| Total fat: 22g| Saturated fat: 6.5g| Carbohydrates: 24g| Fiber: 3.5g| Protein: 68g| Sodium: 1,165mg

Apricot-glazed Turkey Tenderloin

Servings: 4
Cooking Time: 30 Minutes
Ingredients:
- Olive oil
- 80 g sugar-free apricot preserves
- ½ tablespoon spicy brown mustard
- 680 g turkey breast tenderloin
- Salt and freshly ground black pepper, to taste

Directions:
1. Spray the two air fryer drawers lightly with olive oil.
2. In a small bowl, combine the apricot preserves and mustard to make a paste.
3. Season the turkey with salt and pepper. Spread the apricot paste all over the turkey.
4. Place the turkey in the two air fryer drawers and lightly spray with olive oil.
5. Air fry at 190°C for 15 minutes. Flip the turkey over and lightly spray with olive oil. Air fry until the internal temperature reaches at least 80°C, an additional 10 to 15 minutes.
6. Let the turkey rest for 10 minutes before slicing and serving.

Crispy Fried Quail

Servings: 8
Cooking Time: 6 Minutes

Ingredients:

- 8 boneless quail breasts
- 2 tablespoons Sichuan pepper dry rub mix
- ¾ cup rice flour
- ¼ cup all-purpose flour
- 2-3 cups peanut oil
- Garnish
- Sliced jalapenos
- Fresh lime wedges
- Fresh coriander

Directions:

1. Split the quail breasts in half.
2. Mix Sichuan mix with flours in a bowl.
3. Coat the quail breasts with flour mixture and place in the air fryer baskets.
4. Return the air fryer basket 1 to Zone 1, and basket 2 to Zone 2 of the Ninja Foodi 2-Basket Air Fryer.
5. Choose the "Air Fry" mode for Zone 1 at 300 degrees F and 6 minutes of cooking time.
6. Select the "MATCH COOK" option to copy the settings for Zone 2.
7. Initiate cooking by pressing the START/PAUSE BUTTON.
8. Flip the quail breasts once cooked halfway through.
9. Serve warm.

Nutrition:

- (Per serving) Calories 351 | Fat 11g |Sodium 150mg | Carbs 3.3g | Fiber 0.2g | Sugar 1g | Protein 33.2g

Chicken Wings

Servings:3
Cooking Time:20

Ingredients:

- 1 cup chicken batter mix, Louisiana
- 9 Chicken wings
- ½ teaspoon of smoked paprika
- 2 tablespoons of Dijon mustard
- 1 tablespoon of cayenne pepper
- 1 teaspoon of meat tenderizer, powder
- oil spray, for greasing

Directions:

1. Pat dry chicken wings and add mustard, paprika, meat tenderizer, and cayenne pepper.
2. Dredge it in the chicken batter mix.
3. Oil sprays the chicken wings.
4. Grease both baskets of the air fryer.

5. Divide the wings between the two zones of the air fryer.
6. Set zone 1 to AR FRY mode at 400 degrees F for 20 minutes
7. Select MATCH for zone 2.
8. Hit start to begin with the cooking.
9. Once the cooking cycle complete, serve, and enjoy hot.

Nutrition:

- (Per serving) Calories621 | Fat 32.6g| Sodium 2016mg | Carbs 46.6g | Fiber 1.1g | Sugar 0.2g | Protein 32.1g

Cornish Hen With Baked Potatoes

Servings:2
Cooking Time:45

Ingredients:

- Salt, to taste
- 1 large potato
- 1 tablespoon of avocado oil
- 1.5 pounds of Cornish hen, skinless and whole
- 2-3 teaspoons of poultry seasoning, dry rub

Directions:

1. Take a fork and pierce the large potato.
2. Rub the potato with avocado oil and salt.
3. Now put the potatoes in the first basket.
4. Now pick the Cornish hen and season the hen with poultry seasoning (dry rub) and salt.
5. Remember to coat the whole Cornish hen well.
6. Put the potato in zone 1 basket.
7. Now place the hen into zone 2 baskets.
8. Now hit 1 for the first basket and set it to AIR FRY mode at 350 degrees F, for 45 minutes.
9. For the second basket hit 2 and set the time to 45 minutes at 350 degrees F.
10. To start cooking, hit the smart finish button and press hit start.
11. Once the cooking cycle complete, turn off the air fryer and take out the potatoes and Cornish hen from both air fryer baskets.
12. Serve hot and enjoy.

Nutrition:

- (Per serving) Calories 612 | Fat14.3 g| Sodium 304mg | Carbs33.4 g | Fiber 4.5 g | Sugar 1.5g | Protein 83.2 g

Nashville Hot Chicken

Servings: 8
Cooking Time: 24 To 28 Minutes
Ingredients:
- 1.4 kg bone-in, skin-on chicken pieces, breasts halved crosswise
- 1 tablespoon sea salt
- 1 tablespoon freshly ground black pepper
- 140 g finely ground blanched almond flour
- 130 g grated Parmesan cheese
- 1 tablespoon baking powder
- 2 teaspoons garlic powder, divided
- 120 g heavy (whipping) cream
- 2 large eggs, beaten
- 1 tablespoon vinegar-based hot sauce
- Avocado oil spray
- 115 g unsalted butter
- 120 ml avocado oil
- 1 tablespoon cayenne pepper (more or less to taste)
- 2 tablespoons Xylitol

Directions:
1. Sprinkle the chicken with the salt and pepper.
2. In a large shallow bowl, whisk together the almond flour, Parmesan cheese, baking powder, and 1 teaspoon of the garlic powder.
3. In a separate bowl, whisk together the heavy cream, eggs, and hot sauce.
4. Dip the chicken pieces in the egg, then coat each with the almond flour mixture, pressing the mixture into the chicken to adhere. Allow to sit for 15 minutes to let the breading set.
5. Set the air fryer to 200°C. Place the chicken in a single layer in the two air fryer baskets, being careful not to overcrowd the pieces. Spray the chicken with oil and roast for 13 minutes.
6. Carefully flip the chicken and spray it with more oil. Reduce the air fryer temperature to 180°C. Roast for another 11 to 15 minutes, until an instant-read thermometer reads 70°C.
7. While the chicken cooks, heat the butter, avocado oil, cayenne pepper, xylitol, and remaining 1 teaspoon of garlic powder in a saucepan over medium-low heat. Cook until the butter is melted and the sugar substitute has dissolved.
8. Remove the chicken from the air fryer. Use tongs to dip the chicken in the sauce. Place the coated chicken on a rack over a baking sheet, and allow it to rest for 5 minutes before serving.

Wings With Corn On The Cob

Servings: 2
Cooking Time: 40 Minutes
Ingredients:
- 6 chicken wings, skinless
- 2 tablespoons coconut amino
- 2 tablespoons brown sugar
- 1 teaspoon ginger, paste
- ½ inch garlic, minced
- Salt and black pepper to taste
- 2 corn on cobs, small
- Oil spray, for greasing

Directions:
1. Spray the corns with oil spray and season them with salt.
2. Coat the chicken wings with coconut amino, brown sugar, ginger, garlic, salt, and black pepper.
3. Spray the wings with a good amount of oil spray.
4. Put the chicken wings in the zone 1 basket.
5. Put the corn into the zone 2 basket.
6. Select ROAST mode for the chicken wings and set the time to 23 minutes at 400 degrees F/ 200 degrees C.
7. Press 2 and select the AIR FRY mode for the corn and set the time to 40 at 300 degrees F/ 150 degrees C.
8. Once it's done, serve and enjoy.

Nutrition:
- (Per serving) Calories 950 | Fat 33.4g | Sodium 592 mg | Carbs 27.4g | Fiber 2.1g | Sugar 11.3 g | Protein 129g

Chipotle Drumsticks

Servings: 4
Cooking Time: 20 Minutes
Ingredients:
- 1 tablespoon tomato paste
- ½ teaspoon chipotle powder
- ¼ teaspoon apple cider vinegar
- ¼ teaspoon garlic powder
- 8 chicken drumsticks
- ½ teaspoon salt
- ⅛ teaspoon ground black pepper

Directions:
1. In a small bowl, combine tomato paste, chipotle powder, vinegar, and garlic powder.
2. Sprinkle drumsticks with salt and pepper, then place into a large bowl and pour in tomato paste mixture. Toss or stir to evenly coat all drumsticks in mixture.
3. Place drumsticks into two ungreased air fryer baskets. Adjust the temperature to 200°C and air fry for 25 minutes, turning drumsticks halfway through cooking. Drumsticks will be dark red with an internal temperature of at least 75°C when done. Serve warm.

Almond Chicken

Servings: 4
Cooking Time: 25 Minutes
Ingredients:

- 2 large eggs
- ½ cup buttermilk
- 2 teaspoons garlic salt
- 1 teaspoon pepper
- 2 cups slivered almonds, finely chopped
- 4 boneless, skinless chicken breast halves (6 ounces each)

Directions:

1. Whisk together the egg, buttermilk, garlic salt, and pepper in a small bowl.
2. In another small bowl, place the almonds.
3. Dip the chicken in the egg mixture, then roll it in the almonds, patting it down to help the coating stick.
4. Install a crisper plate in both drawers. Place half the chicken breasts in the zone 1 drawer and half in zone 2's, then insert the drawers into the unit.
5. Select zone 1, select AIR FRY, set temperature to 390 degrees F/ 200 degrees C, and set time to 22 minutes. Select MATCH to match zone 2 settings to zone 1. Press the START/STOP button to begin cooking.
6. When the time reaches 11 minutes, press START/STOP to pause the unit. Remove the drawers and flip the chicken. Re-insert the drawers into the unit and press START/STOP to resume cooking.
7. When cooking is complete, remove the chicken.

Nutrition:

- (Per serving) Calories 353 | Fat 18g | Sodium 230mg | Carbs 6g | Fiber 2g | Sugar 3g | Protein 41g

Whole Chicken

Servings: 8
Cooking Time: 20 Minutes
Ingredients:

- 1 whole chicken (about 2.8 pounds), cut in half
- 4 tablespoons olive oil
- 2 teaspoons paprika
- 1 teaspoon garlic powder
- 1 teaspoon onion powder
- Salt and pepper, to taste

Directions:

1. Mix the olive oil, paprika, garlic powder, and onion powder together in a bowl.
2. Place the chicken halves, breast side up, on a plate. Spread a teaspoon or two of the oil mix all over the halves using either your hands or a brush. Season with salt and pepper.

3. Flip the chicken halves over and repeat on the other side. You'll want to reserve a little of the oil mix for later, but other than that, use it liberally.
4. Install a crisper plate in both drawers. Place one half of the chicken in the zone 1 drawer and the other half in the zone 2 drawer, then insert the drawers into the unit.
5. Select zone 1, select AIR FRY, set temperature to 390 degrees F/ 200 degrees C, and set time to 20 minutes. Select MATCH to match zone 2 settings to zone 1. Press the START/STOP button to begin cooking.
6. When cooking is done, check the internal temperature of the chicken. It should read 165°F. If the chicken isn't done, add more cooking time.

Nutrition:

- (Per serving) Calories 131 | Fat 8g | Sodium 51mg | Carbs 0g | Fiber 0g | Sugar 0g | Protein 14g

Chicken Tenders And Curly Fries

Servings: 4
Cooking Time: 35 Minutes
Ingredients:

- 1-pound frozen chicken tenders
- 1-pound frozen curly French fries
- Dipping sauces of your choice

Directions:

1. Place a crisper plate in each drawer. In the zone 1 drawer, place the chicken tenders, then place the drawer into the unit.
2. Fill the zone 2 drawer with the curly French fries, then place the drawer in the unit.
3. Select zone 1, then AIR FRY, and set the temperature to 390 degrees F/ 200 degrees C with a 22-minute timer. Select zone 2, then AIR FRY, and set the temperature to 400 degrees F/ 200 degrees C with a 30-minute timer. Select SYNC. To begin cooking, press the START/STOP button.
4. Press START/STOP to pause the device when the zone 1 and 2 times reach 8 minutes. Shake the drawers for 10 seconds after removing them from the unit. To resume cooking, re-insert the drawers into the unit and press START/STOP.
5. Enjoy!

Nutrition:

- (Per serving) Calories 500 | Fat 19.8g | Sodium 680mg | Carbs 50.1g | Fiber 4.1g | Sugar 0g | Protein 27.9g

Chicken Parmesan With Roasted Lemon-parmesan Broccoli

Servings: 4
Cooking Time: 18 Minutes
Ingredients:

- FOR THE CHICKEN PARMESAN
- 2 tablespoons all-purpose flour
- 2 large eggs
- 1 cup panko bread crumbs
- 2 tablespoons grated Parmesan cheese
- 2 teaspoons Italian seasoning
- 4 thin-sliced chicken cutlets (4 ounces each)
- 2 tablespoons vegetable oil
- ½ cup marinara sauce
- ½ cup shredded part-skim mozzarella cheese
- FOR THE BROCCOLI
- 4 cups broccoli florets
- 2 tablespoons olive oil, divided
- ¼ teaspoon kosher salt
- ¼ teaspoon freshly ground black pepper
- 2 teaspoons fresh lemon juice
- 2 tablespoons grated Parmesan cheese

Directions:

1. To prep the chicken Parmesan:
2. Set up a breading station with 3 small shallow bowls. Place the flour in the first bowl. In the second bowl, beat the eggs. Combine the panko, Parmesan, and Italian seasoning in the third bowl.
3. Bread the chicken cutlets in this order: First, dip them into the flour, coating both sides. Then, dip into the beaten egg. Finally, place in the panko mixture, coating both sides of the cutlets. Drizzle the oil over the cutlets.
4. To prep the broccoli: In a large bowl, combine the broccoli, 1 tablespoon of olive oil, the salt, and black pepper.
5. To cook the chicken and broccoli:
6. Install a crisper plate in the Zone 1 basket. Place the chicken in the basket and insert the basket in the unit. Place the broccoli in the Zone 2 basket and insert the basket in the unit.
7. Select Zone 1, select AIR FRY, set the temperature to 390°F, and set the time to 18 minutes.
8. Select Zone 2, select ROAST, set the temperature to 390°F, and set the time to 15 minutes. Select SMART FINISH.
9. Press START/PAUSE to begin cooking.
10. When the Zone 1 timer reads 10 minutes, press START/PAUSE. Remove the basket and use silicone-tipped tongs to flip the chicken. Reinsert the basket and press START/PAUSE to resume cooking.
11. When the Zone 1 timer reads 2 minutes, press START/PAUSE. Remove the basket and spoon 2 tablespoons of marinara sauce over each chicken cutlet. Sprinkle the mozzarella on top. Reinsert the basket and press START/PAUSE to resume cooking.
12. When cooking is complete, the cheese will be melted and the chicken cooked through . Transfer the broccoli to a large bowl. Add the lemon juice and Parmesan and toss to coat. Serve the chicken and broccoli warm.

Thai Curry Chicken Kabobs

Servings: 4
Cooking Time: 15 Minutes
Ingredients:

- 900g skinless chicken thighs
- 120ml Tamari
- 60ml coconut milk
- 3 tablespoons lime juice
- 3 tablespoons maple syrup
- 2 tablespoons Thai red curry

Directions:

1. Mix red curry paste, honey, lime juice, coconut milk, soy sauce in a bowl.
2. Add this sauce and chicken to a Ziplock bag.
3. Seal the bag and shake it to coat well.
4. Refrigerate the chicken for 2 hours then thread the chicken over wooden skewers.
5. Divide the skewers in the air fryer baskets.
6. Return the air fryer basket 1 to Zone 1, and basket 2 to Zone 2 of the Ninja Foodi 2-Basket Air Fryer.
7. Choose the "Air Fry" mode for Zone 1 at 350 degrees F and 15 minutes of cooking time.
8. Select the "MATCH COOK" option to copy the settings for Zone 2.
9. Initiate cooking by pressing the START/PAUSE BUTTON.
10. Flip the skewers once cooked halfway through.
11. Serve warm.

Nutrition:

- (Per serving) Calories 353 | Fat 5g |Sodium 818mg | Carbs 53.2g | Fiber 4.4g | Sugar 8g | Protein 17.3g

Chicken And Broccoli

Servings: 4
Cooking Time: 15 Minutes
Ingredients:
- 1-pound boneless, skinless chicken breast or thighs, cut into 1-inch bite-sized pieces
- ¼ –½ pound broccoli, cut into florets (1–2 cups)
- ½ medium onion, cut into thick slices
- 3 tablespoons olive oil or grape seed oil
- ½ teaspoon garlic powder
- 1 tablespoon fresh minced ginger
- 1 tablespoon low-sodium soy sauce
- 1 tablespoon rice vinegar
- 1 teaspoon sesame oil
- 2 teaspoons hot sauce (optional)
- ½ teaspoon sea salt, or to taste
- Black pepper, to taste
- Lemon wedges, for serving (optional)

Directions:
1. Combine the oil, garlic powder, ginger, soy sauce, rice vinegar, sesame oil, optional spicy sauce, salt, and pepper in a large mixing bowl.
2. Put the chicken in a separate bowl.
3. In a separate bowl, combine the broccoli and onions.
4. Divide the marinade between the two bowls and toss to evenly coat each.
5. Install a crisper plate into both drawers. Place the broccoli in the zone 1 drawer, then insert the drawer into the unit. Place the chicken breasts in the zone 2 drawer, then insert the drawer into the unit.
6. Select zone 1, select AIR FRY, set temperature to 390 degrees F/ 200 degrees C, and set time to 10 minutes. Select zone 2, select AIR FRY, set temperature to 390 degrees F/ 200 degrees C, and set time to 20 minutes. Select SYNC. Press the START/STOP button to begin cooking.
7. When zone 2 time reaches 9 minutes, press START/STOP to pause the unit. Remove the drawer and toss the chicken. Re-insert the drawer into the unit and press START/STOP to resume cooking.
8. When cooking is complete, serve the chicken breasts and broccoli while still hot.
9. Add additional salt and pepper to taste. Squeeze optional fresh lemon juice on top and serve warm.

Nutrition:
- (Per serving) Calories 224 | Fat 15.8g | Sodium 203mg | Carbs 4g | Fiber 1g | Sugar 1g | Protein 25g

Chicken Ranch Wraps

Servings: 4
Cooking Time: 22 Minutes
Ingredients:
- 1½ ounces breaded chicken breast tenders
- 4 (12-inch) whole-wheat tortilla wraps
- 2 heads romaine lettuce, chopped
- ½ cup shredded mozzarella cheese
- 4 tablespoons ranch dressing

Directions:
1. Place a crisper plate in each drawer. Place half of the chicken tenders in one drawer and half in the other. Insert the drawers into the unit.
2. Select zone 1, then AIR FRY, and set the temperature to 390 degrees F/ 200 degrees C with a 22-minute timer. To match zone 2 settings to zone 1, choose MATCH. To begin cooking, press the START/STOP button.
3. To pause the unit, press START/STOP when the timer reaches 11 minutes. Remove the drawers from the unit and flip the tenders over. To resume cooking, re-insert the drawers into the device and press START/STOP.
4. Remove the chicken from the drawers when they're done cooking and chop them up.
5. Divide the chopped chicken between warmed-up wraps. Top with some lettuce, cheese, and ranch dressing. Wrap and serve.

Nutrition:
- (Per serving) Calories 212 | Fat 7.8g | Sodium 567mg | Carbs 9.1g | Fiber 34.4g | Sugar 9.7g | Protein 10.6g

Thai Curry Meatballs

Servings: 4
Cooking Time: 10 Minutes
Ingredients:
- 450 g chicken mince
- 15 g chopped fresh coriander
- 1 teaspoon chopped fresh mint
- 1 tablespoon fresh lime juice
- 1 tablespoon Thai red, green, or yellow curry paste
- 1 tablespoon fish sauce
- 2 garlic cloves, minced
- 2 teaspoons minced fresh ginger
- ½ teaspoon kosher salt
- ½ teaspoon black pepper
- ¼ teaspoon red pepper flakes

Directions:
1. Preheat the zone 1 air fryer drawer to 200°C.
2. In a large bowl, gently mix the chicken mince, coriander, mint, lime juice, curry paste, fish sauce, garlic, ginger, salt, black pepper, and red pepper flakes until thoroughly combined.
3. Form the mixture into 16 meatballs. Place the meatballs in a single layer in the zone 1 air fryer drawer. Air fry for 10 minutes, turning the meatballs halfway through the cooking time. Use a meat thermometer to ensure the meatballs have reached an internal temperature of 76°C. Serve immediately.

Goat Cheese–stuffed Chicken Breast With Broiled Zucchini And Cherry Tomatoes

Servings: 4
Cooking Time: 25 Minutes
Ingredients:
- FOR THE STUFFED CHICKEN BREASTS
- 2 ounces soft goat cheese
- 1 tablespoon minced fresh parsley
- ½ teaspoon minced garlic
- 4 boneless, skinless chicken breasts (6 ounces each)
- 1 tablespoon vegetable oil
- ½ teaspoon Italian seasoning
- ½ teaspoon kosher salt
- ½ teaspoon freshly ground black pepper
- FOR THE ZUCCHINI AND TOMATOES
- 1 pound zucchini, diced
- 1 cup cherry tomatoes, halved
- 1 tablespoon vegetable oil
- ½ teaspoon kosher salt
- ¼ teaspoon freshly ground black pepper

Directions:
1. To prep the stuffed chicken breasts:
2. In a small bowl, combine the goat cheese, parsley, and garlic. Mix well.
3. Cut a deep slit into the fatter side of each chicken breast to create a pocket . Stuff each breast with the goat cheese mixture. Use a toothpick to secure the opening of the chicken, if needed.
4. Brush the outside of the chicken breasts with the oil and season with the Italian seasoning, salt, and black pepper.
5. To prep the zucchini and tomatoes: In a large bowl, combine the zucchini, tomatoes, and oil. Mix to coat. Season with salt and black pepper.
6. To cook the chicken and vegetables:
7. Install a crisper plate in each of the two baskets. Insert a broil rack in the Zone 2 basket over the crisper plate. Place the chicken in the Zone 1 basket and insert the basket in the unit. Place the vegetables on the broiler rack in the Zone 2 basket and insert the basket in the unit.
8. Select Zone 1, select AIR FRY, set the temperature to 390°F, and set the time to 25 minutes.
9. Select Zone 2, select AIR BROIL, set the temperature to 450°F, and set the time to 10 minutes. Select SMART FINISH.
10. Press START/PAUSE to begin cooking.
11. When cooking is complete, the chicken will be golden brown and cooked through and the zucchini will be soft and slightly charred. Serve hot.

Easy Chicken Thighs

Servings: 8
Cooking Time: 12 Minutes
Ingredients:
- 900g chicken thighs, boneless & skinless
- 2 tsp chilli powder
- 2 tsp olive oil
- 1 tsp garlic powder
- 1 tsp ground cumin
- Pepper
- Salt

Directions:
1. In a bowl, mix chicken with remaining ingredients until well coated.
2. Insert a crisper plate in the Ninja Foodi air fryer baskets.
3. Place chicken thighs in both baskets.
4. Select zone 1 then select "air fry" mode and set the temperature to 390 degrees F for 12 minutes. Press "match" to match zone 2 settings to zone 1. Press "start/stop" to begin. Turn halfway through.

Nutrition:
- (Per serving) Calories 230 | Fat 9.7g |Sodium 124mg | Carbs 0.7g | Fiber 0.3g | Sugar 0.2g | Protein 33g

Honey-glazed Chicken Thighs

Servings: 4
Cooking Time: 14 Minutes
Ingredients:
- Oil, for spraying
- 4 boneless, skinless chicken thighs, fat trimmed
- 3 tablespoons soy sauce
- 1 tablespoon balsamic vinegar
- 2 teaspoons honey
- 2 teaspoons minced garlic
- 1 teaspoon ground ginger

Directions:
1. Preheat the zone 1 air fryer drawer to 200°C. Line the zone 1 air fryer drawer with parchment and spray lightly with oil.
2. Place the chicken in the prepared drawer.
3. Cook for 7 minutes, flip, and cook for another 7 minutes, or until the internal temperature reaches 76°C and the juices run clear.
4. In a small saucepan, combine the soy sauce, balsamic vinegar, honey, garlic, and ginger and cook over low heat for 1 to 2 minutes, until warmed through.
5. Transfer the chicken to a serving plate and drizzle with the sauce just before serving.

Chili Chicken Wings

Servings: 4
Cooking Time: 43 Minutes
Ingredients:

- 8 chicken wings drumettes
- cooking spray
- ⅛ cup low-fat buttermilk
- ¼ cup almond flour
- McCormick Chicken Seasoning to taste
- Thai Chili Marinade
- 1 ½ tablespoons low-sodium soy sauce
- ½ teaspoon ginger, minced
- 1 ½ garlic cloves
- 1 green onion
- ½ teaspoon rice wine vinegar
- ½ tablespoon Sriracha sauce
- ½ tablespoon sesame oil

Directions:

1. Put all the ingredients for the marinade in the blender and blend them for 1 minute.
2. Keep this marinade aside. Pat dry the washed chicken and place it in the Ziploc bag.
3. Add buttermilk, chicken seasoning, and zip the bag.
4. Shake the bag well, then refrigerator for 30 minutes for marination.
5. Remove the chicken drumettes from the marinade, then dredge them through dry flour.
6. Spread the drumettes in the two crisper plate and spray them with cooking oil.
7. Return the crisper plate to the Ninja Foodi Dual Zone Air Fryer.
8. Choose the Air Fry mode for Zone 1 and set the temperature to 390 degrees F and the time to 43 minutes|
9. Select the "MATCH" button to copy the settings for Zone 2.
10. Initiate cooking by pressing the START/STOP button.
11. Toss the drumettes once cooked halfway through.
12. Now brush the chicken pieces with Thai chili sauce and then resume cooking.
13. Serve warm.

Bbq Cheddar-stuffed Chicken Breasts

Servings: 2
Cooking Time: 25 Minutes
Ingredients:

- 3 strips cooked bacon, divided
- 2 ounces cheddar cheese, cubed, divided
- ¼ cup BBQ sauce, divided
- 2 (4-ounces) skinless, boneless chicken breasts
- Salt and ground black pepper, to taste

Directions:

1. In a mixing bowl, combine the cooked bacon, cheddar cheese, and 1 tablespoon BBQ sauce.
2. Make a horizontal 1-inch cut at the top of each chicken breast with a long, sharp knife, producing a little interior pouch. Fill each breast with an equal amount of the bacon-cheese mixture. Wrap the remaining bacon strips around each chicken breast. Coat the chicken breasts with the leftover BBQ sauce and lay them in a baking dish.
3. Install a crisper plate in both drawers. Place half the chicken breasts in zone 1 and half in zone 2, then insert the drawers into the unit.
4. Select zone 1, select AIR FRY, set temperature to 390 degrees F/ 200 degrees C, and set time to 22 minutes. Select MATCH to match zone 2 settings to zone 1. Press the START/STOP button to begin cooking.
5. When the time reaches 11 minutes, press START/STOP to pause the unit. Remove the drawers and flip the chicken. Re-insert drawers into the unit and press START/STOP to resume cooking.
6. When cooking is complete, remove the chicken breasts.

Nutrition:

- (Per serving) Calories 379 | Fat 12.8g | Sodium 906mg | Carbs 11.1g | Fiber 0.4g | Sugar 8.3g | Protein 37.7g

Hawaiian Chicken Bites

Servings: 4

Cooking Time: 15 Minutes

Ingredients:

- 120 ml pineapple juice
- 2 tablespoons apple cider vinegar
- ½ tablespoon minced ginger
- 120 g ketchup
- 2 garlic cloves, minced
- 110 g brown sugar
- 2 tablespoons sherry
- 120 ml soy sauce
- 4 chicken breasts, cubed
- Cooking spray

Directions:

1. Combine the pineapple juice, cider vinegar, ginger, ketchup, garlic, and sugar in a saucepan. Stir to mix well. Heat over low heat for 5 minutes or until thickened. Fold in the sherry and soy sauce.

2. Dunk the chicken cubes in the mixture. Press to submerge. Wrap the bowl in plastic and refrigerate to marinate for at least an hour.

3. Preheat the air fryer to 180ºC. Spritz the two air fryer drawers with cooking spray.

4. Remove the chicken cubes from the marinade. Shake the excess off and put in the preheated air fryer. Spritz with cooking spray.

5. Air fry for 15 minutes or until the chicken cubes are glazed and well browned. Shake the drawer at least three times during the frying.

6. Serve immediately.

Chicken Shawarma

Servings: 4

Cooking Time: 15 Minutes

Ingredients:

- Shawarma Spice:
- 2 teaspoons dried oregano
- 1 teaspoon ground cinnamon
- 1 teaspoon ground cumin
- 1 teaspoon ground coriander
- 1 teaspoon kosher salt
- ½ teaspoon ground allspice
- ½ teaspoon cayenne pepper
- Chicken:
- 450 g boneless, skinless chicken thighs, cut into large bite-size chunks
- 2 tablespoons vegetable oil
- For Serving:
- Tzatziki
- Pita bread

Directions:

1. For the shawarma spice: In a small bowl, combine the oregano, cayenne, cumin, coriander, salt, cinnamon, and allspice. 2. For the chicken: In a large bowl, toss together the chicken, vegetable oil, and shawarma spice to coat. Marinate at room temperature for 30 minutes or cover and refrigerate for up to 24 hours. 3. Place the chicken in the zone 1 air fryer basket. Set the air fryer to 180ºC for 15 minutes, or until the chicken reaches an internal temperature of 75ºC. 4. Transfer the chicken to a serving platter. Serve with tzatziki and pita bread.

Coriander Lime Chicken Thighs

Servings: 4

Cooking Time: 22 Minutes

Ingredients:

- 4 bone-in, skin-on chicken thighs
- 1 teaspoon baking powder
- ½ teaspoon garlic powder
- 2 teaspoons chili powder
- 1 teaspoon cumin
- 2 medium limes
- 5 g chopped fresh coriander

Directions:

1. Pat chicken thighs dry and sprinkle with baking powder.

2. In a small bowl, mix garlic powder, chili powder, and cumin and sprinkle evenly over thighs, gently rubbing on and under chicken skin.

3. Cut one lime in half and squeeze juice over thighs. Place chicken into the zone 1 air fryer drawer.

4. Adjust the temperature to 190ºC and roast for 22 minutes.

5. Cut other lime into four wedges for serving and garnish cooked chicken with wedges and coriander.

Chicken Kebabs

Servings: 4
Cooking Time: 9 Minutes

Ingredients:

- 455g boneless chicken breast, cut into 1-inch pieces
- 1 tablespoon avocado oil
- 1 tablespoon Tamari soy sauce
- 1 teaspoon garlic powder
- 1 teaspoon ground ginger
- 1 teaspoon chili powder
- 1 tablespoon honey
- 1 green capsicum, cut into 1-inch pieces
- 1 red capsicum, cut into 1-inch pieces
- 1 yellow capsicum, cut into 1-inch pieces
- 1 courgette, cut into 1-inch pieces
- 1 small red onion, cut into 1-inch pieces
- cooking spray

Directions:

1. Rub chicken with oil and place in a bowl.
2. Mix honey, chili powder, ginger, garlic and soy sauce in a bowl.
3. Pour this mixture over the chicken.
4. Cover and marinate the chicken for 15 minutes.
5. Thread the marinated chicken with veggies on wooden skewers alternately.
6. Divide the skewers and place in the air fryer baskets.
7. Return the air fryer basket 1 to Zone 1, and basket 2 to Zone 2 of the Ninja Foodi 2-Basket Air Fryer.
8. Choose the "Air Fry" mode for Zone 1 at 350 degrees F and 9 minutes of cooking time.
9. Select the "MATCH COOK" option to copy the settings for Zone 2.
10. Initiate cooking by pressing the START/PAUSE BUTTON.
11. Flip the skewers once cooked halfway through.
12. Serve warm.

Nutrition:

- (Per serving) Calories 546 | Fat 33.1g |Sodium 1201mg | Carbs 30g | Fiber 2.4g | Sugar 9.7g | Protein 32g

Air Fried Chicken Potatoes With Sun-dried Tomato

Servings: 2
Cooking Time: 25 Minutes

Ingredients:

- 2 teaspoons minced fresh oregano, divided
- 2 teaspoons minced fresh thyme, divided
- 2 teaspoons extra-virgin olive oil, plus extra as needed
- 450 g fingerling potatoes, unpeeled
- 2 (340 g) bone-in split chicken breasts, trimmed
- 1 garlic clove, minced
- 15 g oil-packed sun-dried tomatoes, patted dry and chopped
- 1½ tablespoons red wine vinegar
- 1 tablespoon capers, rinsed and minced
- 1 small shallot, minced
- Salt and ground black pepper, to taste

Directions:

1. Preheat the zone 1 air fryer drawer to 180°C.
2. Combine 1 teaspoon of oregano, 1 teaspoon of thyme, ¼ teaspoon of salt, ¼ teaspoon of ground black pepper, 1 teaspoons of olive oil in a large bowl. Add the potatoes and toss to coat well.
3. Combine the chicken with remaining thyme, oregano, and olive oil. Sprinkle with garlic, salt, and pepper. Toss to coat well.
4. Place the potatoes in the preheated air fryer drawer, then arrange the chicken on top of the potatoes.
5. Air fry for 25 minutes or until the internal temperature of the chicken reaches at least 76°C and the potatoes are wilted. Flip the chicken and potatoes halfway through.
6. Meanwhile, combine the sun-dried tomatoes, vinegar, capers, and shallot in a separate large bowl. Sprinkle with salt and ground black pepper. Toss to mix well.
7. Remove the chicken and potatoes from the air fryer and allow to cool for 10 minutes. Serve with the sun-dried tomato mix.

Chicken Breast Strips

Servings:2
Cooking Time:22
Ingredients:
- 2 large organic egg
- 1-ounce buttermilk
- 1 cup of cornmeal
- ¼ cup all-purpose flour
- Salt and black pepper, to taste
- 1 pound of chicken breasts, cut into strips
- 2 tablespoons of oil bay seasoning
- oil spray, for greasing

Directions:
1. Take a medium bowl and whisk eggs with buttermilk.
2. In a separate large bowl mix flour, cornmeal, salt, black pepper, and oil bay seasoning.
3. First, dip the chicken breast strip in egg wash and then dredge into the flour mixture.
4. Coat the strip all over and layer on both the baskets that are already grease with oil spray.
5. Grease the chicken breast strips with oil spray as well.
6. Set the zone 1 basket to AIR FRY mode at 400 degrees F for 22 minutes.
7. Select the MATCH button for zone 2.
8. Hit the start button to let the cooking start.
9. Once the cooking cycle is done, serve.

Nutrition:
- (Per serving) Calories 788| Fat25g| Sodium835 mg | Carbs60g | Fiber 4.9g| Sugar1.5g | Protein79g

Sweet-and-sour Chicken With Pineapple Cauliflower Rice

Servings: 4
Cooking Time: 30 Minutes
Ingredients:
- FOR THE CHICKEN
- ¼ cup cornstarch, plus 2 teaspoons
- ¼ teaspoon kosher salt
- 2 large eggs
- 1 tablespoon sesame oil
- 1½ pounds boneless, skinless chicken breasts, cut into 1-inch pieces
- Nonstick cooking spray
- 6 tablespoons ketchup
- ¾ cup apple cider vinegar
- 1½ tablespoons soy sauce
- 1 tablespoon sugar
- FOR THE CAULIFLOWER RICE
- 1 cup finely diced fresh pineapple
- 1 red bell pepper, thinly sliced
- 1 small red onion, thinly sliced
- 1 tablespoon vegetable oil
- 2 cups frozen cauliflower rice, thawed
- 2 tablespoons soy sauce
- 1 teaspoon sesame oil
- 2 scallions, sliced

Directions:
1. To prep the chicken:
2. Set up a breading station with two small shallow bowls. Combine ¼ cup of cornstarch and the salt in the first bowl. In the second bowl, beat the eggs with the sesame oil.
3. Dip the chicken pieces in the cornstarch mixture to coat, then into the egg mixture, then back into the cornstarch mixture to coat. Mist the coated pieces with cooking spray.
4. In a small bowl, whisk together the ketchup, vinegar, soy sauce, sugar, and remaining 2 teaspoons of cornstarch.
5. To prep the cauliflower rice: Blot the pineapple dry with a paper towel. In a large bowl, combine the pineapple, bell pepper, onion, and vegetable oil.
6. To cook the chicken and cauliflower rice: Install a crisper plate in each of the two baskets. Place the chicken in the Zone 1 basket and insert the basket in the unit. Place a piece of aluminum foil over the crisper plate in the Zone 2 basket and add the pineapple mixture. Insert the basket in the unit.
7. Select Zone 1, select AIR FRY, set the temperature to 400°F, and set the time to 30 minutes.
8. Select Zone 2, select AIR BROIL, set the temperature to 450°F, and set the time to 12 minutes. Select SMART FINISH.
9. Press START/PAUSE to begin cooking.
10. When the Zone 2 timer reads 4 minutes, press START/PAUSE. Remove the basket and stir in the cauliflower rice, soy sauce, and sesame oil. Reinsert the basket and press START/PAUSE to resume cooking.
11. When cooking is complete, the chicken will be golden brown and cooked through and the rice warmed through. Stir the scallions into the rice and serve.

Chicken Legs With Leeks

Servings: 6
Cooking Time: 18 Minutes
Ingredients:

- 2 leeks, sliced
- 2 large-sized tomatoes, chopped
- 3 cloves garlic, minced
- ½ teaspoon dried oregano
- 6 chicken legs, boneless and skinless
- ½ teaspoon smoked cayenne pepper
- 2 tablespoons olive oil
- A freshly ground nutmeg

Directions:

1. In a mixing dish, thoroughly combine all ingredients, minus the leeks. Place in the refrigerator and let it marinate overnight.
2. Lay the leeks onto the bottom of the two air fryer drawers. Top with the chicken legs.
3. Roast chicken legs at 190ºC for 18 minutes, turning halfway through. Serve with hoisin sauce.

Chicken With Pineapple And Peach

Servings: 4
Cooking Time: 14 To 15 Minutes
Ingredients:

- 1 (450 g) low-sodium boneless, skinless chicken breasts, cut into 1-inch pieces
- 1 medium red onion, chopped
- 1 (230 g) can pineapple chunks, drained, 60 ml juice reserved
- 1 tablespoon peanut oil or safflower oil
- 1 peach, peeled, pitted, and cubed
- 1 tablespoon cornflour
- ½ teaspoon ground ginger
- ¼ teaspoon ground allspice
- Brown rice, cooked (optional)

Directions:

1. Preheat the air fryer to 195ºC.
2. In a medium metal bowl, mix the chicken, red onion, pineapple, and peanut oil. Bake in the air fryer for 9 minutes. Remove and stir.
3. Add the peach and return the bowl to the air fryer. Bake for 3 minutes more. Remove and stir again.
4. In a small bowl, whisk the reserved pineapple juice, the cornflour, ginger, and allspice well. Add to the chicken mixture and stir to combine.

5. Bake for 2 to 3 minutes more, or until the chicken reaches an internal temperature of 75ºC on a meat thermometer and the sauce is slightly thickened.
6. Serve immediately over hot cooked brown rice, if desired.

Chicken With Bacon And Tomato

Servings: 4
Cooking Time: 10 Minutes
Ingredients:

- 4 medium-sized skin-on chicken drumsticks
- 1½ teaspoons herbs de Provence
- Salt and pepper, to taste
- 1 tablespoon rice vinegar
- 2 tablespoons olive oil
- 2 garlic cloves, crushed
- 340 g crushed canned tomatoes
- 1 small-size leek, thinly sliced
- 2 slices smoked bacon, chopped

Directions:

1. Sprinkle the chicken drumsticks with herbs de Provence, salt and pepper; then, drizzle them with rice vinegar and olive oil.
2. Cook in the baking pan at 180ºC for 8 to 10 minutes. Pause the air fryer; stir in the remaining ingredients and continue to cook for 15 minutes longer; make sure to check them periodically. Bon appétit!

Juicy Duck Breast

Servings: 1
Cooking Time: 20 Minutes
Ingredients:

- ½ duck breast
- Salt and black pepper, to taste
- 2 tablespoons plum sauce

Directions:

1. Rub the duck breast with black pepper and salt.
2. Place the duck breast in air fryer basket 1 and add plum sauce on top.
3. Return the basket to the Ninja Foodi 2 Baskets Air Fryer.
4. Choose the "Air Fry" mode for Zone 1 and set the temperature to 400 degrees F and 20 minutes of cooking time.
5. Initiate cooking by pressing the START/PAUSE BUTTON.
6. Flip the duck breast once cooked halfway through.
7. Serve warm.

Nutrition:

- (Per serving) Calories 379 | Fat 19g |Sodium 184mg | Carbs 12.3g | Fiber 0.6g | Sugar 2g | Protein 37.7g

Bang-bang Chicken

Servings: 2
Cooking Time: 20 Minutes
Ingredients:

- 1 cup mayonnaise
- ½ cup sweet chili sauce
- 2 tablespoons Sriracha sauce
- ⅓ cup flour
- 1 lb. boneless chicken breast, diced
- 1 ½ cups panko bread crumbs
- 2 green onions, chopped

Directions:

1. Mix mayonnaise with Sriracha and sweet chili sauce in a large bowl.
2. Keep ¾ cup of the mixture aside.
3. Add flour, chicken, breadcrumbs, and remaining mayo mixture to a resealable plastic bag.
4. Zip the bag and shake well to coat.
5. Divide the chicken in the two crisper plates in a single layer.
6. Return the crisper plate to the Ninja Foodi Dual Zone Air Fryer.
7. Choose the Air Fry mode for Zone 1 and set the temperature to 390 degrees F and the time to 20 minutes|
8. Select the "MATCH" button to copy the settings for Zone 2.
9. Initiate cooking by pressing the START/STOP button.
10. Flip the chicken once cooked halfway through.
11. Top the chicken with reserved mayo sauce.
12. Garnish with green onions and serve warm.

Brazilian Chicken Drumsticks

Servings: 6
Cooking Time: 47 Minutes
Ingredients:

- 2 teaspoons cumin seeds
- 2 teaspoons dried parsley
- 2 teaspoons turmeric powder
- 2 teaspoons dried oregano leaves
- 2 teaspoons salt
- 1 teaspoon coriander seeds
- 1 teaspoon black peppercorns
- 1 teaspoon cayenne pepper
- ½ cup lime juice
- 4 tablespoons vegetable oil
- 3 lbs. chicken drumsticks

Directions:

1. Grind cumin, parsley, salt, coriander seeds, cayenne pepper, peppercorns, oregano, and turmeric in a food processor.
2. Add this mixture to lemon juice and oil in a bowl and mix well.
3. Rub the spice paste over the chicken drumsticks and let them marinate for 30 minutes|

4. Divide the chicken drumsticks in both the crisper plates.
5. Return the crisper plates to the Ninja Foodi Dual Zone Air Fryer.
6. Choose the Air Fry mode for Zone 1 and set the temperature to 390 degrees F and the time to 47 minutes|
7. Select the "MATCH" button to copy the settings for Zone 2.
8. Initiate cooking by pressing the START/STOP button.
9. Flip the drumsticks when cooked halfway through, then resume cooking.
10. Serve warm.

Teriyaki Chicken Skewers

Servings: 4
Cooking Time: 16 Minutes
Ingredients:

- 455g boneless chicken thighs, cubed
- 237ml teriyaki marinade
- 16 small wooden skewers
- Sesame seeds for rolling
- Teriyaki Marinade
- ⅓ cup soy sauce
- 59ml chicken broth
- ½ orange, juiced
- 2 tablespoons brown sugar
- 1 teaspoon ginger, grated
- 1 clove garlic, grated

Directions:

1. Blend teriyaki marinade ingredients in a blender.
2. Add chicken and its marinade to a Ziplock bag.
3. Seal this bag, shake it well and refrigerate for 30 minutes.
4. Thread the chicken on the wooden skewers.
5. Place these skewers in the air fryer baskets.
6. Return the air fryer basket 1 to Zone 1, and basket 2 to Zone 2 of the Ninja Foodi 2-Basket Air Fryer.
7. Choose the "Air Fry" mode for Zone 1 at 350 degrees F and 16 minutes of cooking time.
8. Select the "MATCH COOK" option to copy the settings for Zone 2.
9. Initiate cooking by pressing the START/PAUSE BUTTON.
10. Flip the skewers once cooked halfway through.
11. Garnish with sesame seeds.
12. Serve warm.

Nutrition:

- (Per serving) Calories 456 | Fat 16.4g |Sodium 1321mg | Carbs 19.2g | Fiber 2.2g | Sugar 4.2g | Protein 55.2g

Chicken With Bacon And Tomato & Bacon-wrapped Stuffed Chicken Breasts

Servings: 8
Cooking Time: 30 Minutes
Ingredients:
- Chicken with Bacon and Tomato:
- 4 medium-sized skin-on chicken drumsticks
- 1½ teaspoons herbs de Provence
- Salt and pepper, to taste
- 1 tablespoon rice vinegar
- 2 tablespoons olive oil
- 2 garlic cloves, crushed
- 340 g crushed canned tomatoes
- 1 small-size leek, thinly sliced
- 2 slices smoked bacon, chopped
- Bacon-Wrapped Stuffed Chicken Breasts:
- 80 g chopped frozen spinach, thawed and squeezed dry
- 55 g cream cheese, softened
- 20 g grated Parmesan cheese
- 1 jalapeño, seeded and chopped
- ½ teaspoon kosher salt
- 1 teaspoon black pepper
- 2 large boneless, skinless chicken breasts, butterflied and pounded to ½-inch thickness
- 4 teaspoons salt-free Cajun seasoning
- 6 slices bacon

Directions:
1. Make the Chicken with Bacon and Tomato :
2. Sprinkle the chicken drumsticks with herbs de Provence, salt and pepper; then, drizzle them with rice vinegar and olive oil.
3. Place into a baking pan and cook in the zone 1 basket at 180ºC for 8 to 10 minutes. Pause the air fryer; stir in the remaining ingredients and continue to cook for 15 minutes longer; make sure to check them periodically. Bon appétit!
4. Make the Bacon-Wrapped Stuffed Chicken Breasts :
5. In a small bowl, combine the spinach, cream cheese, Parmesan cheese, jalapeño, salt, and pepper. Stir until well combined.
6. Place the butterflied chicken breasts on a flat surface. Spread the cream cheese mixture evenly across each piece of chicken. Starting with the narrow end, roll up each chicken breast, ensuring the filling stays inside. Season chicken with the Cajun seasoning, patting it in to ensure it sticks to the meat.
7. Wrap each breast in 3 slices of bacon. Place in the zone 2 air fryer basket. Set the air fryer to 180ºC for 30 minutes. Use a meat thermometer to ensure the chicken has reached an internal temperature of 75ºC.
8. Let the chicken stand 5 minutes before slicing each rolled-up breast in half to serve.

Chicken Patties And One-dish Chicken Rice

Servings: 8
Cooking Time: 40 Minutes
Ingredients:
- Chicken Patties:
- 450 g chicken thigh mince
- 110 g shredded Mozzarella cheese
- 1 teaspoon dried parsley
- ½ teaspoon garlic powder
- ¼ teaspoon onion powder
- 1 large egg
- 60 g pork rinds, finely ground
- One-Dish Chicken and Rice:
- 190 g long-grain white rice, rinsed and drained
- 120 g cut frozen green beans (do not thaw)
- 1 tablespoon minced fresh ginger
- 3 cloves garlic, minced
- 1 tablespoon toasted sesame oil
- 1 teaspoon kosher salt
- 1 teaspoon black pepper
- 450 g chicken wings, preferably drumettes

Directions:
1. Make the Chicken Patties :
2. In a large bowl, mix chicken mince, Mozzarella, parsley, garlic powder, and onion powder. Form into four patties.
3. Place patties in the freezer for 15 to 20 minutes until they begin to firm up.
4. Whisk egg in a medium bowl. Place the ground pork rinds into a large bowl.
5. Dip each chicken patty into the egg and then press into pork rinds to fully coat. Place patties into the zone 1 air fryer drawer.
6. Adjust the temperature to 180ºC and air fry for 12 minutes.
7. Patties will be firm and cooked to an internal temperature of 76ºC when done. Serve immediately.
8. Make the One-Dish Chicken and Rice :
9. In a baking pan, combine the rice, green beans, ginger, garlic, sesame oil, salt, and pepper. Stir to combine. Place the chicken wings on top of the rice mixture.
10. Cover the pan with foil. Make a long slash in the foil to allow the pan to vent steam. Place the pan in the zone 2 air fryer drawer. Set the air fryer to 190ºC for 30 minutes.
11. Remove the foil. Set the air fryer to 200ºC for 10 minutes, or until the wings have browned and rendered fat into the rice and vegetables, turning the wings halfway through the cooking time.

Chicken Leg Piece

Servings:1
Cooking Time:25
Ingredients:

- 1 teaspoon of onion powder
- 1 teaspoon of paprika powder
- 1 teaspoon of garlic powder
- Salt and black pepper, to taste
- 1 tablespoon of Italian seasoning
- 1 teaspoon of celery seeds
- 2 eggs, whisked
- 1/3 cup buttermilk
- 1 cup of corn flour
- 1 pound of chicken leg

Directions:

1. Take a bowl and whisk egg along with pepper, salt, and buttermilk.
2. Set it aside for further use.
3. Mix all the spices in a small separate bowl.
4. Dredge the chicken in egg wash then dredge it in seasoning.
5. Coat the chicken legs with oil spray.
6. At the end dust it with the corn flour.
7. Divide the leg pieces into two zones.
8. Set zone 1 basket to 400 degrees F, for 25 minutes.
9. Select MATCH for zone 2 basket.
10. Let the air fryer do the magic.
11. Once it's done, serve and enjoy.

Nutrition:

- (Per serving) Calories 1511| Fat 52.3g| Sodium615 mg | Carbs 100g | Fiber 9.2g | Sugar 8.1g | Protein 154.2g

Herbed Turkey Breast With Simple Dijon Sauce

Servings: 4
Cooking Time: 30 Minutes
Ingredients:

- 1 teaspoon chopped fresh sage
- 1 teaspoon chopped fresh tarragon
- 1 teaspoon chopped fresh thyme leaves
- 1 teaspoon chopped fresh rosemary leaves
- 1½ teaspoons sea salt
- 1 teaspoon ground black pepper
- 1 (900 g) turkey breast
- 3 tablespoons Dijon mustard
- 3 tablespoons butter, melted
- Cooking spray

Directions:

1. Preheat the air fryer to 200ºC. Spritz the two air fryer drawers with cooking spray.
2. Combine the herbs, salt, and black pepper in a small bowl. Stir to mix well. Set aside.
3. Combine the Dijon mustard and butter in a separate bowl. Stir to mix well.

4. Rub the turkey with the herb mixture on a clean work surface, then brush the turkey with Dijon mixture.
5. Arrange the turkey in the two preheated air fryer drawers. Air fry for 30 minutes or until an instant-read thermometer inserted in the thickest part of the turkey breast reaches at least 76ºC.
6. Transfer the cooked turkey breast on a large plate and slice to serve.

Honey-cajun Chicken Thighs

Servings: 6
Cooking Time: 25 Minutes
Ingredients:

- ½ cup buttermilk
- 1 teaspoon hot sauce
- 1½ pounds skinless, boneless chicken thighs
- ¼ cup all-purpose flour
- ⅓ cup tapioca flour
- 2 ½ teaspoons Cajun seasoning
- ½ teaspoon garlic salt
- ½ teaspoon honey powder
- ¼ teaspoon ground paprika
- ⅛ teaspoon cayenne pepper
- 4 teaspoons honey

Directions:

1. In a resealable plastic bag, combine the buttermilk and hot sauce. Marinate the chicken thighs in the bag for 30 minutes.
2. Combine the flour, tapioca flour, Cajun spice, garlic salt, honey powder, paprika, and cayenne pepper in a small mixing bowl.
3. Remove the thighs from the buttermilk mixture and dredge them in the flour. Remove any excess flour by shaking it off.
4. Install a crisper plate in both drawers. Place half the chicken thighs in the zone 1 drawer and half in zone 2's, then insert the drawers into the unit.
5. Select zone 1, select AIR FRY, set temperature to 390 degrees F/ 200 degrees C, and set time to 25 minutes. Select MATCH to match zone 2 settings to zone 1. Press the START/STOP button to begin cooking.
6. When the time reaches 11 minutes, press START/STOP to pause the unit. Remove the drawers and flip the chicken. Re-insert the drawers into the unit and press START/STOP to resume cooking.
7. When cooking is complete, remove the chicken and serve.

Nutrition:

- (Per serving) Calories 243 | Fat 11.8g | Sodium 203mg | Carbs 16.1g | Fiber 0.4g | Sugar 5.1g | Protein 19g

Snacks And Appetizers Recipes

Parmesan Crush Chicken

Servings:4
Cooking Time:18
Ingredients:

- 4 chicken breasts
- 1 cup parmesan cheese
- 1 cup bread crumb
- 2 eggs, whisked
- Salt, to taste
- Oil spray, for greasing

Directions:

1. Whisk egg in a large bowl and set aside.
2. Season the chicken breast with salt and then put it in egg wash.
3. Next, dredge it in breadcrumb then parmesan cheese.
4. Line both the basket of the air fryer with parchment paper.
5. Divided the breast pieces between the backsets, and oil spray the breast pieces.
6. Set zone 1 basket to air fry mode at 350 degrees F for 18 minutes.
7. Select the MATCH button for the zone 2 basket.
8. Once it's done, serve.

Nutrition:

- (Per serving) Calories574 | Fat25g | Sodium848 mg | Carbs 21.4g | Fiber 1.2g| Sugar 1.8g | Protein 64.4g

Grill Cheese Sandwich

Servings:2
Cooking Time:10
Ingredients:

- 4 slices of white bread slices
- 2 tablespoons of butter, melted
- 2 slices of sharp cheddar
- 2 slices of Swiss cheese
- 2 slices of mozzarella cheese

Directions:

1. Brush melted butter on one side of all the bread slices and then top the 2 bread slices with slices of cheddar, Swiss, and mozzarella, one slice per bread.
2. Top it with the other slice to make a sandwich.
3. Divide it between two baskets of the air fryer.
4. Turn on AIR FRY mode for zone 1 basket at 350 degrees F for 10 minutes.
5. Use the MATCH button for the second zone.

6. Once done, serve.
Nutrition:

- (Per serving) Calories 577 | Fat38g | Sodium 1466mg | Carbs 30.5g | Fiber 1.1g| Sugar 6.5g | Protein 27.6g

Kale Chips

Servings: 4
Cooking Time: 3 Minutes
Ingredients:

- 1 head fresh kale, stems and ribs removed and cut into 4cm pieces
- 1 tablespoon olive oil
- 1 teaspoon soy sauce
- ⅛ teaspoon cayenne pepper
- Pinch of freshly ground black pepper

Directions:

1. In a large bowl, add all the ingredients and mix well.
2. Grease basket of Ninja Foodi 2-Basket Air Fryer.
3. Press your chosen zone - "Zone 1" or "Zone 2" and then rotate the knob to select "Air Fry".
4. Set the temperature to 200 degrees C and then set the time for 5 minutes to preheat.
5. After preheating, arrange the kale pieces into the basket of each zone.
6. Slide the basket into the Air Fryer and set the time for 3 minutes.
7. While cooking, toss the kale pieces once halfway through.
8. After cooking time is completed, remove the kale chips and baking pans from Air Fryer.
9. Place the kale chips onto a wire rack to cool for about 10 minutes before serving.

Tangy Fried Pickle Spears

Servings: 6
Cooking Time: 15 Minutes
Ingredients:
- 2 jars sweet and sour pickle spears, patted dry
- 2 medium-sized eggs
- 80 ml milk
- 1 teaspoon garlic powder
- 1 teaspoon sea salt
- ½ teaspoon shallot powder
- ⅓ teaspoon chilli powder
- 80 ml plain flour
- Cooking spray

Directions:
1. Preheat the air fryer to 195°C. Spritz the zone 1 air fryer basket with cooking spray.
2. In a bowl, beat together the eggs with milk. In another bowl, combine garlic powder, sea salt, shallot powder, chilli powder and plain flour until well blended.
3. One by one, roll the pickle spears in the powder mixture, then dredge them in the egg mixture. Dip them in the powder mixture a second time for additional coating.
4. Arrange the coated pickles in the prepared basket. Air fry for 15 minutes until golden and crispy, shaking the basket halfway through to ensure even cooking.
5. Transfer to a plate and let cool for 5 minutes before serving.

Taco-spiced Chickpeas And Black Bean Corn Dip

Servings: 7
Cooking Time: 17 Minutes
Ingredients:
- Taco-Spiced Chickpeas:
- Oil, for spraying
- 1 (439 g) can chickpeas, drained
- 1 teaspoon chilli powder
- ½ teaspoon ground cumin
- ½ teaspoon salt
- ½ teaspoon granulated garlic
- 2 teaspoons lime juice
- Black Bean Corn Dip:
- ½ (425 g) can black beans, drained and rinsed
- ½ (425 g) can corn, drained and rinsed
- 60 ml chunky salsa
- 57 g low-fat soft white cheese
- 60 ml shredded low-fat Cheddar cheese
- ½ teaspoon ground cumin
- ½ teaspoon paprika
- Salt and freshly ground black pepper, to taste

Directions:
1. Make the Taco-Spiced Chickpeas :
2. Line the zone 1 air fryer basket with parchment and spray lightly with oil. Place the chickpeas in the prepared basket.
3. Air fry at 200°C for 17 minutes, shaking or stirring the chickpeas and spraying lightly with oil every 5 to 7 minutes.
4. In a small bowl, mix together the chilli powder, cumin, salt, and garlic.
5. When 2 to 3 minutes of cooking time remain, sprinkle half of the seasoning mix over the chickpeas. Finish cooking.
6. Transfer the chickpeas to a medium bowl and toss with the remaining seasoning mix and the lime juice. Serve immediately.
7. Make the Black Bean Corn Dip :
8. Preheat the air fryer to 165°C.
9. In a medium bowl, mix together the black beans, corn, salsa, soft white cheese, Cheddar cheese, cumin, and paprika. Season with salt and pepper and stir until well combined.
10. Spoon the mixture into a baking dish.
11. Place baking dish in the zone 2 air fryer basket and bake until heated through, about 10 minutes.
12. Serve hot.

Tasty Sweet Potato Wedges

Servings: 4
Cooking Time: 20 Minutes
Ingredients:
- 2 sweet potatoes, peel & cut into wedges
- 1 tbsp BBQ spice rub
- ½ tsp sweet paprika
- 1 tbsp olive oil
- Pepper
- Salt

Directions:
1. In a bowl, toss sweet potato wedges with sweet paprika, oil, BBQ spice rub, pepper, and salt.
2. Insert a crisper plate in the Ninja Foodi air fryer baskets.
3. Add sweet potato wedges in both baskets.
4. Select zone 1 then select "air fry" mode and set the temperature to 390 degrees F for 20 minutes. Press "match" to match zone 2 settings to zone 1. Press "start/stop" to begin. Turn halfway through.

Cauliflower Gnocchi

Servings: 5
Cooking Time: 17 Minutes.
Ingredients:

- 1 bag frozen cauliflower gnocchi
- 1 ½ tablespoons olive oil
- 1 teaspoon garlic powder
- 3 tablespoons parmesan, grated
- ½ teaspoon dried basil
- Salt to taste
- Fresh chopped parsley for topping

Directions:

1. Toss gnocchi with olive oil, garlic powder, 1 tablespoon of parmesan, salt, and basil in a bowl.
2. Divide the gnocchi in the two crisper plate.
3. Return the crisper plate to the Ninja Foodi Dual Zone Air Fryer.
4. Choose the Air Fry mode for Zone 1 and set the temperature to 400 degrees F and the time to 10 minutes.
5. Select the "MATCH" button to copy the settings for Zone 2.
6. Initiate cooking by pressing the START/STOP button.
7. Toss the gnocchi once cooked halfway through, then resume cooking.
8. Drizzle the remaining parmesan on top of the gnocchi and cook again for 7 minutes.
9. Serve warm.

Nutrition:

- (Per serving) Calories 134 | Fat 5.9g |Sodium 343mg | Carbs 9.5g | Fiber 0.5g | Sugar 1.1g | Protein 10.4g

Jalapeño Popper Dip With Tortilla Chips

Servings:6
Cooking Time: 15 Minutes
Ingredients:

- FOR THE DIP
- 8 ounces cream cheese, at room temperature
- ½ cup sour cream
- 1 cup shredded Cheddar cheese
- ¼ cup shredded Parmesan cheese
- ¼ cup roughly chopped pickled jalapeños
- ½ teaspoon kosher salt
- ½ cup panko bread crumbs
- 2 tablespoons olive oil
- ½ teaspoon dried parsley
- FOR THE TORTILLA CHIPS
- 10 corn tortillas
- 2 tablespoons fresh lime juice
- 1 tablespoon olive oil
- ½ teaspoon kosher salt

Directions:

1. To prep the dip: In a medium bowl, mix the cream cheese, sour cream, Cheddar, Parmesan, jalapeños, and salt until smooth.
2. In a small bowl, combine the panko, olive oil, and parsley.
3. Pour the dip into a 14-ounce ramekin and top with the panko mixture.
4. To prep the chips: Brush both sides of each tortilla with lime juice, then with oil. Sprinkle with the salt. Using a sharp knife or a pizza cutter, cut each tortilla into 4 wedges.
5. To cook the dip and chips: Install a crisper plate in each of the two baskets. Place the ramekin of dip in the Zone 1 basket and insert the basket in the unit. Layer the tortillas in the Zone 2 basket and insert the basket in the unit.
6. Select Zone 1, select BAKE, set the temperature to 350°F, and set the time to 15 minutes.
7. Select Zone 2, select AIR FRY, set the temperature to 375°F, and set the time to 5 minutes. Select SMART FINISH.
8. Press START/PAUSE to begin cooking.
9. When the Zone 2 timer reads 3 minutes, press START/PAUSE. Remove the basket from the unit and give the basket a good shake to redistribute the chips. Reinsert the basket and press START/PAUSE to resume cooking.
10. When cooking is complete, the dip will be bubbling and golden brown and the chips will be crispy. Serve warm.

Nutrition:

- (Per serving) Calories: 406; Total fat: 31g; Saturated fat: 14g; Carbohydrates: 22g; Fiber: 1g; Protein: 11g; Sodium: 539mg

Avocado Fries With Sriracha Dip

Servings: 4

Cooking Time: 6 Minutes

Ingredients:

- Avocado Fries
- 4 avocados, peeled and cut into sticks
- ¾ cup panko breadcrumbs
- ¼ cup flour
- 2 eggs, beaten
- ½ teaspoon garlic powder
- ½ teaspoon salt
- SRIRACHA-RANCH SAUCE
- ¼ cup ranch dressing
- 1 teaspoon sriracha sauce

Directions:

1. Mix flour with garlic powder and salt in a bowl.
2. Dredge the avocado sticks through the flour mixture.
3. Dip them in the eggs and coat them with breadcrumbs.
4. Place the coated fries in the air fryer baskets.
5. Return the air fryer basket 1 to Zone 1, and basket 2 to Zone 2 of the Ninja Foodi 2-Basket Air Fryer.
6. Choose the "Air Fry" mode for Zone 1 at 400 degrees F and 6 minutes of cooking time.
7. Select the "MATCH COOK" option to copy the settings for Zone 2.
8. Initiate cooking by pressing the START/PAUSE BUTTON.
9. Flip the fries once cooked halfway through.
10. Mix all the dipping sauce ingredients in a bowl.
11. Serve the fries with dipping sauce.

Cheese Corn Fritters

Servings: 6

Cooking Time: 15 Minutes

Ingredients:

- 1 egg
- 164g corn
- 2 green onions, diced
- 45g flour
- 29g breadcrumbs
- 117g cheddar cheese, shredded
- ½ tsp onion powder
- ½ tsp garlic powder
- 15g sour cream
- Pepper
- Salt

Directions:

1. In a large bowl, add all ingredients and mix until well combined.
2. Insert a crisper plate in the Ninja Foodi air fryer baskets.
3. Make patties from the mixture and place them in both baskets.
4. Select zone 1, then select "air fry" mode and set the temperature to 370 degrees F for 12 minutes. Press "match" to match zone 2 settings to zone 1. Press "start/stop" to begin. Turn halfway through.

Spicy Chicken Tenders

Servings:2

Cooking Time:12

Ingredients:

- 2 large eggs, whisked
- 2 tablespoons lemon juice
- Salt and black pepper
- 1 pound of chicken tenders
- 1 cup Panko breadcrumbs
- 1/2 cup Italian bread crumb
- 1 teaspoon smoked paprika
- 1/4 teaspoon garlic powder
- 1/4 teaspoon onion powder
- 1/2 cup fresh grated parmesan cheese

Directions:

1. Take a bowl and whisk eggs in it and set aside for further use.
2. In a large bowl add lemon juice, paprika, salt, black pepper, garlic powder, onion powder
3. In a separate bowl mix Panko breadcrumbs, Italian bread crumbs, and parmesan cheese.
4. Dip the chicken tender in the spice mixture and coat the entire tender well.
5. Let the tenders sit for 1 hour.
6. Then dip each chicken tender in egg and then in bread crumbs.
7. Line both the basket of the air fryer with parchment paper.
8. Divide the tenders between the baskets.
9. Set zone 1 basket to air fry mode at 350 degrees F for 12 minutes.
10. Select the MATCH button for the zone 2 basket.
11. Once it's done, serve.

Nutrition:

- (Per serving) Calories 836| Fat 36g| Sodium1307 mg | Carbs 31.3g | Fiber 2.5g| Sugar3.3 g | Protein 95.3g

Zucchini Chips

Servings: 4

Cooking Time: 15 Minutes

Ingredients:

- 1 medium-sized zucchini
- ½ cup panko breadcrumbs
- ½ teaspoon garlic powder
- ¼ teaspoon onion powder
- 1 egg
- 3 tablespoons flour

Directions:

1. Slice the zucchini into thin slices, about ¼-inch thick.

2. In a mixing bowl, combine the panko breadcrumbs, garlic powder, and onion powder.

3. The egg should be whisked in a different bowl, while the flour should be placed in a third bowl.

4. Dip the zucchini slices in the flour, then in the egg, and finally in the breadcrumbs.

5. Place a crisper plate in each drawer. Put the zucchini slices into each drawer in a single layer. Insert the drawers into the unit.

6. Select zone 1, then AIR FRY, then set the temperature to 360 degrees F/ 180 degrees C with a 6-minute timer. To match zone 2 settings to zone 1, choose MATCH. To begin, select START/STOP.

7. Remove the zucchini from the drawers after the timer has finished.

Nutrition:

- (Per serving) Calories 82 | Fat 1.5g | Sodium 89mg | Carbs 14.1g | Fiber 1.7g | Sugar 1.2g | Protein 3.9g

Chicken Crescent Wraps

Servings: 6

Cooking Time: 12 Minutes.

Ingredients:

- 3 tablespoons chopped onion
- 3 garlic cloves, peeled and minced
- ¾ (8 ounces) package cream cheese
- 6 tablespoons butter
- 2 boneless chicken breasts, cubed, cooked
- 3 (10 ounces) cans refrigerated crescent roll dough

Directions:

1. Heat oil in a skillet and add onion and garlic to sauté until soft.

2. Add cooked chicken, sautéed veggies, butter, and cream cheese to a blender.

3. Blend well until smooth. Spread the crescent dough over a flat surface.

4. Slice the dough into 12 rectangles.

5. Spoon the chicken mixture at the center of each rectangle.

6. Roll the dough to wrap the mixture and form a ball.

7. Divide these balls into the two crisper plate.

8. Return the crisper plate to the Ninja Foodi Dual Zone Air Fryer.

9. Choose the Air Fry mode for Zone 1 and set the temperature to 390 degrees F and the time to 12 minutes.

10. Select the "MATCH" button to copy the settings for Zone 2.

11. Initiate cooking by pressing the START/STOP button.

12. Serve warm.

Nutrition:

- (Per serving) Calories 100 | Fat 2g |Sodium 480mg | Carbs 4g | Fiber 2g | Sugar 0g | Protein 18g

Chicken Tenders

Servings:3

Cooking Time:12

Ingredients:

- 1 pound of chicken tender
- Salt and black pepper, to taste
- 1 cup Panko bread crumbs
- 2 cups Italian bread crumbs
- 1 cup parmesan cheese
- 2 eggs
- Oil spray, for greasing

Directions:

1. Sprinkle the tenders with salt and black pepper.

2. In a medium bowl mix Panko bread crumbs with Italian breadcrumbs.

3. Add salt, pepper, and parmesan cheese.

4. Crack two eggs in a bowl.

5. First, put the chicken tender in eggs.

6. Now dredge the tender in a bowl and coat the tender well with crumbs.

7. Line both of the baskets of the air fryer with parchment paper.

8. At the end spray the tenders with oil spray.

9. Divided the tenders between the baskets of Ninja Foodie 2-Basket Air Fryer.

10. Set zone 1 basket to AIR FRY mode at 350 degrees F for 12 minutes.

11. Select the MATCH button for the zone 2 basket.

12. Once it's done, serve.

Nutrition:

- (Per serving) Calories558 | Fat23.8g | Sodium872 mg | Carbs 20.9g | Fiber1.7 g| Sugar2.2 g | Protein 63.5g

Crunchy Basil White Beans And Artichoke And Olive Pitta Flatbread

Servings: 6
Cooking Time: 19 Minutes
Ingredients:
* Crunchy Basil White Beans:
* 1 (425 g) can cooked white beans
* 2 tablespoons olive oil
* 1 teaspoon fresh sage, chopped
* ¼ teaspoon garlic powder
* ¼ teaspoon salt, divided
* 1 teaspoon chopped fresh basil
* Artichoke and Olive Pitta Flatbread:
* 2 wholewheat pittas
* 2 tablespoons olive oil, divided
* 2 garlic cloves, minced
* ¼ teaspoon salt
* 120 ml canned artichoke hearts, sliced
* 60 ml Kalamata olives
* 60 ml shredded Parmesan
* 60 ml crumbled feta
* Chopped fresh parsley, for garnish (optional)

Directions:
1. Make the Crunchy Basil White Beans :
2. Preheat the air fryer to 190ºC.
3. In a medium bowl, mix together the beans, olive oil, sage, garlic, ⅛ teaspoon salt, and basil.
4. Pour the white beans into the air fryer and spread them out in a single layer.
5. Bake in zone 1 basket for 10 minutes. Stir and continue cooking for an additional 5 to 9 minutes, or until they reach your preferred level of crispiness.
6. Toss with the remaining ⅛ teaspoon salt before serving.
7. Make the Artichoke and Olive Pitta Flatbread :
8. Preheat the air fryer to 190ºC.
9. Brush each pitta with 1 tablespoon olive oil, then sprinkle the minced garlic and salt over the top.
10. Distribute the artichoke hearts, olives, and cheeses evenly between the two pittas, and place both into the zone 2 air fryer basket to bake for 10 minutes.
11. Remove the pittas and cut them into 4 pieces each before serving. Sprinkle parsley over the top, if desired.

Mozzarella Arancini

Servings: 16 Arancini
Cooking Time: 8 To 11 Minutes
Ingredients:
* 475 ml cooked rice, cooled
* 2 eggs, beaten
* 355 ml panko breadcrumbs, divided
* 120 ml grated Parmesan cheese
* 2 tablespoons minced fresh basil
* 16 ¾-inch cubes Mozzarella cheese
* 2 tablespoons olive oil

Directions:
1. Preheat the air fryer to 205ºC.
2. In a medium bowl, combine the rice, eggs, 120 ml of the breadcrumbs, Parmesan cheese, and basil. Form this mixture into 16 1½-inch balls.
3. Poke a hole in each of the balls with your finger and insert a Mozzarella cube. Form the rice mixture firmly around the cheese.
4. On a shallow plate, combine the remaining 240 ml of the breadcrumbs with the olive oil and mix well. Roll the rice balls in the breadcrumbs to coat.
5. Air fry the arancini in two baskets for 8 to 11 minutes or until golden brown.
6. Serve hot.

Crispy Filo Artichoke Triangles

Servings: 18 Triangles
Cooking Time: 9 To 12 Minutes
Ingredients:
* 60 ml Ricotta cheese
* 1 egg white
* 80 ml minced and drained artichoke hearts
* 3 tablespoons grated Mozzarella cheese
* ½ teaspoon dried thyme
* 6 sheets frozen filo pastry, thawed
* 2 tablespoons melted butter

Directions:
1. Preheat the air fryer to 205ºC.
2. In a small bowl, combine the Ricotta cheese, egg white, artichoke hearts, Mozzarella cheese, and thyme, and mix well.
3. Cover the filo pastry with a damp kitchen towel while you work so it doesn't dry out. Using one sheet at a time, place on the work surface and cut into thirds lengthwise.
4. Put about 1½ teaspoons of the filling on each strip at the base. Fold the bottom right-hand tip of phyllo over the filling to meet the other side in a triangle, then continue folding in a triangle. Brush each triangle with butter to seal the edges. Repeat with the remaining phyllo dough and filling.
5. Place the triangles in the two air fryer baskets. Bake, 6 at a time, in two baskets for about 3 to 4 minutes, or until the filo is golden brown and crisp.
6. Serve hot.

Pretzels Hot Dog

Servings: 8
Cooking Time: 15 Minutes
Ingredients:
- 180ml warm water
- 2¼ teaspoons instant yeast
- 1 teaspoon sugar
- 2 teaspoons olive oil
- 250g plain flour
- ½ teaspoon salt
- 1 large egg
- 1 tablespoon water
- 8 hot dogs

Directions:
1. Combine warm water, yeast, sugar, and olive oil in a large mixing basin to make the dough.
2. Stir everything together and leave aside for about 5 minutes.
3. Mix in roughly 125g flour and a pinch of salt. Add 125g of flour at a time until the dough comes together into a ball and pulls away from the bowl's sides.
4. On a floured board, pour the dough. Knead the dough for 3 to 5 minutes, adding extra flour until it is no longer sticky.
5. Cut the dough into eight pieces.
6. Roll the dough between your hands, and roll each piece into an 20 cm to 25 cm rope.
7. Pat, the hot dogs, dry with paper towels to make wrapping the dough around them easier.
8. Begin wrapping the dough around one end of each hot dog in a spiral. To seal the ends, pinch them together.
9. In a small mixing dish, whisk together an egg and a tablespoon of water. Coat the dough in egg wash from all sides.
10. Press your chosen zone - "Zone 1" or "Zone 2" and then rotate the knob to select "Air Fryer".
11. Set the temperature to 200 degrees C, and then set the time for 5 minutes to preheat.
12. After preheating, arrange pretzels into the basket of each zone.
13. Slide the baskets into Air Fryer and set the time for 8 minutes.
14. After cooking time is completed, place on a wire rack for a few minutes, then transfer onto serving plates and serve.

Crispy Calamari Rings

Servings: 4
Cooking Time: 10 Minutes
Ingredients:
- 455g calamari rings, patted dry
- 3 tablespoons lemon juice
- 60g plain flour
- 1 teaspoon garlic powder
- 2 egg whites
- 60ml milk
- 220g panko breadcrumbs
- 1½ teaspoon salt
- 1½ teaspoon ground black pepper

Directions:
1. Allow the squid rings to marinade for at least 30 minutes in a bowl with lemon juice. Drain the water in a colander.
2. In a shallow bowl, combine the flour and garlic powder.
3. In a separate bowl, whisk together the egg whites and milk.
4. In a third bowl, combine the panko breadcrumbs, salt, and pepper.
5. Floured first the calamari rings, then dip in the egg mixture, and finally in the panko breadcrumb mixture.
6. Press either "Zone 1" or "Zone 2" and then rotate the knob to select "Air Fry".
7. Set the temperature to 200 degrees C, and then set the time for 5 minutes to preheat.
8. After preheating, spray the Air-Fryer basket with cooking spray and line with parchment paper. Arrange in a single layer and spritz them with cooking spray.
9. Slide the basket into the Air Fryer and set the time for 10 minutes.
10. After cooking time is completed, transfer them onto serving plates and serve.

Garlic Bread

Servings: 8
Cooking Time: 10 Minutes
Ingredients:
- 60g butter, softened
- 3 tablespoons grated Parmesan cheese
- 2 garlic cloves, minced
- 2 teaspoons minced fresh parsley
- 8 slices of French bread

Directions:
1. Press either "Zone 1" or "Zone 2" and then rotate the knob to select "Bake".
2. Set the temperature to 175 degrees C, and then set the time for 5 minutes to preheat.
3. After preheating, combine the first four ingredients in a small mixing bowl| spread on bread. Arrange bread slices onto basket.
4. Slide the basket into the Air Fryer and set the time for 3 minutes.
5. After cooking time is completed, transfer them onto serving plates and serve.

Mozzarella Sticks

Servings: 6
Cooking Time: 6 Minutes
Ingredients:

- 150g block Mozzarella cheese or string cheese
- 6 slices of white bread
- 1 large egg
- 1 tablespoon water
- 55g panko breadcrumbs
- 1 tablespoon olive oil

Directions:

1. Remove the crust from the bread. Discard or save for breadcrumbs.
2. Roll the bread into thin slices with a rolling pin.
3. Slice mozzarella into 30 cm x 10 cm -long sticks, nearly the same size as your bread slices.
4. In a small bowl, whisk together the egg and the water.
5. Fill a shallow pie plate halfway with panko.
6. Wrap a bread slice around each mozzarella stick.
7. Brush the egg wash around the edge of the bread and push to seal it. Brush all over the bread outside.
8. Dredge in Panko and push to coat on all sides.
9. Line basket with parchment paper.
10. Press either "Zone 1" or "Zone 2" and then rotate the knob to select "Air Fryer".
11. Set the temperature to 200 degrees C, and then set the time for 5 minutes to preheat.
12. After preheating, arrange sticks into the basket.
13. Slide the basket into the Air Fryer and set the time for 6 minutes.
14. After cooking time is completed, place on a wire rack for a few minutes, then transfer onto serving plates and serve.

Dried Apple Chips Dried Banana Chips

Servings:6
Cooking Time: 6 To 10 Hours
Ingredients:

- FOR THE APPLE CHIPS
- ½ teaspoon ground cinnamon
- ¼ teaspoon ground nutmeg
- ⅛ teaspoon ground allspice
- ⅛ teaspoon ground ginger
- 2 Gala apples, cored and cut into ⅛-inch-thick rings
- FOR THE BANANA CHIPS
- 2 firm-ripe bananas, cut into ¼-inch slices

Directions:

1. To prep the apple chips: In a small bowl, mix the cinnamon, nutmeg, allspice, and ginger until combined. Sprinkle the spice mixture over the apple slices.
2. To dehydrate the fruit: Arrange half of the apple slices in a single layer in the Zone 1 basket. It is okay if the edges overlap a bit as they will shrink as they cook. Place a crisper plate on top of the apples. Arrange the remaining apple slices on top of the crisper plate and insert the basket in the unit.
3. Repeat this process with the bananas in the Zone 2 basket and insert the basket in the unit.
4. Select Zone 1, select DEHYDRATE, set the temperature to 135°F, and set the time to 8 hours.
5. Select Zone 2, select DEHYDRATE, set the temperature to 135°F, and set the time to 10 hours. Select SMART FINISH.
6. Press START/PAUSE to begin cooking.
7. When both timers read 2 hours, press START/PAUSE. Remove both baskets and check the fruit for doneness; note that juicier fruit will take longer to dry than fruit that starts out drier. Reinsert the basket and press START/PAUSE to continue cooking if necessary.

Nutrition:

- (Per serving) Calories: 67; Total fat: 0g; Saturated fat: 0g; Carbohydrates: 16g; Fiber: 3g; Protein: 0g; Sodium: 1mg

Healthy Chickpea Fritters

Servings: 6
Cooking Time: 5 Minutes
Ingredients:

- 1 egg
- 425g can chickpeas, rinsed & drained
- ½ tsp ground ginger
- ½ tsp garlic powder
- 1 tsp ground cumin
- 2 green onions, sliced
- 15g fresh cilantro, chopped
- ½ tsp baking soda
- ½ tsp salt

Directions:

1. Add chickpeas and remaining ingredients into the food processor and process until well combined.
2. Insert a crisper plate in the Ninja Foodi air fryer baskets.
3. Make patties from the mixture and place them in both baskets.
4. Select zone 1, then select "air fry" mode and set the temperature to 390 degrees F for 5 minutes. Press "match" to match zone 2 settings to zone 1. Press "start/stop" to begin.

Beef Taquitos

Servings: 8
Cooking Time: 6 Minutes
Ingredients:

- 455g lean beef mince
- 1 teaspoon salt
- 70g salsa
- ½ teaspoon granulated garlic
- ½ teaspoon chili powder
- ½ teaspoon cumin
- 100g shredded cheese
- 12 mini corn tortillas

Directions:

1. Season beef mince with salt in a frying pan and cook over medium-high heat.
2. Cook until the meat is nicely browned, stirring frequently and breaking it into fine crumbles. Remove from the heat and drain any remaining grease.
3. Stir in the salsa, garlic, chili powder, cumin, and cheese until all ingredients are completely incorporated, and the cheese has melted.
4. Warm tortillas on a grill or iron frying pan to make them flexible. Allow them to warm rather than crisp and brown.
5. Fill each tortilla with about 1 to 2 tablespoons of the meat mixture and roll it up.
6. Press either "Zone 1" or "Zone 2" and then rotate the knob to select "Air Fryer".
7. Set the temperature to 175 degrees C, and then set the time for 5 minutes to preheat.
8. After preheating, arrange them into the basket.
9. Slide the basket into the Air Fryer and set the time for 6 minutes.
10. After cooking time is completed, place on a wire rack for a few minutes, then transfer onto serving plates and serve.

Croquettes

Servings: 6
Cooking Time: 10 Minutes
Ingredients:

- 460g mashed potatoes
- 50g grated Parmesan cheese
- 50g shredded Swiss cheese
- 1 shallot, finely chopped
- 2 teaspoons minced fresh rosemary
- ½ teaspoon salt
- ¼ teaspoon pepper
- 420g finely chopped cooked turkey
- 1 large egg

- 2 tablespoons water
- 110g panko bread crumbs
- Cooking spray

Directions:

1. Combine mashed potatoes, cheeses, shallot, rosemary, salt, and pepper in a large mixing bowl| stir in turkey.
2. Lightly but completely combine the ingredients. Form into twelve 5cm thick patties.
3. Whisk the egg and water together in a small basin. In a shallow bowl, place the bread crumbs.
4. Dip the croquettes in the egg mixture, then in the bread crumbs, patting them down.
5. Press either "Zone 1" or "Zone 2" and then rotate the knob to select "Air Fry".
6. Set the temperature to 190 degrees C, and then set the time for 5 minutes to preheat.
7. After preheating, spray the Air-Fryer basket with cooking spray and line with parchment paper. Arrange in a single layer and spritz them with cooking spray.
8. Slide the basket into the Air Fryer and set the time for 5 minutes.
9. After that, turn them and again cook for 5 minutes longer.
10. After cooking time is completed, transfer them onto serving plates and serve.

Dijon Cheese Sandwich

Servings:2
Cooking Time:10
Ingredients:

- 4 large slices sourdough, whole grain
- 4 tablespoons of Dijon mustard
- 1-1/2 cup grated sharp cheddar cheese
- 2 teaspoons green onion, chopped the green part
- 2 tablespoons of butter melted

Directions:

1. Brush the melted butter on one side of all the bread slices.
2. Then spread Dijon mustard on other sides of slices.
3. Then top the 2 bread slices with cheddar cheese and top it with green onions.
4. Cover with the remaining two slices to make two sandwiches.
5. Divide it between two baskets of the air fryer.
6. Turn on the air fry mode for zone 1 basket at 350 degrees f, for 10 minutes.
7. Use the match button for the second zone.
8. Once it's done, serve.

Nutrition:

- (Per serving) calories 617| fat 38 g| sodium 1213mg | carbs40.8 g | fiber 5g| sugar 5.6g | protein 29.5g

Chicken Stuffed Mushrooms

Servings: 6
Cooking Time: 15 Minutes.
Ingredients:

- 6 large fresh mushrooms, stems removed
- Stuffing:
- ½ cup chicken meat, cubed
- 1 (4 ounces) package cream cheese, softened
- ¼ lb. imitation crabmeat, flaked
- 1 cup butter
- 1 garlic clove, peeled and minced
- Black pepper and salt to taste
- Garlic powder to taste
- Crushed red pepper to taste

Directions:

1. Melt and heat butter in a skillet over medium heat.
2. Add chicken and sauté for 5 minutes.
3. Add in all the remaining ingredients for the stuffing.
4. Cook for 5 minutes, then turn off the heat.
5. Allow the mixture to cool. Stuff each mushroom with a tablespoon of this mixture.
6. Divide the stuffed mushrooms in the two crisper plates.
7. Return the crisper plate to the Ninja Foodi Dual Zone Air Fryer.
8. Choose the Air Fry mode for Zone 1 and set the temperature to 375 degrees F and the time to 15 minutes.
9. Select the "MATCH" button to copy the settings for Zone 2.
10. Initiate cooking by pressing the START/STOP button.
11. Serve warm.

Nutrition:

- (Per serving) Calories 180 | Fat 3.2g |Sodium 133mg | Carbs 32g | Fiber 1.1g | Sugar 1.8g | Protein 9g

Pumpkin Fries

Servings: 4
Cooking Time: 15 Minutes
Ingredients:

- 120g plain Greek yoghurt
- 2 to 3 teaspoons minced chipotle peppers
- ⅛ teaspoon plus ½ teaspoon salt, divided
- 1 medium pie pumpkin
- ¼ teaspoon garlic powder
- ¼ teaspoon ground cumin
- ¼ teaspoon chili powder
- ¼ teaspoon pepper

Directions:

1. Combine yoghurt, chipotle peppers, and ⅛ teaspoon salt in a small bowl. Refrigerate until ready to serve, covered.
2. Peeled the pumpkin and split it in half lengthwise. Discard the seeds. Cut pumpkin into 1 cm strips.
3. Place in a large mixing bowl. Toss with ½ teaspoon salt, garlic powder, cumin, chili powder, and pepper.
4. Press either "Zone 1" or "Zone 2" and then rotate the knob to select "Air Fry".
5. Set the temperature to 200 degrees C, and then set the time for 5 minutes to preheat.
6. After preheating, spray the Air-Fryer basket with cooking spray and line with parchment paper. Arrange pumpkin fries and spritz cooking spray on them.
7. Slide the basket into the Air Fryer and set the time for 8 minutes.
8. After that, toss them and again cook for 3 minutes longer.
9. After cooking time is completed, transfer them onto serving plates and serve.

Spinach Patties

Servings: 4
Cooking Time: 10 Minutes
Ingredients:

- 2 large eggs
- 250g frozen spinach, thawed, squeezed dry and chopped
- 185g crumbled feta cheese
- 2 garlic cloves, minced
- ¼ teaspoon pepper
- 1 tube (345g) refrigerated pizza crust

Directions:

1. Whisk eggs in a mixing bowl, reserving 1 tbsp. Combine the spinach, feta cheese, garlic, pepper, and the rest of the beaten eggs in a mixing bowl.
2. Roll out the pizza crust into a 30cm square. Cut each square into four 15cm squares.
3. Place about ⅓ cup of spinach mixture on each square. Fold them into a triangle and pinch them together to seal the edges. Make slits on the top and brush with the remaining egg.
4. Press either "Zone 1" and "Zone 2" and then rotate the knob to select "Air Fry".
5. Set the temperature to 220 degrees C, and then set the time for 5 minutes to preheat.
6. After preheating, spray the Air-Fryer basket with cooking spray and line with parchment paper. Arrange in a single layer and spritz them with cooking spray.
7. Slide the basket into the Air Fryer and set the time for 10 minutes.
8. After cooking time is completed, transfer them onto serving plates and serve.

Avocado Fries

Servings: 8
Cooking Time: 10 Minutes
Ingredients:

- 60g plain flour
- Salt and ground black pepper, as required
- 2 eggs
- 1 teaspoon water
- 100g seasoned breadcrumbs
- 2 avocados, peeled, pitted and sliced into 8 pieces
- Non-stick cooking spray

Directions:

1. In a shallow bowl, mix together the flour, salt, and black pepper.
2. In a second bowl, add the egg and water and beat well.
3. In a third bowl, place the breadcrumbs.
4. Coat the avocado slices with flour mixture, then dip into egg mixture and finally, coat evenly with the breadcrumbs.
5. Now, spray the avocado slices with cooking spray evenly.
6. Grease one basket of Ninja Foodi 2-Basket Air Fryer.
7. Press either "Zone 1" and "Zone 2" and then rotate the knob to select "Air Fry".
8. Set the temperature to 200 degrees C and then set the time for 5 minutes to preheat.
9. After preheating, arrange the avocado slices into the basket.
10. Slide basket into Air Fryer and set the time for 10 minutes.
11. After cooking time is completed, remove the fries from Air Fryer and serve warm.

Crispy Plantain Chips

Servings: 4
Cooking Time: 20 Minutes.
Ingredients:

- 1 green plantain
- 1 teaspoon canola oil
- ½ teaspoon sea salt

Directions:

1. Peel and cut the plantains into long strips using a mandolin slicer.
2. Grease the crisper plates with ½ teaspoon of canola oil.
3. Toss the plantains with salt and remaining canola oil.
4. Divide these plantains in the two crisper plates.

5. Return the crisper plate to the Ninja Foodi Dual Zone Air Fryer.
6. Choose the Air Fry mode for Zone 1 and set the temperature to 350 degrees F and the time to 20 minutes.
7. Select the "MATCH" button to copy the settings for Zone 2.
8. Initiate cooking by pressing the START/STOP button.
9. Toss the plantains after 10 minutes and resume cooking.
10. Serve warm.

Nutrition:

- (Per serving) Calories 122 | Fat 1.8g |Sodium 794mg | Carbs 17g | Fiber 8.9g | Sugar 1.6g | Protein 14.9g

Cinnamon-apple Crisps

Servings: 4
Cooking Time: 32 Minutes
Ingredients:

- Oil, for spraying
- 2 Red Delicious or Honeycrisp apples
- ¼ teaspoon ground cinnamon, divided

Directions:

1. Line the two air fryer baskets with parchment and spray lightly with oil.
2. Trim the uneven ends off the apples. Using a mandoline slicer on the thinnest setting or a sharp knife, cut the apples into very thin slices. Discard the cores.
3. Place the apple slices in a single layer in the two prepared baskets and sprinkle with the cinnamon.
4. Place two metal air fryer trivets on top of the apples to keep them from flying around while they are cooking.
5. Air fry at 150°C for 16 minutes, flipping every 5 minutes to ensure even cooking.
6. Let cool to room temperature before serving. The crisps will firm up as they cool.

Crispy Popcorn Shrimp

Servings: 4
Cooking Time: 10 Minutes
Ingredients:
- 170g shrimp, peeled and diced
- ½ cup breadcrumbs
- Salt and black pepper to taste
- 2 eggs, beaten

Directions:
1. Mix breadcrumbs with black pepper and salt in a bowl.
2. Dip the shrimp pieces in the eggs and coat each with breadcrumbs.
3. Divide the shrimp popcorn into the 2 Air Fryer baskets.
4. Return the air fryer basket 1 to Zone 1, and basket 2 to Zone 2 of the Ninja Foodi 2-Basket Air Fryer.
5. Choose the "Air Fry" mode for Zone 1 at 400 degrees F and 6 minutes of cooking time.
6. Select the "MATCH COOK" option to copy the settings for Zone 2.
7. Initiate cooking by pressing the START/PAUSE BUTTON.
8. Serve warm.

Tater Tots

Servings: 4
Cooking Time: 8 Minutes
Ingredients:
- 16 ounces tater tots
- ½ cup shredded cheddar cheese
- 1½ teaspoons bacon bits
- 2 green onions, chopped
- Sour cream (optional)

Directions:
1. Place a crisper plate in each drawer. Put the tater tots into the drawers in a single layer. Insert the drawers into the unit.
2. Select zone 1, then AIR FRY, then set the temperature to 360 degrees F/ 180 degrees C with a 6-minute timer. To match zone 2 settings to zone 1, choose MATCH. To begin, select START/STOP.
3. When the cooking time is over, add the shredded cheddar cheese, bacon bits, and green onions over the tater tots. Select zone 1, AIR FRY, 360 degrees F/ 180 degrees C, for 4 minutes. Select MATCH. Press START/STOP.
4. Drizzle sour cream over the top before serving.
5. Enjoy!
Nutrition:

- (Per serving) Calories 335 | Fat 19.1g | Sodium 761mg | Carbs 34.1g | Fiber 3g | Sugar 0.6g | Protein 8.9g

Waffle Fries

Servings: 2
Cooking Time: 15 Minutes
Ingredients:
- 2 russet potatoes
- ½ teaspoon seasoning salt

Directions:
1. If desired, peel the potatoes.
2. With Wave-Waffle Cutter, slice potatoes by turning them one-quarter turn after each pass over the blade.
3. In a mixing dish, toss the potato pieces with the seasoning salt. Toss the potatoes in the seasoning to ensure that it is uniformly distributed.
4. Place a baking sheet on the baskets.
5. Press either "Zone 1" or "Zone 2" and then rotate the knob to select "Air Fryer".
6. Set the temperature to 200 degrees C, and then set the time for 5 minutes to preheat.
7. After preheating, arrange them into the basket.
8. Slide the basket into the Air Fryer and set the time for 15 minutes.
9. After cooking time is completed, place on a wire rack for a few minutes, then transfer onto serving plates and serve.

Kale Potato Nuggets

Servings: 4
Cooking Time: 15 Minutes
Ingredients:
- 279g potatoes, chopped, boiled & mashed
- 268g kale, chopped
- 1 garlic clove, minced
- 30ml milk
- Pepper
- Salt

Directions:
1. In a bowl, mix potatoes, kale, milk, garlic, pepper, and salt until well combined.
2. Insert a crisper plate in the Ninja Foodi air fryer baskets.
3. Make small balls from the potato mixture and place them both baskets.
4. Select zone 1 then select "air fry" mode and set the temperature to 390 degrees F for 15 minutes. Press "match" to match zone 2 settings to zone 1. Press "start/stop" to begin. Turn halfway through.

Blueberries Muffins

Servings:2
Cooking Time:15
Ingredients:
- Salt, pinch
- 2 eggs
- 1/3 cup sugar
- 1/3 cup vegetable oil
- 4 tablespoons of water
- 1 teaspoon of lemon zest
- ¼ teaspoon of vanilla extract
- ½ teaspoon of baking powder
- 1 cup all-purpose flour
- 1 cup blueberries

Directions:
1. Take 4 one-cup sized ramekins that are oven safe and layer them with muffin papers.
2. Take a bowl and whisk the egg, sugar, oil, water, vanilla extract, and lemon zest.
3. Whisk it all very well.
4. Now, in a separate bowl, mix the flour, baking powder, and salt.
5. Now, add dry ingredients slowly to wet ingredients.
6. Now, pour this batter into ramekins and top it with blueberries.
7. Now, divide it between both zones of the Ninja Foodie 2-Basket Air Fryer.
8. Set the time for zone 1 to 15 minutes at 350 degrees F.
9. Select the MATCH button for the zone 2 basket.
10. Check if not done, and let it AIR FRY for one more minute.
11. Once it is done, serve.

Nutrition:
- (Per serving) Calories 781| Fat41.6g | Sodium 143mg | Carbs 92.7g | Fiber 3.5g| Sugar41.2 g | Protein 0g

Sweet Bites

Servings:4
Cooking Time:12
Ingredients:
- 10 sheets of Phyllo dough, (filo dough)
- 2 tablespoons of melted butter
- 1 cup walnuts, chopped
- 2 teaspoons of honey
- Pinch of cinnamon
- 1 teaspoon of orange zest

Directions:

1. First, layer together 10 Phyllo dough sheets on a flat surface.
2. Then cut it into 4 *4-inch squares.
3. Now, coat the squares with butter, drizzle some honey, orange zest, walnuts, and cinnamon.
4. Bring all 4 corners together and press the corners to make a little like purse design.
5. Divide it amongst air fryer basket and select zone 1 basket using AIR fry mode and set it for 7 minutes at 375 degrees F.
6. Select the MATCH button for the zone 2 basket.
7. Once done, take out and serve.

Nutrition:
- (Per serving) Calories 397| Fat 27.1 g| Sodium 271mg | Carbs31.2 g | Fiber 3.2g| Sugar3.3g | Protein 11g

Veggie Shrimp Toast

Servings: 4
Cooking Time: 3 To 6 Minutes
Ingredients:
- 8 large raw shrimp, peeled and finely chopped
- 1 egg white
- 2 garlic cloves, minced
- 3 tablespoons minced red pepper
- 1 medium celery stalk, minced
- 2 tablespoons cornflour
- ¼ teaspoon Chinese five-spice powder
- 3 slices firm thin-sliced no-salt wholemeal bread

Directions:
1. Preheat the air fryer to 175ºC.
2. In a small bowl, stir together the shrimp, egg white, garlic, red pepper, celery, cornflour, and five-spice powder. Top each slice of bread with one-third of the shrimp mixture, spreading it evenly to the edges. With a sharp knife, cut each slice of bread into 4 strips.
3. Place the shrimp toasts in the two air fryer baskets in a single layer. Air fry for 3 to 6 minutes, until crisp and golden brown.
4. Serve hot.

Tofu Veggie Meatballs

Servings: 4
Cooking Time: 15 Minutes
Ingredients:

- 122g firm tofu, drained
- 50g breadcrumbs
- 37g bamboo shoots, thinly sliced
- 22g carrots, shredded & steamed
- 1 tsp garlic powder
- 1 ½ tbsp soy sauce
- 2 tbsp cornstarch
- 3 dried shitake mushrooms, soaked & chopped
- Pepper
- Salt

Directions:

1. Add tofu and remaining ingredients into the food processor and process until well combined.
2. Insert a crisper plate in the Ninja Foodi air fryer baskets.
3. Make small balls from the tofu mixture and place them in both baskets.
4. Select zone 1, then select "air fry" mode and set the temperature to 380 degrees F for 10 minutes. Press "match" to match zone 2 settings to zone 1. Press "start/stop" to begin. Turn halfway through.

Desserts Recipes

Chocolate Mug Cakes

Servings: 4
Cooking Time: 20 Minutes
Ingredients:

- 1 cup flour
- 8 tablespoons sugar
- 1 teaspoon baking powder
- ½ teaspoon baking soda
- ¼ teaspoon salt
- 8 tablespoons milk
- 8 tablespoons applesauce
- 2 tablespoons vegetable oil
- 1 teaspoon vanilla extract
- 8 tablespoons chocolate chips

Directions:

1. Press "Zone 1" and "Zone 2" and then rotate the knob for each zone to select "Bake".
2. Set the temperature to 375 degrees F/ 190 degrees C for both zones and then set the time for 5 minutes to preheat.
3. In a bowl, mix together the flour, sugar, baking powder, baking soda and salt.
4. Add the milk, applesauce, oil and vanilla extract and mix until well combined.
5. Gently fold in the chocolate chips.
6. Divide the mixture into 4 heatproof mugs.
7. After preheating, arrange 2 mugs into the basket of each zone.
8. Slide each basket into Air Fryer and set the time for 17 minutes.
9. After cooking time is completed, remove the mugs from Air Fryer.
10. Place the mugs onto a wire rack to cool for about 10 minutes before serving.

Grilled Peaches

Servings: 4
Cooking Time: 10 Minutes
Ingredients:

- 2 yellow peaches
- ¼ cup graham cracker crumbs
- ¼ cup brown sugar
- ¼ cup butter, diced into tiny cubes
- Whipped cream or ice cream, for serving.

Directions:

1. Cut the peaches into wedges and pull out their pits.
2. Install a crisper plate in both drawers. Put half of the peach wedges into the drawer in zone 1 and half in zone 2's. Sprinkle the tops of the wedges with the crumbs, sugar, and butter. Insert the drawers into the unit.
3. Select zone 1, select AIR FRY, set the temperature to 390°F, and set the time to 10 minutes. Select MATCH to match zone 2 settings to zone 1. Press the START/STOP button to begin cooking.

Chocolate Muffins

Servings: 12
Cooking Time: 20 Minutes
Ingredients:

- 2 cup all-purpose flour
- 4 tablespoons cocoa powder
- ½ teaspoon baking soda
- 2 teaspoons baking powder
- ½ teaspoon salt
- 1 cup coconut milk
- ½ cup granulated sugar
- 6 tablespoons coconut oil, melted
- 1 teaspoon vanilla extract
- 1 cup dark chocolate chips
- ½ cup pistachios, chopped

Directions:

1. In a bowl, add the flour, cocoa powder, baking powder, baking soda, and salt and mix well.
2. In another bowl, add the coconut milk, sugar, coconut oil and vanilla extract and beat until well combined.
3. Add the flour mixture and mix until just combined.
4. Fold in the chocolate chips and pistachios.
5. Grease 2 silicone muffin tins.
6. Place the mixture into prepared muffin cups about ¾ full.
7. Press "Zone 1" and "Zone 2" and then rotate the knob for each zone to select "Air Fry".
8. Set the temperature to 300 degrees F/ 150 degrees C for both zones and then set the time for 5 minutes to preheat.
9. After preheating, arrange 1 muffin tin into the basket of each zone.
10. Slide each basket into Air Fryer and set the time for 15 minutes.
11. After cooking time is completed, remove the muffin tin from Air Fryer.
12. Place the muffin molds onto a wire rack to cool for about 10 minutes.
13. Carefully invert the muffins onto the wire rack to completely cool before serving.

Almond Shortbread

Servings: 8
Cooking Time: 12 Minutes
Ingredients:

- 110 g unsalted butter
- 100 g granulated sugar
- 1 teaspoon pure almond extract
- 125 g plain flour

Directions:

1. In bowl of a stand mixer fitted with the paddle attachment, beat the butter and sugar on medium speed until light and fluffy . Add the almond extract and beat until combined . Turn the mixer to low. Add the flour a little at a time and beat for about 2 minutes more until well-incorporated.
2. Pat the dough into an even layer in a baking pan. Place the pan in the zone 1 air fryer drawer. Set the air fryer to 192ºC and bake for 12 minutes.
3. Carefully remove the pan from air fryer drawer. While the shortbread is still warm and soft, cut it into 8 wedges.
4. Let cool in the pan on a wire rack for 5 minutes. Remove the wedges from the pan and let cool completely on the rack before serving.

Chocolate Chip Cake

Servings: 4
Cooking Time: 15 Minutes
Ingredients:

- Salt, pinch
- 2 eggs, whisked
- ½ cup brown sugar
- ½ cup butter, melted
- 10 tablespoons almond milk
- ¼ teaspoon vanilla extract
- ½ teaspoon baking powder
- 1 cup all-purpose flour
- 1 cup chocolate chips
- ½ cup cocoa powder

Directions:

1. Take 2 round baking pans that fit inside the baskets of the air fryer and line them with baking paper.
2. In a bowl with an electric beater, mix the eggs, brown sugar, butter, almond milk, and vanilla extract.
3. In a second bowl, mix the flour, cocoa powder, baking powder, and salt.
4. Slowly add the dry to the wet Ingredients:.
5. Fold in the chocolate chips and mix well with a spoon or spatula.
6. Divide this batter into the round baking pans.
7. Set the time for zone 1 to 16 minutes at 350 degrees F on AIR FRY mode.
8. Select the MATCH button for the zone 2 basket.
9. After the time is up, check. If they're not done, let them AIR FRY for one more minute.
10. Once it is done, serve.

Coconut-custard Pie And Pecan Brownies

Servings: 9
Cooking Time: 20 To 23 Minutes
Ingredients:
- Coconut-Custard Pie:
- 240 ml milk
- 50 g granulated sugar, plus 2 tablespoons
- 30 g scone mix
- 1 teaspoon vanilla extract
- 2 eggs
- 2 tablespoons melted butter
- Cooking spray
- 50 g desiccated, sweetened coconut
- Pecan Brownies:
- 50 g blanched finely ground almond flour
- 55 g powdered sweetener
- 2 tablespoons unsweetened cocoa powder
- ½ teaspoon baking powder
- 55 g unsalted butter, softened
- 1 large egg
- 35 g chopped pecans
- 40 g low-carb, sugar-free chocolate chips

Directions:
1. Make the Coconut-Custard Pie :
2. Place all ingredients except coconut in a medium bowl.
3. Using a hand mixer, beat on high speed for 3 minutes.
4. Let sit for 5 minutes.
5. Preheat the air fryer to 164ºC.
6. Spray a baking pan with cooking spray and place pan in the zone 1 air fryer drawer.
7. Pour filling into pan and sprinkle coconut over top.
8. Cook pie for 20 to 23 minutes or until center sets.
9. Make the Pecan Brownies :
10. In a large bowl, mix almond flour, sweetener, cocoa powder, and baking powder. Stir in butter and egg. 2. Fold in pecans and chocolate chips. Scoop mixture into a round baking pan. Place pan into the zone 2 air fryer drawer. 3. Adjust the temperature to 148ºC and bake for 20 minutes. 4. When fully cooked a toothpick inserted in center will come out clean. Allow 20 minutes to fully cool and firm up.

Jelly Donuts

Servings: 4
Cooking Time: 5 Minutes
Ingredients:

- 1 package Pillsbury Grands (Homestyle)
- ½ cup seedless raspberry jelly
- 1 tablespoon butter, melted
- ½ cup sugar

Directions:
1. Install a crisper plate in both drawers. Place half of the biscuits in the zone 1 drawer and half in zone 2's, then insert the drawers into the unit. You may need to cook in batches.
2. Select zone 1, select AIR FRY, set temperature to 390ºF, and set time to 22 minutes. Select MATCH to match zone 2 settings to zone 1. Press the START/STOP button to begin cooking.
3. Place the sugar into a wide bowl with a flat bottom.
4. Baste all sides of the cooked biscuits with the melted butter and roll in the sugar to cover completely.
5. Using a long cake tip, pipe 1–2 tablespoons of raspberry jelly into each biscuit. You've now got raspberry-filled donuts!

Brownies Muffins

Servings: 3
Cooking Time: 10 Minutes
Ingredients:

- ¼ egg
- ⅛ cup walnuts, chopped
- 1 tablespoon vegetable oil
- ¼ package fudge brownie mix
- ½ teaspoon water

Directions:
1. Take a bowl, add all the ingredients. Mix well.
2. Place the mixture into prepared muffin molds evenly.
3. Line each basket of "Zone 1" and "Zone 2" with parchment paper.
4. Press "Zone 1" and "Zone 2" and then rotate the knob for each zone to select "Air Fry".
5. Set the temperature to 300 degrees F/ 150 degrees C for both zones and then set the time for 5 minutes to preheat.
6. After preheating, arrange the muffin molds into the basket of each zone.
7. Slide each basket into Air Fryer and set the time for 10 minutes.
8. After cooking time is completed, remove from Air Fryer.
9. Refrigerate.
10. Serve and enjoy!

Dehydrated Peaches

Servings: 4
Cooking Time: 8 Hours
Ingredients:

- 300g canned peaches

Directions:

1. Insert a crisper plate in the Ninja Foodi air fryer baskets.
2. Place peaches in both baskets.
3. Select zone 1, then select "dehydrate" mode and set the temperature to 135 degrees F for 8 hours. Press "start/stop" to begin.

Nutrition:

- (Per serving) Calories 30 | Fat 0.2g |Sodium 0mg | Carbs 7g | Fiber 1.2g | Sugar 7g | Protein 0.7g

Lime Bars

Servings: 12 Bars
Cooking Time: 33 Minutes
Ingredients:

- 140 g blanched finely ground almond flour, divided
- 75 g powdered sweetener, divided
- 4 tablespoons salted butter, melted
- 120 ml fresh lime juice
- 2 large eggs, whisked

Directions:

1. In a medium bowl, mix together 110 g flour, 25 g sweetener, and butter. Press mixture into bottom of an ungreased round nonstick cake pan.
2. Place pan into the zone 1 air fryer drawer. Adjust the temperature to 148°C and bake for 13 minutes. Crust will be brown and set in the middle when done.
3. Allow to cool in pan 10 minutes.
4. In a medium bowl, combine remaining flour, remaining sweetener, lime juice, and eggs. Pour mixture over cooled crust and return to air fryer for 20 minutes. Top will be browned and firm when done.
5. Let cool completely in pan, about 30 minutes, then chill covered in the refrigerator 1 hour. Serve chilled.

Double Chocolate Brownies

Servings: 8
Cooking Time: 15 To 20 Minutes
Ingredients:

- 110 g almond flour
- 50 g unsweetened cocoa powder
- ½ teaspoon baking powder
- 35 g powdered sweetener
- ¼ teaspoon salt
- 110 g unsalted butter, melted and cooled

- 3 eggs
- 1 teaspoon vanilla extract
- 2 tablespoons mini semisweet chocolate chips

Directions:

1. Preheat the air fryer to 175°C. Line a cake pan with baking paper and brush with oil.
2. In a large bowl, combine the almond flour, cocoa powder, baking powder, sweetener, and salt. Add the butter, eggs, and vanilla. Stir until thoroughly combined Spread the batter into the prepared pan and scatter the chocolate chips on top.
3. Air fry in the zone 1 basket for 15 to 20 minutes until the edges are set Let cool completely before slicing. To store, cover and refrigerate the brownies for up to 3 days.

Oreo Rolls

Servings: 9
Cooking Time: 10 Minutes
Ingredients:

- 1 crescent sheet roll
- 9 Oreo cookies
- Cinnamon powder, to serve
- Powdered sugar, to serve

Directions:

1. Spread the crescent sheet roll and cut it into 9 equal squares.
2. Place one cookie at the center of each square.
3. Wrap each square around the cookies and press the ends to seal.
4. Place half of the wrapped cookies in each crisper plate.
5. Return the crisper plates to the Ninja Foodi Dual Zone Air Fryer.
6. Select the Bake mode for Zone 1 and set the temperature to 360 degrees F and the time to 4-6 minutes.
7. Select the "MATCH" button to copy the settings for Zone 2.
8. Initiate cooking by pressing the START/STOP button.
9. Check for the doneness of the cookie rolls if they are golden brown, else cook 1-2 minutes more.
10. Garnish the rolls with sugar and cinnamon.
11. Serve.

Air Fried Bananas

Servings: 4
Cooking Time: 15 Minutes
Ingredients:

- 4 bananas, sliced
- 1 avocado oil cooking spray

Directions:

1. Spread the banana slices in the two crisper plates in a single layer.
2. Drizzle avocado oil over the banana slices.
3. Return the crisper plate to the Ninja Foodi Dual Zone Air Fryer.
4. Choose the Air Fry mode for Zone 1 and set the temperature to 350 degrees F and the time to 13 minutes.
5. Select the "MATCH" button to copy the settings for Zone 2.
6. Initiate cooking by pressing the START/STOP button.
7. Serve.

Dessert Empanadas

Servings: 12
Cooking Time: 10 Minutes
Ingredients:

- 12 empanada wrappers thawed
- 2 apples, chopped
- 2 tablespoons raw honey
- 1 teaspoon vanilla extract
- 1 teaspoon cinnamon
- ⅛ teaspoon nutmeg
- 2 teaspoons cornstarch
- 1 teaspoon water
- 1 egg beaten

Directions:

1. Mix apples with vanilla, honey, nutmeg, and cinnamon in a saucepan.
2. Cook for 3 minutes then mix cornstarch with water and pour into the pan.
3. Cook for 30 seconds.
4. Allow this filling to cool and keep it aside.
5. Spread the wrappers on the working surface.
6. Divide the apple filling on top of the wrappers.
7. Fold the wrappers in half and seal the edges by pressing them.
8. Brush the empanadas with the beaten egg and place them in the air fryer basket 1.
9. Return the air fryer basket 1 to Zone 1 of the Ninja Foodi 2-Basket Air Fryer.
10. Choose the "Air Fry" mode for Zone 1 at 400 degrees F and 10 minutes of cooking time.
11. Initiate cooking by pressing the START/PAUSE BUTTON.
12. Flip the empanadas once cooked halfway through.
13. Serve.

Nutrition:

- (Per serving) Calories 204 | Fat 9g |Sodium 91mg | Carbs 27g | Fiber 2.4g | Sugar 15g | Protein 1.3g

Lava Cake

Servings: 4
Cooking Time: 15 Minutes
Ingredients:

- 1 cup semi-sweet chocolate chips
- 8 tablespoons butter
- 4 eggs
- 2 teaspoons vanilla extract
- ½ teaspoon salt
- 6 tablespoons all-purpose flour
- 1 cup powdered sugar
- For the chocolate filling:
- 2 tablespoons Nutella
- 1 tablespoon butter, softened
- 1 tablespoon powdered sugar

Directions:

1. Heat the chocolate chips and butter in a medium-sized microwave-safe bowl in 30-second intervals until thoroughly melted and smooth, stirring after each interval.
2. Whisk together the eggs, vanilla, salt, flour, and powdered sugar in a mixing bowl.
3. Combine the Nutella, softened butter, and powdered sugar in a separate bowl.
4. Spray 4 ramekins with oil and fill them halfway with the chocolate chip mixture. Fill each ramekin halfway with Nutella, then top with the remaining chocolate chip mixture, making sure the Nutella is well covered.
5. Install a crisper plate in both drawers. Place 2 ramekins in each drawer and insert the drawers into the unit.
6. Select zone 1, select AIR FRY, set temperature to 390°F, and set time to 22 minutes. Select MATCH to match zone 2 settings to zone 1. Press the START/STOP button to begin cooking.
7. Serve hot.

Berry Crumble And Coconut-custard Pie

Servings: 8
Cooking Time: 20 To 23 Minutes
Ingredients:

- Berry Crumble:
- For the Filling:
- 300 g mixed berries
- 2 tablespoons sugar
- 1 tablespoon cornflour
- 1 tablespoon fresh lemon juice
- For the Topping:
- 30 g plain flour
- 20 g rolled oats
- 1 tablespoon granulated sugar
- 2 tablespoons cold unsalted butter, cut into small cubes
- Whipped cream or ice cream (optional)
- Coconut-Custard Pie:
- 240 ml milk
- 50 g granulated sugar, plus 2 tablespoons
- 30 g scone mix
- 1 teaspoon vanilla extract
- 2 eggs
- 2 tablespoons melted butter
- Cooking spray
- 50 g desiccated, sweetened coconut

Directions:

1. Make the Berry Crumble :
2. 1. Preheat the air fryer to 205°C. For the filling: In a round baking pan, gently mix the berries, sugar, cornflour, and lemon juice until thoroughly combined. 3. For the topping: In a small bowl, combine the flour, oats, and sugar. Stir the butter into the flour mixture until the mixture has the consistency of breadcrumbs. 4. Sprinkle the topping over the berries. 5. Put the pan in the zone 1 air fryer basket and air fry for 15 minutes. Let cool for 5 minutes on a wire rack. 6. Serve topped with whipped cream or ice cream, if desired.
3. Make the Coconut-Custard Pie :
4. Place all ingredients except coconut in a medium bowl.
5. Using a hand mixer, beat on high speed for 3 minutes.
6. Let sit for 5 minutes.
7. Preheat the air fryer to 165°C.
8. Spray a baking pan with cooking spray and place pan in the zone 2 air fryer basket.
9. Pour filling into pan and sprinkle coconut over top.
10. Cook pie for 20 to 23 minutes or until center sets.

Spiced Apple Cake

Servings: 6
Cooking Time: 30 Minutes
Ingredients:

- Vegetable oil
- 2 diced & peeled Gala apples
- 1 tablespoon fresh lemon juice
- 55 g unsalted butter, softened
- 65 g granulated sugar
- 2 large eggs
- 155 g plain flour
- 1½ teaspoons baking powder
- 1 tablespoon apple pie spice
- ½ teaspoon ground ginger
- ¼ teaspoon ground cardamom
- ¼ teaspoon ground nutmeg
- ½ teaspoon kosher, or coarse sea salt
- 60 ml whole milk
- Icing sugar, for dusting

Directions:

1. Grease a 0.7-liter Bundt, or tube pan with oil; set aside.
2. In a medium bowl, toss the apples with the lemon juice until well coated; set aside.
3. In a large bowl, combine the butter and sugar. Beat with an electric hand mixer on medium speed until the sugar has dissolved. Add the eggs and beat until fluffy. Add the flour, baking powder, apple pie spice, ginger, cardamom, nutmeg, salt, and milk. Mix until the batter is thick but pourable.
4. Pour the batter into the prepared pan. Top batter evenly with the apple mixture. Place the pan in the zone 1 air fryer drawer. Set the temperature to 176°C and cook for 30 minutes, or until a toothpick inserted in the center of the cake comes out clean. Close the air fryer and let the cake rest for 10 minutes. Turn the cake out onto a wire rack and cool completely.
5. Right before serving, dust the cake with icing sugar.

Sweet Potato Donut Holes

Servings: 18 Donut Holes
Cooking Time: 4 To 5 Minutes
Ingredients:

- 125 g plain flour
- 65 g granulated sugar
- ¼ teaspoon baking soda
- 1 teaspoon baking powder
- ⅛ teaspoon salt
- 125 g cooked & mashed purple sweet potatoes
- 1 egg, beaten
- 2 tablespoons butter, melted
- 1 teaspoon pure vanilla extract
- Coconut, or avocado oil for misting or cooking spray

Directions:

1. Preheat the air fryer to 200ºC.
2. In a large bowl, stir together the flour, sugar, baking soda, baking powder, and salt.
3. In a separate bowl, combine the potatoes, egg, butter, and vanilla and mix well.
4. Add potato mixture to dry ingredients and stir into a soft dough.
5. Shape dough into 1½-inch balls. Mist lightly with oil or cooking spray.
6. Place the donut holes in the two air fryer baskets, leaving a little space in between. Cook for 4 to 5 minutes, until done in center and lightly browned outside.

Mocha Pudding Cake Vanilla Pudding Cake

Servings:8
Cooking Time: 25 Minutes
Ingredients:

- FOR THE MOCHA PUDDING CAKE
- 1 cup all-purpose flour
- ⅔ cup granulated sugar
- 1 cup packed light brown sugar, divided
- 5 tablespoons unsweetened cocoa powder, divided
- 2 teaspoons baking powder
- ¼ teaspoon kosher salt
- ½ cup unsweetened almond milk
- 2 teaspoons vanilla extract
- 2 tablespoons vegetable oil
- 1 cup freshly brewed coffee
- FOR THE VANILLA PUDDING CAKE
- 1 cup all-purpose flour
- ⅔ cup granulated sugar, plus ½ cup
- 2 teaspoons baking powder
- ¼ teaspoon kosher salt
- ½ cup unsweetened almond milk
- 2½ teaspoons vanilla extract, divided
- 2 tablespoons vegetable oil
- ¾ cup hot water
- 2 teaspoons cornstarch

Directions:

1. To prep the mocha pudding cake: In a medium bowl, combine the flour, granulated sugar, ½ cup of brown sugar, 3 tablespoons of cocoa powder, the baking powder, and salt. Stir in the almond milk, vanilla, and oil to form a thick batter.
2. Spread the batter in the bottom of the Zone 1 basket. Sprinkle the remaining ½ cup brown sugar and 2 tablespoons of cocoa powder in an even layer over the batter. Gently pour the hot coffee over the batter (do not mix).
3. To prep the vanilla pudding cake: In a medium bowl, combine the flour, ⅔ cup of granulated sugar, the baking powder, and salt. Stir in the almond milk, 2 teaspoons of vanilla, and the oil to form a thick batter.
4. Spread the batter in the bottom of the Zone 2 basket.
5. In a small bowl, whisk together the hot water, cornstarch, and remaining ½ cup of sugar and ½ teaspoon of vanilla. Gently pour over the batter (do not mix).
6. To cook both pudding cakes: Insert both baskets in the unit.
7. Select Zone 1, select BAKE, set the temperature to 330ºF, and set the timer to 25 minutes. Select MATCH COOK to match Zone 2 settings to Zone 1.
8. Press START/PAUSE to begin cooking.
9. When cooking is complete, the tops of the cakes should be dry and set.
10. Let the cakes rest for 10 minutes before serving. The pudding will thicken as it cools.

Nutrition:

- (Per serving) Calories: 531; Total fat: 8g; Saturated fat: 1g; Carbohydrates: 115g; Fiber: 3.5g; Protein: 5g; Sodium: 111mg

Savory Almond Butter Cookie Balls

Servings: 10 (1 Ball Per Serving)
Cooking Time: 10 Minutes
Ingredients:

- 1 cup almond butter
- 1 large egg
- 1 teaspoon vanilla extract
- ¼ cup low-carb protein powder
- ¼ cup powdered erythritol
- ¼ cup shredded unsweetened coconut
- ¼ cup low-carb, sugar-free chocolate chips
- ½ teaspoon ground cinnamon

Directions:

1. Stir egg and almond butter in a large bowl. Add in protein powder, erythritol, and vanilla.
2. Fold in cinnamon, coconut, and chocolate chips. Roll up into 1&quot| balls. Put balls into 6&quot| round baking pan and place into the air fryer basket.
3. Set the temperature to 320°F, then set the timer for 10 minutes.
4. Let it cool fully. Keep in an airtight container in the refrigerator up to 4 days and serve.

Chocó Lava Cake

Servings: 4
Cooking Time: 10 Minutes
Ingredients:

- 3 eggs
- 3 egg yolks
- 70g dark chocolate, chopped
- 168g cups powdered sugar
- 96g all-purpose flour
- 1 tsp vanilla
- 113g butter
- ½ tsp salt

Directions:

1. Add chocolate and butter to a bowl and microwave for 30 seconds. Remove from oven and stir until smooth.
2. Add eggs, egg yolks, sugar, flour, vanilla, and salt into the melted chocolate and stir until well combined.
3. Pour batter into the four greased ramekins.
4. Insert a crisper plate in Ninja Foodi air fryer baskets.
5. Place ramekins in both baskets.
6. Select zone 1 then select "air fry" mode and set the temperature to 390 degrees F for 10 minutes. Press

"match" to match zone 2 settings to zone 1. Press "start/stop" to begin.
Nutrition:

- (Per serving) Calories 687 | Fat 37.3g |Sodium 527mg | Carbs 78.3g | Fiber 1.5g | Sugar 57.4g | Protein 10.7g

Lemon Raspberry Muffins

Servings: 6
Cooking Time: 15 Minutes
Ingredients:

- 220 g almond flour
- 75 g powdered sweetener
- 1¼ teaspoons baking powder
- ⅓ teaspoon ground allspice
- ⅓ teaspoon ground star anise
- ½ teaspoon grated lemon zest
- ¼ teaspoon salt
- 2 eggs
- 240 ml sour cream
- 120 ml coconut oil
- 60 g raspberries

Directions:

1. Preheat the air fryer to 176ºC. Line a muffin pan with 6 paper cases.
2. In a mixing bowl, mix the almond flour, sweetener, baking powder, allspice, star anise, lemon zest, and salt.
3. In another mixing bowl, beat the eggs, sour cream, and coconut oil until well mixed. Add the egg mixture to the flour mixture and stir to combine. Mix in the raspberries.
4. Scrape the batter into the prepared muffin cups, filling each about three-quarters full.
5. Bake for 15 minutes, or until the tops are golden and a toothpick inserted in the middle comes out clean.
6. Allow the muffins to cool for 10 minutes in the muffin pan before removing and serving.

Speedy Chocolate Espresso Mini Cheesecake

Servings: 2
Cooking Time: 15 Minutes
Ingredients:
- ½ cup walnuts
- 2 tablespoons salted butter
- 2 tablespoons granular erythritol
- 4 ounces full-fat cream cheese, softened
- 1 large egg
- ½ teaspoon vanilla extract
- 2 tablespoons powdered erythritol
- 2 teaspoons unsweetened cocoa powder
- 1 teaspoon espresso powder

Directions:
1. Put butter, granular erythritol and walnuts in a food processor. Pulse until all the ingredients stick together to form a dough.
2. Place dough into 4&quot| springform pan and put into the air fryer basket.
3. Set the temperature to 400°F, then set the timer for 5 minutes.
4. When timer goes off, remove crust and allow it to cool.
5. Combine cream cheese with vanilla extract, egg, powdered erythritol, espresso powder and cocoa powder until smooth in a medium bowl.
6. Pour mixture on top of baked walnut crust and put into the air fryer basket.
7. Set the temperature for 300°F, then set the timer for 10 minutes.
8. Once fully cooked, allow to chill for 2 hours before serving.

Simple Pineapple Sticks And Crispy Pineapple Rings

Servings: 9
Cooking Time: 10 Minutes
Ingredients:
- Simple Pineapple Sticks:
- ½ fresh pineapple, cut into sticks
- 25 g desiccated coconut
- Crispy Pineapple Rings:
- 240 ml rice milk
- 85 g plain flour
- 120 ml water
- 25 g unsweetened flaked coconut
- 4 tablespoons granulated sugar
- ½ teaspoon baking soda
- ½ teaspoon baking powder
- ½ teaspoon vanilla essence
- ½ teaspoon ground cinnamon
- ¼ teaspoon ground star anise
- Pinch of kosher, or coarse sea salt
- 1 medium pineapple, peeled and sliced

Directions:
1. Simple Pineapple Sticks :
2. Preheat the air fryer to 204ºC.
3. Coat the pineapple sticks in the desiccated coconut and put in the zone 1 air fryer drawer.
4. Air fry for 10 minutes.
5. Serve immediately
6. Crispy Pineapple Rings :
7. Preheat the air fryer to 204ºC.
8. In a large bowl, stir together all the ingredients except the pineapple.
9. Dip each pineapple slice into the batter until evenly coated.
10. Arrange the pineapple slices in the zone 2 drawer and air fry for 6 to 8 minutes until golden brown.
11. Remove from the drawer to a plate and cool for 5 minutes before serving warm

Easy Mini Chocolate Chip Pan Cookie

Servings: 4
Cooking Time: 7 Minutes
Ingredients:
- ½ cup blanched finely ground almond flour
- ¼ cup powdered erythritol
- 2 tablespoons unsalted butter, softened
- 1 large egg
- ½ teaspoon unflavored gelatin
- ½ teaspoon baking powder
- ½ teaspoon vanilla extract
- 2 tablespoons low-carb, sugar-free chocolate chips

Directions:
1. Combine erythritol and almond flour in a large bowl. Add in egg, gelatin, and butter , stir well.
2. Stir in vanilla and baking powder and then fold in chocolate chips. Spoon batter into 6&quot| round baking pan. Put pan into the air fryer basket.
3. Set the temperature to 300°F, then set the timer for 7 minutes.
4. The top of the cookie will be golden brown and a toothpick inserted in center will come out clean when fully cooked. Allow to rest for more than 10 minutes.

Pumpkin Cookie With Cream Cheese Frosting

Servings: 6
Cooking Time: 7 Minutes
Ingredients:
- 50 g blanched finely ground almond flour
- 50 g powdered sweetener, divided
- 2 tablespoons butter, softened
- 1 large egg
- ½ teaspoon unflavored gelatin
- ½ teaspoon baking powder
- ½ teaspoon vanilla extract
- ½ teaspoon pumpkin pie spice
- 2 tablespoons pure pumpkin purée
- ½ teaspoon ground cinnamon, divided
- 40 g low-carb, sugar-free chocolate chips
- 85 g full-fat cream cheese, softened

Directions:
1. In a large bowl, mix almond flour and 25 gsweetener. Stir in butter, egg, and gelatin until combined. 2. Stir in baking powder, vanilla, pumpkin pie spice, pumpkin purée, and ¼ teaspoon cinnamon, then fold in chocolate chips. 3. Pour batter into a round baking pan. Place pan into the zone 1 air fryer basket. 4. Adjust the temperature to 150°C and bake for 7 minutes. 5. When fully cooked, the top will be golden brown, and a toothpick inserted in center will come out clean. Let cool at least 20 minutes. 6. To make the frosting: mix cream cheese, remaining ¼ teaspoon cinnamon, and remaining 25 g sweetener in a large bowl. Using an electric mixer, beat until it becomes fluffy. Spread onto the cooled cookie. Garnish with additional cinnamon if desired.

Zucchini Bread

Servings: 12
Cooking Time: 40 Minutes
Ingredients:
- 220 g coconut flour
- 2 teaspoons baking powder
- 150 g granulated sweetener
- 120 ml coconut oil, melted
- 1 teaspoon apple cider vinegar
- 1 teaspoon vanilla extract
- 3 eggs, beaten
- 1 courgette, grated
- 1 teaspoon ground cinnamon

Directions:

1. In the mixing bowl, mix coconut flour with baking powder, sweetener, coconut oil, apple cider vinegar, vanilla extract, eggs, courgette, and ground cinnamon.
2. Transfer the mixture into the two air fryer drawers and flatten it in the shape of the bread.
3. Cook the bread at 176°C for 40 minutes.

Glazed Cherry Turnovers

Servings: 8
Cooking Time: 14 Minutes
Ingredients:
- 2 sheets frozen puff pastry, thawed
- 600 g can premium cherry pie filling
- 2 teaspoons ground cinnamon
- 1 egg, beaten
- 90 g sliced almonds
- 120 g icing sugar
- 2 tablespoons milk

Directions:
1. Roll a sheet of puff pastry out into a square that is approximately 10-inches by 10-inches. Cut this large square into quarters.
2. Mix the cherry pie filling and cinnamon together in a bowl. Spoon ¼ cup of the cherry filling into the center of each puff pastry square. Brush the perimeter of the pastry square with the egg wash. Fold one corner of the puff pastry over the cherry pie filling towards the opposite corner, forming a triangle. Seal the two edges of the pastry together with the tip of a fork, making a design with the tines. Brush the top of the turnovers with the egg wash and sprinkle sliced almonds over each one. Repeat these steps with the second sheet of puff pastry. You should have eight turnovers at the end.
3. Preheat the air fryer to 188°C.
4. Air fry turnovers in the two drawers for 14 minutes, carefully turning them over halfway through the cooking time.
5. While the turnovers are cooking, make the glaze by whisking the icing sugar and milk together in a small bowl until smooth. Let the glaze sit for a minute so the sugar can absorb the milk. If the consistency is still too thick to drizzle, add a little more milk, a drop at a time, and stir until smooth.
6. Let the cooked cherry turnovers sit for at least 10 minutes. Then drizzle the glaze over each turnover in a zigzag motion. Serve warm or at room temperature.

Fried Oreos

Servings: 8
Cooking Time: 8 Minutes
Ingredients:

- 1 can Pillsbury Crescent Dough (or equivalent)
- 8 Oreo cookies
- 1–2 tablespoons powdered sugar

Directions:

1. Open the crescent dough up and cut it into the right-size pieces to completely wrap each cookie.
2. Wrap each Oreo in dough. Make sure that there are no air bubbles and that the cookies are completely covered.
3. Install a crisper plate in both drawers. Place half the Oreo cookies in the zone 1 drawer and half in zone 2's. Sprinkle the tops with the powdered sugar, then insert the drawers into the unit.
4. Select zone 1, select AIR FRY, set temperature to 390°F, and set time to 8 minutes. Select MATCH to match zone 2 settings to zone 1. Press the START/STOP button to begin cooking.
5. Serve warm and enjoy!

Baked Brazilian Pineapple

Servings: 4
Cooking Time: 10 Minutes
Ingredients:

- 95 g brown sugar
- 2 teaspoons ground cinnamon
- 1 small pineapple, peeled, cored, and cut into spears
- 3 tablespoons unsalted butter, melted

Directions:

1. In a small bowl, mix the brown sugar and cinnamon until thoroughly combined.
2. Brush the pineapple spears with the melted butter. Sprinkle the cinnamon-sugar over the spears, pressing lightly to ensure it adheres well.
3. Place the spears in the two air fryer drawers in a single layer. Set the air fryer to 204°C and cook for 10 minutes. Halfway through the cooking time, brush the spears with butter.
4. The pineapple spears are done when they are heated through, and the sugar is bubbling. Serve hot.

Olive Oil Cake & Old-fashioned Fudge Pie

Servings: 16
Cooking Time: 30 Minutes
Ingredients:

- Olive Oil Cake:
- 120 g blanched finely ground almond flour
- 5 large eggs, whisked
- 175 ml extra-virgin olive oil
- 75 g granulated sweetener
- 1 teaspoon vanilla extract
- 1 teaspoon baking powder
- Old-Fashioned Fudge Pie:
- 300 g granulated sugar
- 40 g unsweetened cocoa powder
- 70 g self-raising flour
- 3 large eggs, unbeaten
- 12 tablespoons unsalted butter, melted
- 1½ teaspoons vanilla extract
- 1 (9-inch) unbaked piecrust
- 30 g icing sugar (optional)

Directions:

1. Make the Olive Oil Cake :
2. In a large bowl, mix all ingredients. Pour batter into an ungreased round nonstick baking dish.
3. Place dish into the zone 1 air fryer basket. Adjust the temperature to 150°C and bake for 30 minutes. The cake will be golden on top and firm in the center when done.
4. Let cake cool in dish 30 minutes before slicing and serving.
5. Make the Old-Fashioned Fudge Pie :
6. In a medium bowl, stir together the sugar, cocoa powder, and flour. Stir in the eggs and melted butter. Stir in the vanilla.
7. Preheat the air fryer to 175°C.
8. Pour the chocolate filing into the crust.
9. Cook in the zone 2 basket for 25 to 30 minutes, stirring every 10 minutes, until a knife inserted into the middle comes out clean. Let sit for 5 minutes before dusting with icing sugar to serve.

Walnut Baklava Bites
Pistachio Baklava Bites

Servings:12
Cooking Time: 10 Minutes
Ingredients:
- FOR THE WALNUT BAKLAVA BITES
- ¼ cup finely chopped walnuts
- 2 teaspoons cold unsalted butter, grated
- 2 teaspoons granulated sugar
- ½ teaspoon ground cinnamon
- 6 frozen phyllo shells (from a 1.9-ounce package), thawed
- FOR THE PISTACHIO BAKLAVA BITES
- ¼ cup finely chopped pistachios
- 2 teaspoons very cold unsalted butter, grated
- 2 teaspoons granulated sugar
- ¼ teaspoon ground cardamom (optional)
- 6 frozen phyllo shells (from a 1.9-ounce package), thawed
- FOR THE HONEY SYRUP
- ¼ cup hot water
- ¼ cup honey
- 2 teaspoons fresh lemon juice

Directions:
1. To prep the walnut baklava bites: In a small bowl, combine the walnuts, butter, sugar, and cinnamon. Spoon the filling into the phyllo shells.
2. To prep the pistachio baklava bites: In a small bowl, combine the pistachios, butter, sugar, and cardamom (if using). Spoon the filling into the phyllo shells.
3. To cook the baklava bites: Install a crisper plate in each of the two baskets. Place the walnut baklava bites in the Zone 1 basket and insert the basket in the unit. Place the pistachio baklava bites in the Zone 2 basket and insert the basket in the unit.
4. Select Zone 1, select BAKE, set the temperature to 330°F, and set the timer to 10 minutes. Press MATCH COOK to match Zone 2 settings to Zone 1.
5. Press START/PAUSE to begin cooking.
6. When cooking is complete, the shells will be golden brown and crisp.
7. To make the honey syrup: In a small bowl, whisk together the hot water, honey, and lemon juice. Dividing evenly, pour the syrup over the baklava bites (you may hear a crackling sound).
8. Let cool completely before serving, about 1 hour.
Nutrition:

- (Per serving) Calories: 262; Total fat: 16g; Saturated fat: 3g; Carbohydrates: 29g; Fiber: 1g; Protein: 2g; Sodium: 39mg

Chocolate And Rum Cupcakes

Servings: 6
Cooking Time: 15 Minutes
Ingredients:
- 150 g granulated sweetener
- 140 g almond flour
- 1 teaspoon unsweetened baking powder
- 3 teaspoons cocoa powder
- ½ teaspoon baking soda
- ½ teaspoon ground cinnamon
- ¼ teaspoon grated nutmeg
- ⅛ teaspoon salt
- 120 ml milk
- 110 g butter, at room temperature
- 3 eggs, whisked
- 1 teaspoon pure rum extract
- 70 g blueberries
- Cooking spray

Directions:
1. Preheat the air fryer to 175°C. Spray a 6-cup muffin tin with cooking spray.
2. In a mixing bowl, combine the sweetener, almond flour, baking powder, cocoa powder, baking soda, cinnamon, nutmeg, and salt and stir until well blended.
3. In another mixing bowl, mix together the milk, butter, egg, and rum extract until thoroughly combined. Slowly and carefully pour this mixture into the bowl of dry mixture. Stir in the blueberries.
4. Spoon the batter into the greased muffin cups, filling each about three-quarters full.
5. Bake for 15 minutes, or until the center is springy and a toothpick inserted in the middle comes out clean.
6. Remove from the basket and place on a wire rack to cool. Serve immediately.

Berry Crumble And S'mores

Servings: 8
Cooking Time: 15 Minutes
Ingredients:
- Berry Crumble:
- For the Filling:
- 300 g mixed berries
- 2 tablespoons sugar
- 1 tablespoon cornflour
- 1 tablespoon fresh lemon juice
- For the Topping:
- 30 g plain flour
- 20 g rolled oats
- 1 tablespoon granulated sugar
- 2 tablespoons cold unsalted butter, cut into small cubes
- Whipped cream or ice cream (optional)
- S'mores:
- Coconut, or avocado oil, for spraying
- 8 digestive biscuits
- 2 (45 g) chocolate bars
- 4 large marshmallows

Directions:
1. Make the Berry Crumble :
2. 1. Preheat the air fryer to 204°C. For the filling: In a round baking pan, gently mix the berries, sugar, cornflour, and lemon juice until thoroughly combined. 3. For the topping: In a small bowl, combine the flour, oats, and sugar. Stir the butter into the flour mixture until the mixture has the consistency of breadcrumbs. 4. Sprinkle the topping over the berries. 5. Put the pan in the zone 1 air fryer drawer and air fry for 15 minutes. Let cool for 5 minutes on a wire rack. 6. Serve topped with whipped cream or ice cream, if desired.
3. Make the S'mores :
4. Line the zone 2 air fryer drawer with baking paper and spray lightly with oil.
5. Place 4 biscuits into the prepared drawer.
6. Break the chocolate bars in half, and place 1/2 on top of each biscuit. Top with 1 marshmallow.
7. Air fry at 188°C for 30 seconds, or until the marshmallows are puffed, golden brown and slightly melted.
8. Top with the remaining biscuits and serve.

Peanut Butter, Honey & Banana Toast

Servings: 4
Cooking Time: 9 Minutes
Ingredients:
- 2 tablespoons unsalted butter, softened
- 4 slices white bread
- 4 tablespoons peanut butter
- 2 bananas, peeled and thinly sliced
- 4 tablespoons honey
- 1 teaspoon ground cinnamon

Directions:
1. Spread butter on one side of each slice of bread, then peanut butter on the other side. Arrange the banana slices on top of the peanut butter sides of each slice . Drizzle honey on top of the banana and sprinkle with cinnamon.
2. Cut each slice in half lengthwise so that it will better fit into the air fryer basket. Arrange the bread slices, butter sides down, in the two air fryer baskets. Set the air fryer to 190°C cooking for 5 minutes. Then set the air fryer to 205°C and cook for an additional 4 minutes, or until the bananas have started to brown. Serve hot.

Fluffy Layered Peanut Butter Cheesecake Brownies

Servings: 6
Cooking Time: 35 Minutes
Ingredients:
- ½ cup blanched finely ground almond flour
- 1 cup powdered erythritol, divided
- 2 tablespoons unsweetened cocoa powder
- ½ teaspoon baking powder
- ¼ cup unsalted butter, softened
- 2 large eggs, divided
- 8 ounces full-fat cream cheese, softened
- ¼ cup heavy whipping cream
- 1 teaspoon vanilla extract
- 2 tablespoons no-sugar-added peanut butter

Directions:
1. In a large bowl, combine ½ cup erythritol, almond flour, baking powder and cocoa powder. Add in butter and one egg, stir well.
2. Spoon mixture into 6&quot| round baking pan. Put pan into the air fryer basket.
3. Set the temperature to 300°F, then set the timer for 20 minutes.
4. A toothpick inserted in center will come out clean when fully cooked. Allow to completely cool for 20 minutes and firm up.
5. In a large bowl, beat heavy cream, cream cheese, remaining ½ cup erythritol, peanut butter, remaining egg, and vanilla until turns fluffy.
6. Spoon mixture over cooled brownies. Return the pan into the air fryer basket.
7. Set the temperature to 300°F, then set the timer for 15 minutes.
8. When fully done, cheesecake will be slightly browned and mostly firm with
9. a slight jiggle. Let it rest and refrigerate for at least 2 hours before serving.

Chocolate Pudding

Servings: 2
Cooking Time: 12 Minutes
Ingredients:
- 1 egg
- 32g all-purpose flour
- 35g cocoa powder
- 50g sugar
- 57g butter, melted
- ½ tsp baking powder

Directions:
1. In a bowl, mix flour, cocoa powder, sugar, and baking powder.
2. Add egg and butter and stir until well combined.
3. Pour batter into the two greased ramekins.
4. Insert a crisper plate in Ninja Foodi air fryer baskets.
5. Place ramekins in both baskets.
6. Select zone 1 then select "bake" mode and set the temperature to 375 degrees F for 12 minutes. Press match cook to match zone 2 settings to zone 1. Press "start/stop" to begin.

Nutrition:
- (Per serving) Calories 512 | Fat 27.3g |Sodium 198mg | Carbs 70.6g | Fiber 4.7g | Sugar 50.5g | Protein 7.2g

Crispy Pineapple Rings

Servings: 6
Cooking Time: 6 To 8 Minutes
Ingredients:
- 240 ml rice milk
- 85 g plain flour
- 120 ml water
- 25 g unsweetened flaked coconut
- 4 tablespoons granulated sugar
- ½ teaspoon baking soda
- ½ teaspoon baking powder
- ½ teaspoon vanilla essence
- ½ teaspoon ground cinnamon
- ¼ teaspoon ground star anise
- Pinch of kosher, or coarse sea salt
- 1 medium pineapple, peeled and sliced

Directions:
1. Preheat the air fryer to 190°C.
2. In a large bowl, stir together all the ingredients except the pineapple.
3. Dip each pineapple slice into the batter until evenly coated.
4. Arrange the pineapple slices in the zone 1 basket and air fry for 6 to 8 minutes until golden brown.
5. Remove from the basket to a plate and cool for 5 minutes before serving warm

Delicious Apple Fritters

Servings: 10

Cooking Time: 8 Minutes
Ingredients:
- 236g Bisquick
- 2 apples, peel & dice
- 158ml milk
- 30ml butter, melted
- 1 tsp cinnamon
- 24g sugar

Directions:
1. In a bowl, mix Bisquick, cinnamon, and sugar.
2. Add milk and mix until dough forms. Add apple and stir well.
3. Insert a crisper plate in Ninja Foodi air fryer baskets.
4. Make fritters from the mixture and place in both baskets. Brush fritters with melted butter.
5. Select zone 1 then select "air fry" mode and set the temperature to 360 degrees F for 10 minutes. Press "match" to match zone 2 settings to zone 1. Press "start/stop" to begin.

Nutrition:
- (Per serving) Calories 171 | Fat 6.7g |Sodium 352mg | Carbs 25.8g | Fiber 1.7g | Sugar 10.8g | Protein 2.7g

Pineapple Wontons

Servings: 5
Cooking Time: 15 To 18 Minutes
Ingredients:
- 225 g cream cheese
- 170 g finely chopped fresh pineapple
- 20 wonton wrappers
- Cooking oil spray

Directions:
1. In a small microwave-safe bowl, heat the cream cheese in the microwave on high power for 20 seconds to soften.
2. In a medium bowl, stir together the cream cheese and pineapple until mixed well.
3. Lay out the wonton wrappers on a work surface. A clean table or large cutting board works well.
4. Spoon 1½ teaspoons of the cream cheese mixture onto each wrapper. Be careful not to overfill.
5. Fold each wrapper diagonally across to form a triangle. Bring the 2 bottom corners up toward each other. Do not close the wrapper yet. Bring up the 2 open sides and push out any air. Squeeze the open edges together to seal.
6. Preheat the air fryer to 200°C.
7. Place the wontons into the two drawers. Spray the wontons with the cooking oil.
8. Cook wontons for 10 minutes, then remove the drawers, flip each wonton, and spray them with more oil. Reinsert the drawers to resume cooking for 5 to 8 minutes more until the wontons are light golden brown and crisp.
9. When the cooking is complete, cool for 5 minutes before serving.

RECIPES INDEX

Hard Boiled Eggs 8
Hawaiian Chicken Bites 71
Healthy Chickpea Fritters 85
Herb And Lemon Cauliflower 28
Herb Lemon Mussels 51
Herb Tuna Patties 54
Herbed Turkey Breast With Simple Dijon Sauce 77
Honey Banana Oatmeal 19
Honey Glazed Bbq Pork Ribs 33
Honey Pecan Shrimp 52
Honey-cajun Chicken Thighs 77
Honey-glazed Chicken Thighs 69

I

Italian Baked Cod 60
Italian-style Meatballs With Garlicky Roasted Broccoli 40

J

Jalapeño Popper Dip With Tortilla Chips 80
Jelly Donuts 93
Jerk-rubbed Pork Loin With Carrots And Sage 47
Juicy Duck Breast 74

K

Kale Chips 78
Kale Potato Nuggets 89

L

Lamb Chops With Dijon Garlic 38
Lava Cake 95
Lemon Herb Cauliflower 29
Lemon Pepper Fish Fillets 57
Lemon Raspberry Muffins 98
Lime Bars 94
Lime Glazed Tofu 25

M

Meat And Rice Stuffed Peppers 43
Meatloaf 40
Mexican Breakfast Pepper Rings 10
Mixed Air Fry Veggies 23
Mocha Pudding Cake Vanilla Pudding Cake 97
Morning Patties 7
Mozzarella Arancini 83
Mozzarella Sticks 85
Mushroom-and-tomato Stuffed Hash Browns 15

Mustard Pork Chops 33

N

Nashville Hot Chicken 65
New York Strip Steak 35
Nigerian Peanut-crusted Bavette Steak 46

O

Olive Oil Cake & Old-fashioned Fudge Pie 101
Orange-mustard Glazed Salmon 48
Orange-mustard Glazed Salmon And Cucumber And Salmon Salad 58
Oreo Rolls 94

P

Panko Crusted Calf's Liver Strips 37
Panko-crusted Fish Sticks 61
Parmesan Crush Chicken 78
Parmesan Mackerel With Coriander And Garlic Butter Prawns Scampi 53
Parmesan Pork Chops 47
Parmesan Sausage Egg Muffins 9
Parmesan-crusted Fish Sticks With Baked Macaroni And Cheese 56
Peanut Butter, Honey & Banana Toast 103
Pepper Egg Cups 16
Pineapple Wontons 104
Pork Chops With Broccoli 47
Pork Katsu With Seasoned Rice 45
Pork Sausage Eggs With Mustard Sauce 9
Pork With Green Beans And Potatoes 44
Potato And Parsnip Latkes With Baked Apples 30
Prawns Curry And Paprika Crab Burgers 57
Pretzels Hot Dog 84
Pumpkin Cookie With Cream Cheese Frosting 100
Pumpkin Fries 87

R

Red Pepper And Feta Frittata 15
Red Pepper And Feta Frittata And Bacon Eggs On The Go 19
Roast Beef 37
Roast Beef With Yorkshire Pudding 42
Roast Souvlaki-style Pork With Lemon-feta Baby Potatoes 34
Roasted Halibut Steaks With Parsley 54

Roasted Oranges 10

Roasted Salmon And Parmesan Asparagus 59

S

Salmon Fritters With Courgette & Cajun And Lemon Pepper Cod 61

Salmon With Coconut 49

Sausage And Cheese Balls 11

Sausage And Pork Meatballs 42

Sausage Breakfast Casserole 14

Sausage With Eggs 13

Savory Almond Butter Cookie Balls 98

Scallops 51

Scallops And Spinach With Cream Sauce And Confetti Salmon Burgers 55

Seasoned Lamb Steak 39

Sesame Bagels 7

Shrimp Po'boys With Sweet Potato Fries 62

Shrimp Skewers 53

Simple Pineapple Sticks And Crispy Pineapple Rings 99

Smoked Salmon 53

Smothered Chops 45

Snapper With Fruit 55

Speedy Chocolate Espresso Mini Cheesecake 99

Spiced Apple Cake 96

Spice-rubbed Pork Loin 34

Spicy Chicken Tenders 81

Spicy Lamb Chops 38

Spinach Omelet And Bacon, Egg, And Cheese Roll Ups 13

Spinach Patties 87

Steak Fajitas With Onions And Peppers 44

Stuffed Beef Fillet With Feta Cheese 44

Stuffed Mushrooms With Crab 59

Stuffed Sweet Potatoes 27

Stuffed Tomatoes 25

Sweet & Spicy Fish Fillets 55

Sweet Bites 90

Sweet Potato Donut Holes 97

Sweet Potatoes & Brussels Sprouts 22

Sweet Potatoes Hash 17

Sweet Potatoes With Honey Butter 24

Sweet-and-sour Chicken With Pineapple Cauliflower Rice 73

T

Taco-spiced Chickpeas And Black Bean Corn Dip 79

Tangy Fried Pickle Spears 79

Tasty Sweet Potato Wedges 79

Tater Tots 89

Teriyaki Chicken Skewers 75

Thai Curry Chicken Kabobs 67

Thai Curry Meatballs 68

Tilapia Sandwiches With Tartar Sauce 49

Tofu Veggie Meatballs 91

Tuna-stuffed Quinoa Patties 60

Two-way Salmon 58

V

Veggie Burgers With "fried" Onion Rings 29

Veggie Shrimp Toast 90

W

Waffle Fries 89

Walnut Baklava Bites Pistachio Baklava Bites 102

Whole Chicken 66

Wings With Corn On The Cob 65

Z

Zucchini Bread 100

Zucchini Cakes 22

Zucchini Chips 82

Zucchini Pork Skewers 41

Printed in Great Britain
by Amazon

33225934R00062